Laura Ingalls Wilder
and Rose Wilder Lane

Laura Ingalls Wilder and Rose Wilder Lane

Authorship, Place, Time, and Culture

John E. Miller

University of Missouri Press   Columbia and London

Copyright © 2008 by
The Curators of the University of Missouri
University of Missouri Press, Columbia, Missouri 65201
Printed and bound in the United States of America
All rights reserved
5 4 3 2 1   12 11 10 09 08

Library of Congress Cataloging-in-Publication Data

Miller, John E., 1945–
    Laura Ingalls Wilder and Rose Wilder Lane : authorship, place, time, and
culture / John E. Miller.
        p. cm.
    Includes bibliographical references and index.
    Summary: "One of America's leading authorities on Laura Ingalls Wilder
and Rose Wilder Lane combines analyses of both women to explore their
collaborative process and how their books reflect the authors' view of place,
time, and culture, expanding the critical discussion of Wilder and Lane
beyond the Little House"—Provided by publisher.
    ISBN 978-0-8262-1823-0 (alk. paper)
    1. Wilder, Laura Ingalls, 1867–1957—Criticism and interpretation.
2. Lane, Rose Wilder, 1886–1968—Criticism and interpretation.
3. Authorship—Collaboration.   4. Wilder, Laura Ingalls, 1867–1957.
Little house on the prairie.   5. Historical fiction, American—History
and criticism.   6. Autobiographical fiction, American—History and
criticism.   7. Frontier and pioneer life in literature. 8. Frontier and
pioneer life—United States.   I. Title.
    PS3545.I342Z7695 2008
    813'.52—dc22
                                                              2008028185

∞™ This paper meets the requirements of the American National Standard
for Permanence of Paper for Printed Library Materials, Z39.48, 1984.

Designer: Jennifer Cropp
Typesetter: The Composing Room of Michigan, Inc.
Printer and binder: Thomson-Shore, Inc.
Typefaces: Palatino and Garamond

*To Paul W. Glad, whose dedication to the historical craft
and whose wise and generous counsel have served as a model
and inspiration for me and countless other students.*

Contents

Acknowledgments

A book like this cannot be written without the kind assistance and support of many people. I would like to thank generous and unstinting archivists and librarians at the Herbert Hoover Presidential Library, South Dakota State University, the University of Wisconsin, the University of Missouri, the National Archives, the State Historical Society of Missouri, the South Dakota State Historical Society, and the State Historical Society of Wisconsin. Special thanks also to the staff at the Laura Ingalls Wilder Memorial Society in De Smet, South Dakota, and at the Laura Ingalls Wilder Home and Museum in Mansfield, Missouri. I also wish to thank the Little House Heritage Trust for its assistance and encouragement in making available the Rose Wilder Lane papers at the Hoover Presidential Library.

I am grateful for the penetrating comments and advice of Gary Kass, for the careful editorial assistance of Jane Lago and Julianna Schroeder, and for the helpful suggestions made by three anonymous readers at the University of Missouri Press. They have made this book immeasurably better than it was in the beginning. I am particularly grateful to Bill Anderson and Dwight Miller, who were generous and astute in answering my questions and helping me think through my ideas about Wilder and Lane. To every other person and organization providing assistance to me, I extend my heartfelt gratitude.

For permission to revise and expand essays that became chapters

4, 6, 7, and 8 of the book, I thank the following publications in which they originally appeared:

"Laura Ingalls Wilder: A Perspective from 1932, the Year of Publication of Her First 'Little House' Book," *Big Muddy: A Journal of the Mississippi River Valley* 2, no. 1 (2002): 38–54.

"Rose Wilder Lane and Thomas Hart Benton: A Turn toward History during the 1930s," *American Studies* 37, no. 2 (fall 1996): 83–101.

"Laura Ingalls Wilder's Apprenticeship as a Farm Author," *Papers of the Twenty-sixth Annual Dakota History Conference*, ed. Arthur R. Huseboe and Harry F. Thompson, 481–88. Sioux Falls, S.D.: Center for Western Studies, 1994.

"American Indians in the Fiction of Laura Ingalls Wilder," *South Dakota History* 30, no. 3 (fall 2000): 303–20.

Laura Ingalls Wilder and Rose Wilder Lane

1

Writing the Self

Approaching the Biographies of
Laura Ingalls Wilder and Rose Wilder Lane

When I told a friend of mine that I was writing another book about Laura Ingalls Wilder, a surprised expression came over her face. "What?" she asked wonderingly. "Is there anything else we need to know about her?" I tried to explain to her what it was I was planning to do, but I wonder now whether what I told her sounded very convincing. That there is plenty of room for further study of one of the twentieth century's most popular children's authors, however, is a given. Adding to that is the success of her daughter, Rose Wilder Lane, as a novelist, short-story writer, and literary journalist and her crucial assistance to Wilder in the production of her Little House novels. As I argue in the next chapter, future studies of Wilder's literary output will have to be conducted with full recognition of the close collaboration that occurred between mother and daughter in the writing of the books, and therefore it makes eminent sense to treat the two in tandem, which is what I have done in this book.

Although Lane had worked previously with her mother on several writing projects and had attempted to tutor her in the writing of articles for national magazines, it was only in 1930 that an intense collaboration began between the two as they set to work to produce autobiographical novels of the frontier aimed at children's audiences. Wilder's original autobiography, "Pioneer Girl," never found a publisher, but it served as a resource for seven of the eight Little House books, which appeared regularly between 1932 and 1943 (*Farmer Boy*, the second in the series, was based upon the boyhood experiences of Wilder's husband). The decade of the thirties, which witnessed the publication of Wilder's first five books as well as of Lane's two most important novels, was a time of tremendous social, political, and cultural ferment and conflict, and most of the chapters in this book grapple with issues emerging out of this creative and conflicted environment.

Lane not only collaborated with her mother on the texts of all of the Little House books, but also actually lived at Rocky Ridge farm in a house just a few hundred yards away from her parents until the middle of 1935. While the two were in essential agreement in their views about politics, which found expression to varying degrees in the books of both, they frequently found themselves enervated by the intense, multisided, and contradictory mother-daughter relationship that simultaneously drew them together and drove them apart. Both of them, while highly individualistic and creative in their own ways, were very much products of their times, so any analysis of Wilder and Lane as authors must be, in part at least, a discussion of the depression decade and the powerful cultural and political forces that coursed through it.

The Stock Market Crash of 1929, while not directly causing the economic debacle of the thirties, set in motion a series of events that collectively brought into being the worst economic calamity in American history. Not only was capitalism in crisis, but also American democracy appeared to be in danger. Wilder's Little House books and much of Lane's writing during the 1930s were, to one degree or another, responses to the challenges that people all around the United States were experiencing. Ironically, the man in the White House, Franklin D. Roosevelt, elicited Wilder and Lane's scorn and ire, although he, more than anyone else, was responsible for saving capitalism at a time when extremists of the right and left, not to mention totalitarians, were taking over in other parts of the world. In Lane's case, the hatred the president inspired in her was close to pathological.

Added to their growing political concerns were constant worries about money. Lane, in addition, seemed to be going through a prolonged midlife crisis, unsure of where to concentrate her writing talents, haunted by the effects of the aging process, uncertain about her identity, and beset by philosophical anxieties. Psychologists suggest that people commonly respond to anxiety by resorting to various defense mechanisms, such as regression, repression, identification, and projection. Lane longed to escape from Rocky Ridge and from the confining embrace of her mother, which she finally managed to do in 1935 at age forty-eight. Beyond that, she was looking for a comfortable philosophical home, one she eventually discovered in extreme right-wing libertarian politics. Her relationship with her parents, her writing career, and her psychological and philosophical needs, thus, were all bound up together.

Wilder's personality, while much less tortured and complex than her daughter's, was likewise highly charged and ambitious. With regard to her political and social views, she too sought to find a home of a sort that resembled the treasured farmhouse at Rocky Ridge that she and her husband, Almanzo, had so energetically and lovingly built and expanded over a period of almost two decades. She had no desire to leave Mansfield, the small town in Missouri where she had resided since 1894, but she also was able to find an intellectual refuge during a time of troubles. In her case, that was the remembered frontier of her childhood, imagined through the lens of memory as she tried to reconstruct scenes that had occurred five or six decades earlier. Lane's two frontier novels written during the period—*Let the Hurricane Roar* and *Free Land*—also hearkened back to frontier history to relate tales of heroic individualism and fierce courage in the face of unremitting hardship and challenge. Wilder's and Lane's responses to the thirties, in other words, involved both physical escape and metaphorical escape into the safe havens of libertarian political philosophy and mythologized history.

If mother and daughter were writing a kind of history as they constructed their fictional accounts, they also engaged in two other major literary genres during their writing careers: biography and autobiography. Lane, a basically self-trained journalist and writer of fiction, advanced her career as a writer for the *San Francisco Bulletin* and then as a freelancer by writing biographical sketches as well as full-scale biographical treatments of Henry Ford, Herbert Hoover, and Jack London. In 1919, she also wrote a thinly veiled autobiographical novel, *Diverging Roads,* which was based loosely upon her life in California as a career woman during the teens. It was she who in 1930 got her mother going on writing her autobiography, which they hoped to serialize in a national magazine. When that project failed and a children's book editor suggested that Wilder draw upon some of her stories to write a fictionalized account for children, her career as a children's novelist was born.

The appeals of biography and autobiography for readers are apparent in any bookstore or library in America, where long shelves and whole sections bulge with the incredibly large and varied output of authors who have chosen to write about their own lives or those of others. We cannot seem to get our fill of reading about other people's experiences, and increasing numbers of us seem compelled to write about our own. Literary critics and scholars have not been so convinced of the allure and benefits of the genres. Poststructuralist theorists, beginning in the late 1960s, proclaimed "the death of the author," and they and postmodernists argued that there are no stable identities to be discovered, no grand narratives to relate, no essential realities to pass on to others. Postmodernist theories from the seventies onward, with their notions of the self as fragmented, discontinuous, and ephemeral, challenged the assumptions of traditional biography. Earlier, during the reign of the New Critics in the forties and fifties, the connection between author and text was severed, and later efforts by New Historicists and others to reinject historical context and biographical information into the analysis of literature did not fully satisfy those who believe that knowledge about an author's background and intentions in writing a text may be highly relevant to interpreting it.

I, as a historian, am biased toward treating historical context and personal history with care and consideration. But, like others of my ilk, I am constantly aware of the difficulties, ambiguities, lacunae, false leads, misimpressions, slanted assumptions, and downright errors that often inject themselves into the process and crop up in the historical and biographical record. Historians do not need to be reminded of their own weaknesses and failures and those of other researchers in their attempts to ferret out the evidence, apply correct theoretical concepts and assumptions, and make judicious interpretations. While aiming at the truth, we realize that we often fall short of it. Most of us are not yet ready to abandon the notion of correspondence between "what happened" and the records we produce of it. What we are willing to admit is that our reconstructions of the past are always imperfect and subject to revision, as new evidence, methods, conceptual schemes, and interpretive tools are advanced. We recognize that many different stories can be told about the same phenomenon, but we also know in our bones that some stories are better (that is, more accurate, more truthful, or productive of warranted assertable belief) than others and that some are so far off the mark that they don't deserve anybody's time or energy.

"Biography is apparently prosperous," literary critic Catherine Peters writes, "but it is also uneasy. Modern critical theory, we know, is scornful of the idea that the text can be related to its author's life in any useful or significant way." Weighing in from the writer's point of view, John Updike opines, "The main question concerning literary biography is, surely, Why do we need it at all? When an author has devoted his life to expressing himself, and, if a poet or a writer of fiction, has used the sensations and critical events of his life as his basic material, what of significance can a biographer add to the record? Most writers lead quiet lives or, even if they don't, are of interest to us because of the words they set down in what had to be quiet moments."[1]

But avid consumers are not put off by such comments or by warnings that such works can be misleading, untrue, basely motivated, or just plain dull. "Biographers can only be unauthentic, can only get it wrong, can only lie, can only substitute their own story for the story of their announced subject," cautions literary critic Stanley Fish. Readers of biographies, in turn, take their lumps from Elizabeth Hardwick, who chides "the contemporary appetite for tawdry revelation." Going one step further, Joyce Carol Oates attaches the label "pathography" to works intended to tear down their subjects, usually dead and unable to answer back.[2]

The biographer's task is never a simple one. Arnold Rampersad, a practitioner of the craft, admits that "all aspects of biography are problematical, with biography itself being problematical in that it purports to do something—recover a life—that is patently impossible to do." Attempting to understand other times and cultures, searching for elusive facts, remaining unaware of many if not most of the people, places, and events that structured their subjects' lives, lacking access to the interior recesses of their minds, usually lacking expertise in psychological theory and practice, and limited in the space available to them to tell their stories, biographers necessarily have to settle for something less than "the truth, the whole truth, and nothing but the truth." Furthermore, as Jay Parini, author of several literary biographies, notes, "I know I do bring my own perception of reality, my own prejudices and predilections, my deepest fears and fondest hopes, to bear on my subject." None of that, he asserts, has distorted the truth of his work.[3] I am not sure how he can be certain of that, but at least if a biographer is aware of the dangers and pitfalls surrounding the task, he or she has a better chance of transcending them and arriving at an approximation of the truth.

Autobiography poses its own special difficulties. While the autobiographer does have the advantage of writing about his or her own life, which should be as well known to the person as to anybody else, imperfect memories, failure to pay attention all the time, inability to understand the social forces operating and the social contexts in which one was living, as well as self-interested motives, dreams, delusions, and the urge to wreak revenge on one's enemies constitute a few of the impediments to truth-telling. "Because the autobiographer often dresses up in fictions and disguises himself in slanted fact," cautions Herbert Leibowitz, "the reader must pass like a secret agent across the borders of actuality and myth, following its winding trail of hallowed lies and profane truths." Even for memoirists intent on telling the truth, memory falters. Rather than consisting of a stable, static record of the past, it constantly undergoes unconscious revision, being constructed, as well as behaving like a mirror on the past.[4]

Thus, although many readers may come to autobiography assuming that authors are simply presenting verifiable facts of a life, by now we should have learned the lesson that fictions are inextricably intertwined with facts in any autobiographical presentation. "Obviously, then, there is no such thing as a 'uniquely' true, correct, or even faithful autobiography," observes psychologist Jerome Bruner. Such writings can never be simple statements about a "life as lived," for no such thing exists, he asserts. A life, rather, is always constructed or construed by the act of autobiography: "Construal and reconstrual are interpretive. Like all forms of interpretation, how we construe our lives is subject to our intentions, to the interpretive conventions available to us, and to the meanings imposed upon us by the usages of our culture and language."[5]

Women's autobiography entails its own challenges. While men's lives tend to be focused outward, where records are external and public, women's lives traditionally were directed more inwardly, where less can be known about how they interacted with their fellow human beings or how they made a direct impact upon society.[6] Ultimately, the difference resolves into a matter of power, for in most cultures throughout most of human history men have managed to maintain domination through a wide variety of means, mostly with the complicity of women, forced or unforced. Writing an autobiography makes one vulnerable, especially when the author goes beyond stating bare facts. "Psychologically painful experiences and elusive truths are difficult matters to expose to strangers," writes Estelle C. Jelinek, who goes on to note that when the autobiographer is a woman, it causes even greater trepidation. Women came to sense that they were different from, other than, or outside of the male-dominated world, thus making them a poor fit for it. "This sense of alienation from the male world is very real," Jelinek goes on, "but there also exists the positive delineation of a *female* culture, a *women's* world."[7] It is this women's culture that stands out in Wilder's Little House books and much of Lane's fiction, but both of them also devoted a significant amount of their attention to the more social and political aspects of the outside world, thus establishing a link between the two realms.

A particular hazard in trying to say anything about Laura Ingalls Wilder is the strong sense of attachment that so many of her readers develop toward her. Not content to read her books through once, they often reread them many times, devour anything else about her that they can, visit the sites where she lived, get on Internet chat lines to talk about her, even name daughters after her or have doll collections representing characters in her books. They often develop very firm opinions about how it was living on the frontier and are endlessly curious about the actual figures behind the fictional characters and about facts regarding people who are introduced in the books. Many of them are heartbroken to discover that some of the people mentioned in the books did not exist, that names have sometimes been changed, and that episodes have been reconstructed or totally fabricated. Many especially resist having to learn that Wilder's daughter, Rose, played a crucial role in manufacturing the manuscripts that became the books. The phenomenon resembles the never-ending debate among a wide variety of groups who have an investment in Shakespeare's identity and literary output. As Peter Holland notes, "Shakespeare's biography has long been annexed by special-interest groups for their version of the person, for their creation of the Shakespeare that best appeals to them." This temptation for readers to expect and demand certain renditions of their hero's life applies with special force to many fans of Laura Ingalls Wilder. Norman White puts it well when he states, "What often gets in the way of telling truths about someone's life is not the biographer's distortions or myopia, but the reader's preconceptions about what should be there, the way it should be told, and the conclusions which should be drawn."[8]

When it comes to Laura Ingalls Wilder, the chief drawback to achieving a full and penetrating picture of her life is the paucity of sources available informing us about what she was really thinking and feeling. Ironically, her daughter wrote and saved diaries and journals and sent friends and associates hundreds of long, often highly revealing letters over the course of her life. We can indeed ascertain a great deal about the specific traumas, exhilarations, joys, sorrows, challenges, and triumphs that helped make her such a fascinating, complex, and contradictory character. Relatively little of this sort of material is available for Wilder. Included are a few letters, some journals kept during journeys that she took, reports of friends and neighbors, scattered jottings, and notes that have been preserved. Much of what we know about her ideas, values, and personal inclinations must be inferred from her books and other writings. To me, her semimonthly columns published in the *Missouri Ruralist* during the late teens and early twenties are especially revealing. Beyond that, the best information available derives from letters, journals, and diaries of her daughter, Rose, which must be read with a certain amount of care, taking account of their biases and point of view. Clearly, the single most important relationship for each person was that between mother and daughter, so any discussion of either's personality must be one that takes account of both of them.

Biography traditionally formed the backbone of history and was closely allied with it. To Thomas Carlyle, Ralph Waldo Emerson, and others of their persuasion, history *was*, in essence, biography—especially the biography of "great men." Eventually, biography seemed to sever its traditional umbilical cord to history, asserting its independence as an independent genre, but history has never, on that account, been willing to proceed without maintaining an important place for biography within its purview. With the rise of the New Social History during the 1970s, it appeared that biography might be

of ways by their fellows, their situations, and their surroundings, retain considerable leeway to make choices about what they will do to exercise the power they possess to accomplish their ends. If I have a guiding motto as a historian, it is, "Expect the unexpected."

Who would ever have thought that a sixty-five-year-old woman living in the Missouri Ozarks who had never written a significant piece of fiction in her life would emerge a dozen years later as one of the most beloved children's authors in American history and that her books would still be avidly read today, three-quarters of a century later? Who would have predicted that the places where she grew up would become destinations for countless thousands of loyal fans and admirers from all over the globe? Who would have guessed that her daughter, who played a huge role in producing and marketing those books, would abandon her own fiction-writing career immediately after achieving her greatest literary triumph and then devote the rest of her life to a completely different field of endeavor—political philosophy?

Both Wilder and Lane have attracted considerable popular and scholarly critical attention, especially during the past two decades or so. The first investigator to research them in depth was William T. Anderson, who began his studies as a thirteen-year-old schoolboy after spending a summer vacation working at the Wilder homesite in De Smet. His many pamphlets, articles, and books, ranging from popular magazine treatments and books to heavily footnoted scholarly journal articles, have established him as the best-informed student of Wilder's life, and, along with William Holtz, he fits that designation regarding Rose Wilder Lane as well.[13]

Children's literature specialists, not surprisingly, were the first group to publish extensively on Wilder's writings, and they continue to play an important role in extending our knowledge about her. Articles about her and her books have appeared with some frequency in journals such as *Children's Literature, Children's Literature in Education,* and *The Lion and the Unicorn.* Jane M. Subramanian's comprehensive 1997 annotated bibliography of works on Wilder indicates that the 1980s was the decade when scholarly interest in and publication about her picked up significantly in the form of popular magazine articles as well as scholarly articles, books, master's theses, and doctoral dissertations. Meanwhile, articles and edited volumes written by William Holtz paved the way in directing serious attention at Rose Wilder Lane and her work. While there had been some excellent work on the mother-daughter collaboration that produced the Little House books, beginning with Rosa Ann Moore's original articles on the subject, the first of which came out in 1975, Holtz's controversial 1993 biography *The Ghost in the Little House: A Life of Rose Wilder Lane,* which argued that Lane deserved major credit for writing the books, raised the stakes of the debate. Since then, serious discussion of Wilder's work has had to grapple with the issue. My book of essays on Wilder the following year took for granted that a collaboration had occurred between the two and attempted to address a number of questions emanating from that situation.[14]

Before William Anderson produced a brief but authoritative biography of Wilder in 1992, Donald Zochert and Janet Spaeth had published their own studies on her. The former focused upon Wilder's childhood, and the latter was part of the Twayne series on American authors, combining biography and literary analysis. Virginia L. Wolf's *Little House on the Prairie: A Reader's Companion* provided an insightful reading of the entire series, dealing with a variety of questions and themes, including historical context, environment, gender, technology, heroism, and national identity. Toward the end of the decade, two major books appeared within a year of each other, furthering our knowledge of Wilder as a person and of her literary output. Ann Romines's *Constructing the Little House: Gender, Culture, and Laura Ingalls Wilder* provided a creative and provocative interpretation of Wilder's books and brought to the fore several themes and issues that bore further investigation. Referring to herself as a "feminist scholar with gynocritical and (new) historicist leanings," Romines, in her first and fourth chapters, engaged in feminist analysis, just as a growing number of other scholars were beginning to do at the time. Chapter 2, "Indians in the House," discussed a topic that soon attracted increasing attention in scholarly journals, and chapter 3, on materialism and consumerism, reflected a growing scholarly interest in that area. My 1998 biography dealt in some detail with Wilder's last six decades in Mansfield, Missouri, discussing extensively the writing collaboration she worked out with her daughter.[15]

That same year, the Hoover Presidential Library hosted a conference, "Laura Ingalls Wilder and the American Frontier," featuring papers by Romines, Elizabeth Jameson, Anita Clair Fellman, Ann Weller Dahl, and myself. William Anderson presided over the sessions and the ensuing discussions, and Dwight M. Miller of the

Hoover Library edited a volume containing the session papers. In it, Romines and I spoke mainly about our new books. Jameson provided a feminist analysis of Wilder and her writings, a theme she also addressed in scholarly articles. Fellman, also writing from a feminist viewpoint, provided a preview of the book she was working on about the impact of Wilder's writings upon all aspects of American culture, from the book publishing industry and the mass media to education and politics.[16]

Meanwhile, she and Julia Ehrhardt authored two of the most important studies of the cooperative writing process that occurred between Wilder and Lane, in addition dealing with the political implications of that collaboration. Fellman's splendid "Laura Ingalls Wilder and Rose Wilder Lane: The Politics of a Mother-Daughter Relationship" is perhaps the most influential single critical article ever published about Wilder's writing. Drawing upon psychoanalytical theory and feminist scholarship, it deftly links Lane's psychological tensions and the troubled relationship between mother and daughter with the cultural context to illuminate the two women's attitudes, behavior, and writing. Covering some of the same ground, Julia C. Ehrhardt's chapter on Lane in her book *Writers of Conviction* insightfully connects her personal politics to her professional writing career. She locates the roots of her shift to an extreme form of right-wing ideology in the creative malaise Lane suffered during the 1930s and the opportunity afforded by the Great Depression for her to transfer her intellectual energies into anti–New Deal polemics.[17]

Of the many other articles on Wilder and Lane published during the past couple of decades, several merit special mention for the themes and issues with which they grapple. Suzanne Rahn's discussion of *Little Town on the Prairie* is notable for illustrating the importance of the theme of community in Wilder's writing. Claudia Mills takes a frequently discussed subject—the values expressed in the Little House books—and places it within the purview of theories about moral development. Ann Romines notes the architectural theme that weaves its way throughout the Little House series. The subject that has probably been more discussed than any other and which certainly has generated the most controversy is Wilder's treatment of Native Americans in her books. Sharon Smulders, Philip Heldrich, Frances W. Kaye, Penny T. Linsenmayer, and Donna M. Campbell have all weighed in with important discussions on the subject. Regarding Lane, in an edited collection on "middlebrow modern" writers, Campbell establishes Lane's credentials for being included within that group.[18]

In addition to publications already mentioned, many articles, whether written from a feminist viewpoint or not, have thrown light on the gender issue in Wilder's and Lane's writing. Ann Romines, who treats it extensively in her book on Wilder, also takes it up in a piece on *The Long Winter.* Elizabeth Jameson focuses on Wilder's treatment of her mother in her article on the female frontier.[19]

Also noteworthy are two recently published books by Fellman and Pamela Smith Hill. Most students of Lane and Wilder have focused directly upon their lives and writings. Fellman takes up the more elusive task of trying to delineate the impact Wilder had upon her readers and upon the culture in general. Her findings are intriguing, and her contention that the Little House books paved the way for America's conservative shift to Reaganism during the eighties is especially provocative and will no doubt generate considerable discussion and debate. Hill's book on Wilder's writing career succinctly synthesizes what is known about her developing interest in writing and about her maturing skill as an author. Hill's contention that Lane functioned more like an aggressive editor of her mother's writing than like a true collaborator will also no doubt generate further debate.[20]

Two other welcome recent publications are a new, expanded edition of Wilder's farm journalism and a collection of Lane's literary journalism. Compendiums like these help facilitate interest in and the development of new perspectives on the work and lives of the two women.[21]

It is clear that a great deal of progress has been made in uncovering information about and interpreting the lives and careers of both Wilder and Lane. Some of these gains have derived from recent intellectual trends in the disciplines—feminism, multiculturalism, postmodernism, and reader-response or reception theory—as well as from new research on mother-daughter relationships, consumerism and material culture, ideology, and the publishing industry. Much of the progress that has been attained derives from traditional methods—simply slogging away in the texts, manuscript collections, and other conventional sources. Some of it (the most prominent example being the work of Ann Romines) has explicitly aligned itself with postmodernism and other novel approaches.

What should be the direction of further research? I originally turned to Wilder's novels as a way of learning something about small-town social life on the midwestern frontier. Having graduated from high school in Monett, Missouri, which is a hundred miles west of Mansfield on Highway 60, and after living for a decade in Brookings, South Dakota, forty miles east of De Smet on Highway 14, I felt a measure of rapport for the kinds of milieus in which Wilder lived almost all of her life. After completing a book of essays on her and then a biography, I had thought my work was finished, but as time went by I found myself coming back to her as a subject for conference papers and publications. This interest in Wilder naturally spilled over into curiosity about Lane. Only after several years did I realize that my intellectual forays actually possessed an overarching unity to them. Without being guided by any particular methodology or critical perspective, I began to think of what I was doing as a series of probes that centered around several themes: place, time, and culture. The subjects addressed under those rubrics were, for the most part, ones that neither merited book-length treatment nor could be easily squeezed into more conventional thematic treatments. They could stand alone, but they could also be woven together to add to our understanding of the biographies and literary output of mother and daughter. I also understood that any discussion of Wilder and Lane from now on must start from the knowledge of the two women's collaboration in the process of producing the Little House books. In such fashion, the book you hold in your hands gradually evolved.

Thus, in the text that follows, Chapter 2 sets the stage for what is to come by pulling together various strands of the discussion and debate over the issue of authorship of the Little House books as it has been addressed previously by Anderson, Holtz, Fellman, Ehrhardt, Hill, myself, and others. By providing my "take" on this fraught subject, I intend, in brief, concentrated form, to provide a platform for what is to follow.

The rest of the volume is divided into three sections—one devoted to place, one to time, and one to culture—revolving around spatial, temporal, and sociopolitical perspectives. Chapter 3, the single chapter in Section II, takes up one aspect of the general theme of "place" by focusing upon the unusual emotional resonance that "little houses"—or "home"—possessed for both women. In their personal lives and in their writings, houses played a central role, and the attitudes and values surrounding these notions no doubt had much to do with the appeal that their writing (especially Wilder's) had for their readers.

Section III, on the subject of "time," launches three probes into aspects of biography and history. Chapter 4 picks a single year—1932, the year Wilder's first book was published—to pose the question of how a biographical treatment might turn out differently if the biographer possessed the luxury of dwelling at length on a variety of themes and topics that often get left out all together because of space limitations. Chapter 5 compares the lives and historical approaches of Wilder and Frederick Jackson Turner, the United States' most influential historian of the frontier. Both authors placed the settlement process at the center of their writing, relating triumphal stories of European-Americans occupying the land, and in so doing they diminished the importance of Native Americans in the process. This, no doubt, explains in large part why such a surge of criticism has been directed against both authors of late. Chapter 6 redirects attention toward Lane, examining some of her views on history. To do so, it relates her unpublished history book on Missouri to Thomas Hart Benton's vibrant, controversial mural, *A Social History of the State of Missouri,* that he was painting on the walls in the state capitol at the same time that she was working on her book. Lane and Benton shared similar backgrounds, and while their takes on history differed considerably, their works constituted prime examples of the turn toward history that occurred in the United States during the 1930s.

Section IV, on the subject of "culture," focuses upon the values Wilder brought to her writing, the moral dilemmas surrounding her depiction of American Indians in her novels, and the way in which the depression milieu and public reaction against Roosevelt's New Deal influenced Wilder's and Lane's political views and led them to inject some of their political values into their writing. Chapter 7 discusses how Wilder's regular columns in the *Missouri Ruralist* during the late teens and early twenties provided her, in effect, with a useful apprenticeship in writing regularly for a broad audience, an experience that served her well when she began writing children's novels later on. I argue that, as a whole, Wilder's farm journalism helps us to understand that she was a highly capable writer by the time she turned her hand to fiction. The pieces also provide the best picture we have of Wilder's values, worldview, and mode of thinking. Chapter 8 takes up the highly controversial topic of Wilder's treatment of Indians in her books and especially in *Little House on the*

Prairie. I rehearse the positions that have been taken by previous authors on the topic and conclude that Wilder—while deficient by present standards in her views on the subject and not always enlightened in her depiction of Native Americans in her books—made an effort to show the complexities that were involved in the subject and left us with books that can serve as vehicles for further learning. The question of exactly how the books should be used in schools, especially for the youngest readers, needs to be kept separate from an evaluation of Wilder's own views and writing output. Finally, in Chapter 9, I take up one of the most interesting and significant subjects regarding mother and daughter—their conservative or libertarian political views and how these may or may not have found a place in their writings. It is no secret by now that both Wilder and Lane hated Roosevelt and shuddered at the damage they believed he and his New Dealers were doing to the country. I argue that Lane's visceral hatred of FDR transformed itself into a positive identification with libertarian ideology, which largely resulted from its capacity to fill the philosophical void that had haunted her for a long time. The presence of right-wing ideology in Lane's books is obvious and massive. In Wilder's case, the story is more complicated. While undoubtedly conservative in their political slant, the Little House books' political messages remained generally implicit or subtler and are primarily to be found in the last three volumes.

As noted above, these chapters are meant to be probes that allow us to investigate significant questions and issues surrounding Wilder and Lane, both as persons and as writers. If the chapter on 1932 seems somewhat playful, it is meant that way in part. But it also is entirely serious, for after years of researching and thinking about the subject, I am only more convinced of the complexity, mutability, ambiguity, contradictoriness, and downright messiness of history and the shapes of people's lives. If readers wonder what Babe Ruth has to do with Laura Ingalls Wilder, I can answer them that both were examples of the rapidly rising influence of celebrity culture in America and that they were connected to each other and to Mansfield through Ruth's teammate Carl Mays, who also was a resident of the town. But also I see this episode as an example of the endless multiplication of lines of connection and influence that wrap themselves around people in their everyday lives. If we concentrate too heavily upon the obvious and well-trod linkages and causal patterns that connect people with their peers and social surroundings, we may deny ourselves the opportunity to perceive other, less obvious connections and patterns.

I became a historian, in part, because I was a baseball fan and player first. I know that the game isn't over until the last batter is out, that on any given day any team can beat any other team, and that you have to play the game before you print the results. Yes, history reveals many regularities, tendencies, and predictable outcomes. But it also often turns out differently, in the long run at least, than most people would or could have predicated. History is full of surprises, and the writing careers of Laura Ingalls Wilder and Rose Wilder Lane constitute two of its most remarkable surprises.

I

Authorship

Who Wrote the Books?

That two twentieth-century writers as important as Laura Ingalls Wilder and Rose Wilder Lane would emerge from a small country town in the Missouri Ozarks was improbable. That they were mother and daughter adds charm to the story. That the daughter was the first to win recognition for herself as a literary figure increases the tale's attraction. That she deserves credit for inducing her mother to start her novel-writing career, played a crucial role in producing those books, and called upon her talents and literary connections to get the books published makes it irresistible. Finally, it is ironic that the mother retains continuing appeal today as a wildly popular children's author, while the daughter, despite her earlier start in the business, is remembered primarily by a small coterie of literary scholars and specialists.

Literature appeals to people on many different levels. For the novelist Henry James, the only absolute requirement of fiction was that "it be interesting." Other criteria that have been utilized for evaluating fiction include dramatic vividness, conviction, intensity, poetic purity, thematic development, objectivity, detachment, and artfulness. Standing out perhaps above all the rest in the minds of many

19

readers is realism. Stated differently, an author's ability to create an air or illusion of reality appears to rank as the highest test of success in the realm of fiction.[1]

In churning out the eight children's novels that would emerge as the Little House series, Laura Ingalls Wilder managed simultaneously to keep her stories interesting and to make them seem realistic to her young readers. Accomplishing the former, in fact, resulted in large measure from her success at achieving the latter. Her daughter, Rose, also gained recognition for producing interesting stories, but their authenticity and realism seemed slightly suspect to some of her readers and reviewers. What people did not realize for many years was that the writing careers of mother and daughter were closely intertwined. Although rumors sometimes circulated in Mansfield, Missouri, that Lane had assisted with or even bore major responsibility for the books her mother published, few people suspected the true nature of the literary relationship that existed between the two. Only recently have we come to appreciate fully the close collaboration that developed between them over time, as Lane tutored her mother in writing for publication and then edited, revised, and assisted in the publication of her mother's magazine articles and books. Meanwhile, she was able to draw upon stories related to her by her mother and father in writing some of her own novels and short stories.

Wilder's and Lane's greatest achievements as writers derived from their ability to translate personal experience into compelling fiction. Wilder's Little House series related her own story of growing up on the midwestern frontier in seven volumes and her husband Almanzo's boyhood story in an eighth book. Lane's short stories collected in *Old Home Town* drew upon her own experiences and observations while growing up in Mansfield, and *Let the Hurricane Roar* and *Free Land* were based upon family stories passed on to her by her parents.

"All writing is autobiographical, just as all dreaming is," Lane wrote in a letter to a literary friend of hers. "You write out of yourself, that is, *one* of your selves. You detach from your multiple personality—which we all have—one part of it, and make it the whole."[2] This observation applied with special force to her and her mother's literary careers. So different in many ways, they also shared many similarities. One thing they shared was a passion for words and for writing. While their literary output differed considerably, they both found inspiration in the world as they experienced and understood it, and they both, in their own inimitable ways, sought to depict accurately what they had learned about it. The place to start, then, is with their understanding of what authorship entails and to delineate the ways in which they assisted each other in advancing their respective literary careers.

2

The Mother-Daughter Collaboration
That Produced the Little House Series

Generations of schoolchildren, as well as adults, have derived great enjoyment from reading the Little House books, assuming that Laura Ingalls Wilder sat down in her midsixties to write a simple, straightforward story of her childhood based upon her memories of growing up on the frontier. Such a notion was satisfying, reassuring, and encouraging (supporting the idea that it is never too late in life to commence a great task). The stories—full of fortitude, bravery, self-reliance, and generosity—reinforced traditional values, widely held assumptions about the superiority of the American way of life, and patriotic beliefs about the conditions of American society, patterns of opportunity, and democratic governance. A closer look at the actual way in which the books were constructed, however, can provide contemporary readers with a more realistic understanding of their actual making and a better appreciation that their real contribution to our knowledge is as much mythological as historical. For some time now, any realistic assessment of the Little House series has had to start from the proposition that the words on the pages of the books got there as a result of a continuing collaborative process that occurred between Wilder and her daughter, Rose Wilder Lane. Any serious study of Wilder's writing in the future will likewise have to be undertaken in the same spirit. Thus, it makes sense at the outset to set down the outlines of that collaboration and to discuss how the process worked and what it meant.

After arriving in Missouri in 1894, Laura and Almanzo Wilder built up their initial forty-acre farm on Rocky Ridge to almost two hundred acres, transforming it in the process into a paying proposition. Nevertheless, their personal finances remained precarious, and as they advanced into old age they depended upon annual income subsidies from their increasingly famous and successful daughter, Rose. This caused considerable anxiety for both parents as well as their only child. During the early 1920s, both mother and daughter came to believe that the best opportunity for providing for the financial independence of the aging couple, and one that would allow Rose to independently pursue her own writing career, was to enable her mother to develop her writing ability to a point where she could earn a reliable stream of royalties by writing articles for popular magazines. The project never proceeded very far, however, and petered out after 1925. Rose actually lived at Rocky Ridge with or near her parents in 1924 and 1925 and again from 1928 to 1935.

It was at Rose's urging that Wilder in 1930 wrote her autobiography with the hope that it might be salable to a magazine. Lane tried unsuccessfully to peddle this story, "Pioneer Girl," in serial form to several magazines in New York, where she maintained a large acquaintanceship in literary and publishing circles. Only Graeme Lorimer of the *Saturday Evening Post* liked the story very much, terming it "a grand piece of work, fascinating material, and most intelligent writing." But with magazines cutting back their manuscript purchases as the Great Depression settled in and with the *Post* already possessing a backlog of that kind of material on file, he felt compelled to turn it down. Lorimer suggested that the narrative might have a better chance of getting published if Wilder could rework it into fictional form. However, Lane's agent in New York, George T. Bye, was not much impressed by the manuscript. "'Pioneer Girl' didn't warm me enough the first reading," he told Lane. The story lacked drama, he thought, sounding like the work of a "fine old lady" who was "sitting in a rocking chair and telling a story chronologically but with no benefit of perspective or theatre."[1]

But Marion Fiery, children's editor at Alfred A. Knopf, took an interest in a shorter piece that Lane was able to extrude from her mother's manuscript by stringing together some of her grandfather's stories. Lane called it "When Grandma Was a Little Girl." Fiery suggested expanding this story into a picture book for young readers.[2] Although Wilder had written a fair amount of not very memorable poetry, most of her writing experience had been with nonfiction, turning out stories and columns for farm newspapers and in several cases for magazines. Her new assignment did not daunt her, however; she quickly managed to expand the six- or seven-thousand-word manuscript into one closer to twenty-five thousand words. This is what emerged the following year as *Little House in the Big Woods*.

It was not published, however, before Lane did additional work on it, making her own changes and corrections in the manuscript. She typed it up and had her mother send it on to Fiery in New York, maintaining the fiction that her only role in the process was as an intermediary. Unfortunately, the summer of 1931 saw the country slide deeper and deeper into the Great Depression, and the Knopf firm decided to close its children's department as a cost-cutting move. At Fiery's urging, Lane and Wilder then approached Harper and Brothers, which the Knopf editor thought would be better situated than her own firm to promote the book. Virginia Kirkus, an editor at Harper's, was delighted on first reading of the manuscript, impressed by the narrative skill of its author. She thought that "the real magic was in the telling," she later recalled. "One felt that one was listening, not reading." She later considered her "discovery" of Laura Ingalls Wilder to have been one of the milestones of her book-publishing career.[3]

For Wilder, writing her autobiography served as a transitional step between her earlier farm journalism and dilatory efforts at magazine article writing, on the one hand, and the production of her popular series of children's novels, on the other. While of some interest today as a document about life on the post–Civil War frontier, "Pioneer Girl" displayed few of the endearing qualities that would make her books so memorable and compelling.[4] Without Rose's example, encouragement, advice, editing, and—in places—substantial rewriting of her manuscripts, and without her ability to find a publisher for them, Wilder probably never would have been able to extend her reach beyond a limited local and statewide audience.

To get *Little House in the Big Woods* into publishable form in 1931, Lane spent about a week making revisions on it and typing the manuscript for mailing.[5] The other seven novels would take more of her time; in some cases, it required several months to complete the task. Nevertheless, it took a long time for Lane to begin to appreciate fully the true significance of what she was doing for her mother. Concealing her own work in revising the original book manuscript for publication, Lane disingenuously wrote editor Marian Fiery, "I don't know just where or how I come into this, do you? But somehow I do, because my mother naturally consults me about everything concerning her writing."[6] When she originally asked her agent George Bye if he would handle the negotiations with the publisher on her mother's books and collect the royalties for her, Rose indicated just how little importance she attached to them. "It's really awfully decent of you to bother with this small fry; I do appreciate it," she wrote Bye. "And I don't expect you really to bother. I want it to be nothing more than a bit of semi-annual office routine which will adequately pay for itself." She did not take juvenile literature seriously but rather was intent upon her own work as a novelist and short-story writer.[7]

Although Lane mentioned the customary and expected things about her mother's work when she was asked about it, her main interest, in the beginning at least, seems to have been the additional income the books would earn for the family and the reduced dependence her parents consequently would have on her. If they could become financially independent as a result of the royalties her mother earned, Lane would be relieved of that worry. As Anita Clair Fellman points out, she was intent upon getting out of Mansfield and away from her mother so that she could reestablish her independence and pursue her own writing career, while at the same time fulfilling her familial obligations to her parents.[8] Wilder's motives in writing the books, meanwhile, seem to have escalated somewhat as time went by, and what had at first been a single book expanded into an eight-book series. From preserving some of the stories her father had told by putting them down on paper, her ambition evolved into one of earning a little bit of prestige for herself, then obtaining financial independence for her and her husband, and finally telling a frontier story that would add to historical knowledge.[9]

During the early and mid-1930s, while she was collaborating with her mother on the series, Lane underwent a major crisis in her own life and career. In 1928 she had built an English-style stone cottage for her parents across the hill from their original frame house, which she took over for herself as soon as they moved out. Living at Rocky Ridge farm between 1928 and 1935, Lane was running out of ideas for her own fiction and was finding it increasingly difficult to churn out new material. Still able to command good prices for stories, when inspired, she often found herself coming to a dead end, at a loss for suitable subjects to develop.

After the Stock Market crashed in October 1929, demand for Lane's short stories declined dramatically. The ones that did sell commanded smaller payments than she had become accustomed to. She worried constantly about finances. More than merely worrying, she suffered from deep and prolonged depression. Her financial situation, health problems, decaying teeth, the oppressive heat, separation from her literary friends, and psychological anxiety—all of these and other factors contributed to what she herself referred to as a mental illness. In long letters to friends and in gut-spilling diary and journal entries she related the oppressiveness of the Missouri environment, how much she loathed living there, and how she longed to break free from it. She felt trapped, unable to escape. Why she thought it necessary to stay, however, remains something of a mystery. Certainly she felt an obligation to care for her parents. Yet, when she finally did leave Missouri for good in 1937, they managed to get along perfectly well by themselves.[10] Nor did she feel compelled to return to visit them before her father died in 1949.

Rose, who to outsiders always seemed chipper and cheerful, was undergoing a private hell while she was living at Rocky Ridge working on her mother's first three novels. The revisions on the second book, *Farmer Boy*, which was initially rejected by Harper and Brothers, required approximately seventy days of her time between March 1932 and March 1933.[11] Conducting background research for the third volume, *Little House on the Prairie*, Lane and Wilder drove out to look for the spot where Charles and Caroline Ingalls and their daughters had lived on the Osage Indian Reservation in 1869 and 1870 (they never did find it because Laura remembered her family's cabin as being more like forty miles away from Independence, Kansas, rather than the thirteen that it actually had been).[12] While Rose felt obliged to assist her mother in putting her books into publishable form and certainly was pleased about the income that they generated and the satisfaction they brought to her mother, she bridled at the time that working on them took away from her own writing. "Have to finish my mother's goddam juvenile," she resentfully entered in her diary on May 10, 1936.[13] While her mother's popularity continually mounted, her own frustration grew apace.

Two novels that she had written during the late 1920s about life in the Ozarks—*Hill-Billy* and *Cindy*—she considered to be mere trash. Most of the short stories that she published afterward, also deriving from her experiences and observations in Missouri, were churned out relatively quickly for mass-market magazines like *Country Gentleman, Ladies Home Journal,* and *Saturday Evening Post.* She took some real pride in a collection of stories based upon her childhood years in Mansfield, writing an introduction that tied them together and publishing the book under the title of *Old Home Town* in 1935.

This kind of output placed her writing, along with that of writers such as Edna Ferber and Zona Gale, into the category of "middlebrow regionalist" fiction. These authors won success in the marketplace, selling their work to major presses and sometimes hitting the best-seller lists by catering to a rapidly growing middlebrow culture industry during the twenties and thirties.[14] But Lane wanted something more than commercial success; she desired recognition as the kind of serious writer chronicled by some literary historians as exemplars during the period from the midtwenties through the late thirties of "late modernism."[15] She wanted her work to count, to be judged sophisticated, to make a difference. Moving into middle age, she longed increasingly to do something of real significance—work of lasting importance that would elevate her above the level of what she deemed to be mere "hack writing." In 1932, the year that her mother's first book came out, Lane published *Let the Hurricane Roar,* first as a serial in the *Saturday Evening Post* and later in book form. The material in it was inspired by tales passed on to her by her parents. The plot was based loosely upon the experiences of her grandparents Charles and Caroline Ingalls during the Great Dakota Boom of the early 1880s. Having listened often to the harrowing story of the hard winter of 1880–1881, when tiny De Smet had been snowed in and cut off from railroad service for months, Lane also attempted several times without success to convert the material into fiction. (Harrowing blizzard scenes did feature prominently in both *Let the Hurricane Roar* and *Free Land.*) Her most ambitious concept for historical fiction was a plan she sketched out to write a ten-volume historical novel encompassing the entire sweep of American history. She quickly abandoned the idea, however, as impractical.[16]

In April 1935, when an invitation arrived from the McBride Publishing Company to write a historical travelogue of Missouri for a series of state books that the company was publishing, Lane grabbed quickly at the offer, influenced in part by the $1,500 advance that came along with it. Her research quickly took her to the State Historical Society of Missouri in Columbia. Unfortunately, through a series of misunderstandings, the book was never published.[17] In 1937, Lane moved temporarily to New York City, where she took a room in the Grosvenor Hotel on Fifth Avenue while she was writing *Free Land*, a serialized novel based upon stories her father and mother had told her about their experiences of homesteading in Dakota Territory. The book earned $25,000—her largest paycheck. It and *Let the Hurricane Roar*, both based upon stories she had heard from her parents, constituted her greatest achievement as a fiction writer. The following year she bought a farmhouse in Danbury, Connecticut, and moved there, where she could remain close to the New York literary scene. After 1938, Rose came to the conclusion that her fiction-writing career was over and gradually shifted her attention to the subject that would occupy her for the rest of her life—right-wing political philosophy.

The collaborative writing process between mother and daughter that produced the Little House series of children's novels abounds with contradictions and ironies. Lane, who was slow to recognize the significance of the work that she was doing for her mother, was resentful that her mother displayed so little interest in her own work. Although Wilder took obvious pride in her daughter's accomplishments and enjoyed showing her off to neighbors and friends in Mansfield (sometimes holding receptions at Rocky Ridge, where Lane regaled guests with stories about her adventures in Paris, Albania, and other exotic places), Lane believed that her mother seldom, if ever, actually read the stuff that she wrote. "Oh, it isn't hard to keep Mama Bess from reading my books," she informed her writer friend Guy Moyston. "She never reads 'em. She just likes to have 'em around."[18]

In her children's novels, Wilder depicted her family of origin as being very affectionate and tight-knit. But at Rocky Ridge, while Lane was living there during the twenties and thirties, relations were anything but pleasant much of the time. Although she usually appeared happy and gay to others, Lane's moods frequently turned sour. She hated listening to the frequent bickering of her parents. Most of all, there was the constant contest of wills between mother and daughter—a battle for control that seemed to bring out the worst in each of their assertive personalities while they lived elbow-to-elbow near each other at Rocky Ridge. After one run-in with her mother, Lane unburdened herself in her journal: "It's amazing how my mother can make me suffer." Thinking back on her childhood, she wailed, "She made me so miserable when I was a child that I've never gotten over it."[19] Not surprisingly, the state of the mother-daughter bond varied inversely with the distance separating them. When Lane was far away from home, the two came to realize how much, in fact, they really did love each other and tended to forget the petty annoyances as well as the deep-seated strains and differences dividing them, which were only accentuated when they lived close by.

In "Laura Ingalls Wilder and Rose Wilder Lane: The Politics of a Mother-Daughter Relationship," Anita Clair Fellman provides an insightful analysis of the factors contributing to the mutual dependency that rendered the interactions of two such highly independent-minded individuals so volatile. The daughter, troubled by the experience of her mother's controlling behavior while she was a child growing up in the household and exasperated by her continuing efforts to bind her to Rocky Ridge even as she was moving into her fifth decade, bounced back and forth between feelings of love for and obligation to the older woman, on the one hand, and resentment toward and desire to escape from her domineering ways, on the other. Wilder, for her part, was proud of and admired her only child's evident success, sought and depended upon her literary advice and assistance, and wished for her to be happy and contented. But she also chafed at Rose's independent and unorthodox ways, wished her daughter would marry and raise a family, and longed for the time when she would be capable of taking care of her own literary business and not have to rely upon Rose to edit, revise, and market her work. Fellman describes the resultant mercurial relationship with a vivid metaphor: "The two women set up an elaborate dance in which Wilder both sought Lane's assistance with her writing and resisted it, and Lane helped with increasing ambivalence, trying to induce gratitude and guilt for the time and effort she expended. While Wilder never gave up either her expression of anxiety over the work she was causing her daughter or her hopes that she could do the writing wholly on her own, by the early 1930s she came reluctantly to accept her dependence upon Lane's editing."[20]

During the twenties and into the thirties, it was Lane who was the famous author in Mansfield, while her mother seemed to be being carried along on the coattails of her fame. Only later, as Wilder kept churning out new volumes every year or two and Lane abandoned fiction writing, did it begin to appear that the mother, rather than the daughter, was the primary literary achiever. The younger person had been playing the role of mentor, while the older one appeared as a usually appreciative, but sometimes resentful, trainee. Eventually, however, student surpassed teacher. Lane never openly accepted any credit for her mother's work. Wilder, for her part, never acknowledged that anyone else had been involved in the writing of her books. The two continued to maintain this fiction to the end. They had to engage in a complicated rigmarole when submitting material to and communicating with Lane's agent and with the publishing company in New York City so as to eliminate any evidence of Rose's heavy involvement in the production of the books. As late as 1949, Wilder was instructing George Bye to consign 10 percent of her royalties from the Little House books to her daughter, because she owed her "for helping me, at first, in selling my books and for the publicity she gave them." No mention was included of Lane's editing, revising, restructuring, and, in places, composing of significant sections of the books.[21]

Between 1931 and 1935, while working on Wilder's autobiography and on the first three books, the logistics of collaboration were fairly simple, with Lane occupying her parents' old farmhouse and they living on the other side of the hill in the new rock house that she had built for them in 1928. When Lane set aside her own projects to work on the Little House books, she and her mother were able to talk on the telephone any time they wanted, and during some stretches they got together almost every day over breakfast or tea to talk over strategy. Wilder's fourth book, *On the Banks of Plum Creek,* was finished mostly in 1936 after Lane had moved to Columbia to research her book about Missouri. That required that they work separately, communicating with each other by mail.

The collaborative process that they hammered out can be observed most directly in the many letters passing between them that have been preserved from the period in which they were working on *By the Shores of Silver Lake* during 1937 and 1938. By the time they began revisions on that book, Rose was living in the Grosvenor Hotel. Entering her seventies, Wilder discovered that trying to recall people and events from her childhood was becoming a harder and harder task. To help jog her memory, Lane sent some pages from her mother's "Pioneer Girl" manuscript, composed in 1930, and later she instructed George Bye to send her mother a copy of the entire manuscript. Wilder also used a book that her mother had compiled, consisting of fragments of poetry, songs, and other remembrances, to help trigger elusive memories. In addition, she wrote her sister Grace to inquire about the types of wildflowers they had known in Dakota Territory. She had already forgotten many of the things she had written about just seven years earlier. These kinds of devices and activities served as helpful reminders, but Wilder, aware of her fading capacities of memory, wrote her daughter that "the sooner I write my stuff the better."[22]

By then, the two had worked out a rather clear division of labor, although Wilder continued to hope that she could do more of the work on her own without as much intervention from her daughter. Lane was teaching her how to block out a book before beginning to write so that she could envision the final product and see how the parts fit together. That involved much more than Wilder simply sitting down and writing her recollections and then passing them along to Lane for typing up and revising. As she explained in a letter sent in August 1938, "The only way I can write is to wander along with the story, then rewrite and re-arrange and change it everywhere." By then, she had already composed ten chapters of a "first rough, very rough, draft" of "Hard Winter" (the title was later changed to "The Long Winter").[23] Clean, neat drafts of Wilder's books have been preserved in several libraries and archives. They obviously are her carefully handwritten copies, following upon one or more earlier drafts that she had composed in her standard five-cent tablets.

Mother and daughter had a number of issues to resolve as Lane began editing and revising *Silver Lake* toward the end of 1937. Most important was the question of how to begin the book. Wilder wanted to start it at the railroad depot in Tracy, Minnesota, as her family prepared to move to Dakota Territory in 1879. Lane thought it should begin earlier, with Aunt Docia's offer of a job for Pa on the railroad construction crew, so that readers could learn what had happened since the end of *On the Banks of Plum Creek* and about the circumstances of their departure from Minnesota. Lane also was having trouble discerning the central theme of the book: was it the building of the railroad and establishing towns along the line, or was it the homesteading process? Ultimately, the underlying challenge, as she read the manuscript, was structural. By reading carefully, word for

word, other writers' works, or even by copying one of her own previous books, Lane suggested, her mother could begin to get more of
a feel for the rhythm of language and for the structure of sentences,
paragraphs, and chapters. She suggested that "you will see that in
each paragraph there is a rhythm, a sort of broken-tune, underneath,
and that the chapters and the whole book have their rhythms, too."
Wilder's writing in general, she said, was "really lovely," but she
needed to keep working at structure, which was always a problem.[24]

Once Lane had typed up one of her mother's manuscripts, changing words and phraseology along the way, she would go over it with
a pen, making revisions, cutting things in places, adding in others,
inserting dialogue, sometimes rearranging the order of presentation.
Some of it required little more than light editing; in other places, she
constructed entire new scenes or added substantial chunks of material. She queried her mother on many points, trying to clarify facts,
to render the actions of characters understandable and consistent,
and to establish an appropriate tone. She wondered if the point of
view of *Silver Lake* in places was too adultish, and she worried that
there were sometimes too many characters or too few or that readers would not be able to sort them all out in their own minds. Wilder
was grateful for her daughter's close attention to her manuscripts
and for the diligent work that she put into revising them. But she also
stood her ground on many points, insisting that she knew what she
was writing about and that she was reporting what had happened
accurately.

In a letter to her daughter in January 1938, Wilder complained, "To
make the changes you want to make in Silver Lake, it will have to be
practically rewritten." Several paragraphs later, however, she indicated that she no longer cared what changes Lane made in the manuscript, and that her judgment might be best. Further on, frustration
rising again, she grumbled, "From what you wrote, I can't help but
think you didn't read my mss carefully."[25] A few days later, liking
Lane's idea for the beginning of the book less and less the more she
thought about it, Wilder wrote, "I am afraid I am going to insist that
the story starts as I started it."[26] On further consideration, however,
perhaps in acknowledgment of her daughter's superior professional experience as a writer, Wilder gave up: "Change the beginning of
the story if you want. Do anything you please with the dam stuff if
you will fix it up."[27] When the book was finally published, it began
the way Lane had originally suggested.

On most issues, Wilder willingly went along with her daughter's advice and the changes she made in the manuscript. She acknowledged that "without your fine touch, it would be a flop."[28] She wished that Lane did not have to spend so much time on her manuscripts, so that her daughter would have more time to work on her own projects. But since Wilder planned to finish the series with two more books—one about the hard winter of 1880–1881 and one entitled "Prairie Girl," leading up to her marriage to Almanzo in 1885—the task would soon be finished, she reassured Lane.[29] Things did not play out exactly that way, however. Lane probably spent more time on and did more work revising *The Long Winter* than any of the other books.[30] Meanwhile, Wilder realized that she would need more than one volume to finish the story, so "Prairie Girl" metamorphosed into *Little Town on the Prairie* and *These Happy Golden Years.*

Some of the books required more work than others, and, depending upon her circumstances at the time, Lane chose to do more detailed revisions on some of the books than on others. This led William Holtz in his 1993 biography of Lane, *The Ghost in the Little House,* to conclude that she deserved to be recognized as the ghostwriter of the books since she had done so much to revise them and get them into publishable form. Lane, in fact, had considerable experience at the task, having ghosted books for Frederick O'Brien, Lowell Thomas, and others. So she understood what the process involved.[31]

In granting so much credit to Lane, Holtz diminished Wilder's role in the process to one of simply providing the raw materials, including the major story line, for the volumes. She remained "a determined but amateurish writer to the end," he concluded. In his view, "Almost everything we admire about the Little House books—the pace and rhythm of the narrative line, the carefully nuanced flow of feeling, the muted drama of daily life—are created by what Mama Bess called Rose's 'fine touch,' as shining fiction is made from her mother's tangle of fact."[32]

While some readers accepted Holtz's interpretation, others balked, resisting especially the baldness with which he advanced his thesis. Those who examined varying drafts of the books and read the correspondence between mother and daughter readily acknowledged that Lane had played a major role in the process of producing the books. Most of them were ready to call the two "collaborators" on the books. Lane's major role in the project seemed manifest to all but die-hard Wilder fans who refused to believe that their heroine might not have written all of the books entirely by herself. But to reduce her role to that of a collector of stories and provider of raw facts that her daughter took and wove into compelling narratives went too far, in the views of most who weighed in on the controversy.

Caroline Fraser, writing in the *New York Review of Books*, emphasized that, in the absence of detailed evidence of exactly how the language of Wilder's handwritten drafts got transformed into the printed books, readers had to assume from available knowledge of conversations and letters between them while they were working on the last several books that this kind of interactive process occurred for all of the others, too. Fraser also questioned Holtz's contention that Lane was a far better writer than her mother, judging Wilder to have been capable of writing "descriptive and lyrical" prose while deeming Lane's output to have been often clichéd, hackneyed, and sentimental. In calling what occurred between mother and daughter a "collaboration," Fraser followed in the footsteps of William Anderson and Rosa Ann Moore, who had begun to detail how the division of labor had been worked out between the two.[33]

Since then, while most scholars who have weighed in on the subject continue to prefer describing the process as a collaborative one, others have opted for slightly different terminology. "Composite author" is the term preferred by Fred Erisman and Ann Romines, who also used the word *collaboration* to describe a procedure that allowed each to take advantage of strengths and qualities that neither was able to display in works produced on their own. Pamela Smith Hill's careful analysis of Wilder's writing career contends that Lane's role was actually that of a somewhat more active than usual "editor," reserving for Wilder the title of "author." Hill's background as a children's author provides her with an insider's detailed understanding of how the editorial process works in the field of children's books, and she makes a vigorous case for her contention that what Lane was doing was analogous to what energetic editors do all the time.[34] Having compared the published books with Wilder's original handwritten manuscripts and the various draft stages of the manuscripts that have been preserved, I remain struck by how often we simply cannot trace the development of initial draft to final product. Taking notice of the kinds of conversations that went on between the two in letters written while they were working on *On the Banks of Plum Creek*, *By the Shores of Silver Lake*, and *The Long Winter*, however, I continue to think that Lane's work on and the rewriting she did on the books went far beyond what typical editors normally do. This still does not lead me to think that what Lane did was to ghostwrite the books. What happened, in my opinion, constituted a true collaboration under unusual circumstances between a mother and daughter who each brought unique and complimentary talents to the task.

Defending his stance in an article titled "Ghost and Host in the Little House Books," Holtz provides a useful taxonomy of the range of positions that can be taken on the issue of how much Wilder and Lane respectively contributed to the writing of the books. With the spectrum ranging between light and heavy editing on one end to complete or partial ghosting on the other, he opts for a position somewhere in the latter category, where "the ghostwriter's function can, at best, be nothing less than a creative act." In so doing, he continues to argue for Lane's priority of authorship over that of Wilder.[35]

Until someone does a meticulous book-by-book analysis of the writing process utilizing a scheme that weighs the contribution of each author, I think the debate over "who wrote the books?" will remain at an impasse. Some of the questions worth further discussion include: In which books or sections of the books would Wilder's original penciled drafts be able to stand largely as written, with only light copyediting? Which books or sections of books received the most thorough rewriting? Which passages, paragraphs, or entire sections were probably contributed mainly or entirely by Lane? Which of them were likely discussed by Wilder and Lane before deciding upon a final text?

Taking into account the commentaries of William Holtz, William Anderson, Ann Romines, Anita Clair Fellman, Julia Ehrhardt, Pamela Smith Hill, and others, and based upon my own analysis of the manuscripts and book drafts, I offer the following tentative hypotheses: The first book and the last (*Little House in the Big Woods* and *These Happy Golden Years*) received the least amount of editing and rewriting and took the least amount of time to edit and revise. Lane was living in the Rocky Ridge farmhouse during the time that work was done on the first three books, so she and her mother would have gotten together frequently to discuss revising those manuscripts. Lane had moved to Columbia by the time she began to tackle the first draft of *On the Banks of Plum Creek* and was living in New York City or Danbury, Connecticut, during the rewrite phase of the final four volumes. Many letters between the two have been preserved delineating the discussions and frequent disagreements they had over revising four, five, and six. No letters have been discovered illuminating the process by which *Little Town on the Prairie* and *These Happy Golden Years* were edited. This raises the possibility that Lane may have made her revisions on those books with little input from her mother, although the final book in the series took less work than any other volume after the first. The published book stands very much like Wilder's original handwritten version; long sections and whole chapters follow her draft closely, with only a few words being changed.

On the other hand, *Farmer Boy* and *Little House on the Prairie* went through major rewrites from beginning to end, which was reflected in the amount of time that Lane spent in revising them. Some sections of *On the Banks of Plum Creek* read pretty much the way Wilder composed them, but other parts of the book are heavily rewritten. There are modifications all through *By the Shores of Silver Lake*, but for the most part they are minor ones; the text follows the original draft pretty closely. *The Long Winter* appears to be the most heavily rewritten book of all. In it, Lane no doubt was responsible for taking brief accounts of Almanzo Wilder and Cap Garland's dangerous journey out into the wintry countryside to buy wheat for the starving townspeople and the confrontation at Daniel Loftus's store over what to charge for it and for embellishing them into stories that were several times as long as in the original. As William Holtz notes in *The Ghost in the Little House*, Lane was responsible for the elaborated Fourth of July scene in *Little Town on the Prairie*, which stands out as a prime example of the series' conservative ideological slant.[36]

In sum, the basic narrative line of the books was almost completely Wilder's. Some of her writing was capable of standing by itself, with relatively light copyediting, one of the things that demonstrates, in my opinion, that she was more than just an amateurish writer. Lane often expanded, embellished, rearranged, added dialogue to, dramatized, and, in some cases, constructed scenes, but the process was selective. Wilder was fully capable of lyric description, dialogue, and narration. She did not manage to do it consistently, however, and thus was deeply in debt to her daughter, a professional author and expert editor, for fixing up and improving the original drafts of her books. Having said that, trying to determine in many places whether Wilder's original version or Lane's modified one should be judged superior is largely a matter of taste.

The collaborative process was a developmental one in which the daughter, as teacher, sought to instruct the student, her mother, in how to go about writing and revising a work of fiction. It was a mutually beneficial interaction but also an often frustrating one, for the instructor knew a lot more about how to put words on a page in a logical, coherent, and interesting way, but as her mother's daughter she had also stood in a subordinate position her entire life. Yet by the time Lane started the project at age forty-four, she was already successful, famous, well connected in the publishing world, and possessed of skills and experience that her mother lacked. She also had once been financially well-off and retained the potential for earning a large income from her writing. The mother-daughter relationship, alternating between feelings of affection and resentment, had been highly charged from the very beginning, and the frustrations of working together on their big project during the thirties and forties only heightened the potential for conflict. Yet both understood how much each had to gain by their collaboration. "When I go to count up our comfortableness and the luck of the world we have[,] it all leads back to you," Wilder gratefully wrote in January 1939. "Oh Rose my dear, we do thank you so much for being so good to us."[37]

Both writers insisted upon the complete factual accuracy of all of the stories in the Little House series.[38] They went to elaborate lengths to pin down facts and names, places and distances, foods and clothing, wildflowers growing on the prairies, and building construction techniques. Yet from the start, in producing the novels, mother and daughter manipulated facts, changed dates and the names and ages of some people, combined characters, and rewrote history, all in the interest of art. To the degree that they convinced themselves that the stories they were telling were totally true, they were simply kidding themselves. Letters back and forth between mother and daughter after Rose moved away from Mansfield make clear that they both were very well aware of the fact that what they were producing was not history, but fiction.

While not being totally factual or historical then, Wilder's stories were authentic in an important sense. Based upon her own personal experience half a century earlier, they had the ring of truth about them. This struck a deep chord in the minds of the popular author's readers. Placing her own story inside that of her family's, she created a familiar space within which her readers could feel comfortable. Furthermore, by setting her stories on the post–Civil War frontier, carrier of some of the most resonant mythical themes in American culture, she extended her appeal to one of the widest audiences there is for popular literature.

What makes these stories so compelling is not only their basis in fact, which undergirds their realism, and in myth, which touches the emotions, but also their grounding in hope, optimism, and courage, which support their idealism. Wilder instinctively fused realism and idealism, appealing to the heart as well as the head, evoking emotions of fear, joy, love, and affection in stories that, when they were read, could make people think, "This is real!" It is possible to deconstruct these stories as much as we want. For example, we know that in real life Wilder's mother, who in the books thought that working in the fields with men was uncivilized, in fact did help her husband with field labor, when necessary, as did most farm women at the time. We know that Nellie Oleson, one of the most memorable characters in the Little House series, was an amalgam of three actual people—Nellie Owens, Genevieve Masters, and Stella Gilbert. We know that during the hard winter of 1880–1881 the Ingalls family, which was described as living all alone in *The Long Winter,* had a young family living with them, consisting of a husband, wife, and little baby.[39] But this should not concern us overmuch, because once we understand that these stories, while based on actual people, places, and events, are not simple autobiography but rather are autobiographical fiction, we can read behind the words to discover the core truth that is situated there. Something solid remains.

The division of labor that existed between mother and daughter contributed mightily to the appeal of the books. The factual grounding of the narratives—the quotidian details and rituals of family life, the artifacts of farm and home, the routines of farm labor and household chores, and the skeletal chronology of the family's wanderings from place to place throughout the Midwest—derived primarily from the imperfect memory of the books' primary author, Laura Ingalls Wilder. Many of the rhetorical flourishes, some of the more lyrical passages describing the landscape and the weather, much of the dialogue, and a large amount of elaboration of scenes and episodes in the narrative were contributed by her daughter, Rose.

What Lane longed to achieve as a novelist, but never quite managed to attain, was the kind of authenticity that came so naturally to her mother. Part of Lane's despair during the 1930s resulted from the dawning recognition that most of her own work derived from secondhand experience, not the kind of lived experience that her mother was able to transform into fiction. Lane was able to observe and write about her Missouri Ozarks neighbors, but lacking any solid connection to them or much real appreciation for the kinds of lives they led, the stories that she wrote were often satirical, superficial, or inauthentic. Even the stories in *Old Home Town,* deriving from her own girlhood in Mansfield, were written by a woman who felt herself cut off from and not truly a part of the society that she was describing.

Lane, brilliant woman that she was, had grown up as an only child, more intelligent than any of her schoolmates, and she never really felt comfortable with most of the rural, small-town Ozarkians among whom she lived. She found it difficult to truly connect with people living around her. She came to realize that her work lacked a solid foundation in human reality. Ironically, her best works—*Let the Hurricane Roar* and *Free Land*—were based not on her own material but on stories passed on to her by her parents. During the 1940s and 1950s, her intellectual wandering finally came to rest on what she perceived to be the solid ground of right-wing political ideology. After 1938, she never returned to writing fiction.

In the end, the lasting literary legacy remains that of the mother more than that of the daughter. Lane's main literary accomplishment was the contribution that she made to her mother's novels. Lane possessed style; Wilder had substance. Lane led the more exciting life, at least on the surface, traveling all over the world and becoming acquainted with and making friends with people ranging from Sinclair Lewis and Dorothy Thompson to Mary Margaret McBride, Fremont Older, and Clarence Day. But her mother, in a way, had the more interesting life. Life to her played out as moral drama. It was, nevertheless, a complex drama; it could not be reduced to simple political formulas. Lane lived in her head, her thinking ruled by abstract categories; Wilder lived concretely in a world inhabited by real people and difficult moral dilemmas. Wilder's world may have seemed dull and prosaic to some sophisticates, but the stories that she enshrined in her books thrilled her readers. Lane, who tended to see the world in black-and-white terms and who constantly vented her acerbic judgments about other people, often failed to perceive the nuances and the deep dilemmas that inhere in human experience. Wilder, who better recognized moral complexity, drawing her sustenance from the Bible and its reminders of the potential for good and evil in everyone, in the end exerted the greater moral authority. Luckily for us, that moral authority, combined with literary talent and the experienced editorial skill of her daughter, resulted in the Little House series that continues to inform and delight us today.

II

Place

What Attracted Wilder and Lane to Little Houses?

The decade of the Great Depression, which launched Laura Ingalls Wilder's Little House series as well as saw the publication of Rose Wilder Lane's most important novels, bore powerful witness to the significance of place and home in people's lives. Among the indelible images of the thirties were those of Dorothea Lange's migrant mother, John Steinbeck's wandering Joad family, homeless unemployed waiting in soup lines, hoboes riding the rails, Bonus Army veterans bunkered down in the nation's capital, and countless shantytown Hoovervilles in cities and towns across America. Only when people have lost their home can they fully appreciate the comfort and security it affords. In the broadest sense, the American people during the dark days of the Great Depression were searching for a safe harbor from the privations, challenges, and terrors of the economic debacle that had occurred. People hungered for home—for a place where they could find safety and succor.

"'Place' is one of the trickiest words in the English language, a suitcase so overfilled one can never shut the lid," architectural historian Dolores Hayden has written. American novelist and short-story writer Eudora Welty, whose stories were set mostly in the

South, instinctively understood the power of place. "It is by the nature of itself that fiction is all bound up in the local," she writes in *The Eye of the Story.* "The internal reason for that is surely that *feelings* are bound up in place. The human mind is a mass of associations—associations more poetic than actual." Of all the arts, literature is most closely bound to its sources in particular localities. "The truth is, fiction depends for its life on place. Location is the crossroads of circumstance, the proving ground of 'What happened? Who's here? Who's coming?'—and that is the heart's field," Welty observes.[1] Nowhere are these observations truer than in the case of Laura Ingalls Wilder's Little House books. Each one, at its own level of sophistication and targeted audience, is very much tied to place and historical context. This is not to say that the books are geographically or historically accurate in all of their details, but it is to suggest that their characters, settings, and plots emerged naturally out of the remembered life of their author.

For Wilder, place provided the basic backdrop for telling the story of her childhood and adolescence up to the time of her marriage at age eighteen and moving out to the little house her husband had built for them on his tree claim. In making the houses that her family had lived in while she was growing up so central to the construction of her narratives, Wilder was following the practice of all genres of children's literature, as described by Pauline Dewan—spinning out stories of home. The home, she asserts, is "a child's first universe."[2] The enduring popularity of the children's novels Wilder wrote derives heavily from the images of houses and homes that occupy a central position in them as well as from the geographical progression of her family as it is chronicled in the series.

Her daughter, Rose Wilder Lane, left her childhood home as soon as she could and by the time she was forty had lived on each coast and traveled all over Europe and the Near East. For several years she became obsessed with making her home in the tiny, remote country of Albania and invested considerable emotional energy in contemplating building a pretentious dream house there. Though highly successful in the world of popular magazine and novel publishing during the 1920s and 1930s, she grew increasingly frustrated with her failure to find a subject of substantial significance to which she could tie her writing and build her reputation. Much of failure resulted from her inability to root her fiction in geographical locations that possessed a commanding resonance corresponding to that of her mother's.

There are many directions one could take in writing about place in the lives and writing careers of Wilder and Lane. One could trace their moves and their travels, the places where they made their homes, the locations in which they set their stories, the social milieus in which they lived and about which they wrote, and a dozen other topics. In this section I hone in on a topic of particular interest, the profound emotional reverberations of home and houses—in particular, "little houses"—in their lives and writings.

Homes, beyond their more practical, mundane functions, serve as metaphors, according to architectural historian Gwendolyn Wright, "suggesting and justifying social categories, values, and relations." Culture intersects with place, and the dwellings people inhabit are signifiers of their most deeply held values, their internal form being influenced by social, religious, and political traditions. "Houses are shaped not just by materials and tools, but by ideas, values, and norms," writes Daphne Spain. "They should not be regarded simply as utilitarian structures, but as 'designs for living.'"[3] This chapter reminds us of the power of home, and of place in general, in literature and in people's lives.

3

The Place of "Little Houses" in the Lives and Imaginations of Laura Ingalls Wilder and Rose Wilder Lane

In the fictional reconstructions of her childhood that we call the Little House books, Laura Ingalls Wilder always identified emotionally more with her westering "Pa"—he of the itchy foot who always seemed ready to move on to the next location, expecting it to be better than where they were—than with her patient, home-oriented "Ma," who took responsibility for establishing a pleasant, happy, cooperative atmosphere within whatever little house the family happened to be occupying at the moment. Trotting out the symbolic china shepherdess and placing it on its bracket on the wall was always the sign that the family had really arrived in a place and was ready to get on with business.[1] Thus, it is with some irony that we learn of Wilder's enduring fascination with and strong emotional commitment to building houses and simultaneously making them happy homes where people could live meaningful and constructive lives. The adventurous and freedom-loving spirit she attributed to her fictional character "Laura" in her frontier novels she kept largely suppressed as an adult woman, Laura Wilder, transmuting the impulse into strong commitments to personal autonomy and freedom from government control. Doubly ironic is the fact that her daughter, Rose Wilder Lane, who carried her libertarian political convictions to a more extreme level, was just as heavily devoted to houses and building, making them a central element of her daydreams, some of which she actually implemented. For both mother and daughter, we can confidently say, the notion of place occupied a key role in their thinking and everyday actions. Simultaneously, they were also more than commonly historically minded, carrying this inclination over into their writing, just as they did with their fascination for houses.

By the time of her marriage to Almanzo Wilder at age eighteen, Laura Ingalls had lived in more than a dozen houses in half a dozen different places, ranging from log cabins, a dugout, a store building, and a hotel to rented rooms and houses, claim shanties, and more substantial houses. As a married woman during the last seventy-two years of her life, she would inhabit at least eight more dwellings, finally ending up in the farmhouse she and Almanzo built at Rocky Ridge and of which they were so proud. As important as the little houses she had lived in as a girl were for her in plotting the books that she later wrote about her youth, the houses she lived in while writing the books during her sixties and seventies were equally important to her. Their construction and the roles they played in her life, as well as in the life of her daughter, Rose, were equally telling with regard to what kinds of persons they were and what kinds of values and aspirations they adhered to.

Wilder greatly enjoyed living in the distinctive but unostentatious two-story frame house that she and Almanzo had built and expanded over a period of almost two decades after arriving in Mansfield in 1894. Starting as a small log house with a fireplace but no windows, it was added onto several times and finally completed with a major construction project between 1911 and 1913. There had appeared to be little to recommend either the land or the house when they purchased the property. To Almanzo it looked quite rough in comparison with what he had been used to in South Dakota, but Laura took a fancy to it, confident that it could be made into a pretty place. "It needed the eye of faith," she wrote many years later in the *Missouri Ruralist*, "to see that in time it could be made very beautiful."[2] Like her daughter, she was an incurable romantic; the potential of a thing mattered as much as the reality.

In an article published in the *Ruralist* in 1911, Wilder described her and her husband's expansion and improvement of the farm. The first thing they did was to add twenty acres of apple trees to what had already been planted on the only four acres of cleared land on the place. Other fields were later cleared for planting corn, wheat, and oats; rocks were picked; and grass seed was sown to make pastures and meadows for a little herd of cows. Laura, meanwhile, built up her flock of chickens, in the process earning a reputation as an expert on their care. The couple also harnessed water from the five springs located on the property in order to build a three-acre lake and to pipe water into the house, the barn, and the chicken houses. Over time they also planted strawberries, grapes, and other fruits, vegetables, and crops. Contemplating what she and her husband had accomplished, in spite of many obstacles and hardships, Wilder marveled, "I can hardly bring back to my mind the rough, rocky, brushy, ugly place that we first called Rocky Ridge Farm. The name given it then serves to remind us of the battles we have fought and won and gives a touch of sentiment and an added value to the place."[3]

Building and paying for Laura's dream house on Rocky Ridge proved no easier than was the expansion of and paying off of the mortgages on their farm property. Cash income was difficult to come by during the early period, especially during the time the country went through an economic depression during their first four years in Missouri. In 1898, the couple decided to move into town and rent a small, one-story house, where Laura could serve meals to boarders and Almanzo could operate a draying business and later on an oil distributorship. An inheritance from Almanzo's father enabled them to buy the house. Not until around 1910 did they move back to the farm, and during the next several years, with money obtained from the sale of their house in town and the help of some hired labor, they finished their improvements on the farmhouse. Laura had put considerable thought into what she wanted her dream house to be, and now she drew up plans for a two-story structure with ten rooms, four porches, a fireplace, and a library. Especially dear to her were the native stone fireplace and two large picture windows in the parlor looking to the south over the countryside. The cabinets and counters in the kitchen were built to accommodate her diminutive height—four feet, eleven inches—leading the house in that regard to have a rather miniature feel to it. Once completed, the home gained a reputation as something of a showplace in the area.[4]

For Wilder, Rocky Ridge farm and the substantial, self-designed, and (at least in part) personally built farmhouse where she and her husband lived constituted a major part of her identity. It symbolized the success they had achieved up to that time and their triumph over poverty as well as their inventiveness, industriousness, willpower, and goal-orientation. Designed for living in a practical and comfortable manner, it provided the couple not only with a pleasant workplace and a cozy respite for relaxation and enjoyment but also with a welcoming, cheery atmosphere that invited in friends, neighbors, and guests for a friendly chat, pot of coffee, or place to meet. Brief "Local Items" in the *Mansfield Mirror* noted the frequent card parties, get-togethers, and women's club meetings that were held there. When Lane returned to live at Rocky Ridge in 1924 and 1925 and again between 1928 and 1935, she frequently invited writer friends to stay there with her for a time. At one point in 1929, the place took on the appearance of a little writers' colony, with Helen Boylston, Genevieve Parkhurst, Catherine Brody, and Lane herself all working away on their current projects during the daytime and setting them aside to engage in enthusiastic conversation over dinner and late into the evening. At other times, writer friends such as Dorothy Thompson or Guy Moyston stopped over to stay for a few days or a few weeks.[5]

Just as memories of the little houses where she had lived while growing up inspired much of what Wilder later wrote in her Little House novels, the house on Rocky Ridge served as the subject for two of the earliest published pieces she produced for a national audience. Lane's success in helping her mother write and place "Whom Will You Marry?" in *McCall's* magazine in 1919 had not been duplicated afterward, but six years later she again collaborated with her, this time on stories that got taken by the popular *Country Gentleman*. The articles on rooms in the farmhouse—"My Ozark Kitchen" and "The Farm Dining Room"—would be of interest to homemakers who wanted to spruce up their own homes. A professional photographer came in to take pictures of the rooms for illustration purposes, and Lane revised the pieces before they were shipped off to the editor. She assured her mother, who protested that she had put too much work into changing them, that her part in the project had amounted to no more than an "ordinary rewrite job."[6] The articles were thick with detail, just like the descriptions Wilder would later compose concerning the construction of the family's cabin in Kansas in *Little House on the Prairie* and with regard to the appearance of the rooms in the surveyors' shanty in *By the Shores of Silver Lake*. They reflected the huge pride she took in the house she had helped plan and build and the emotional significance she attached to it.

Wilder's life and identity were very much caught up in her position as an equal partner with her husband in owning, managing, and working on Rocky Ridge farm and as an active citizen of a small town in the Missouri Ozarks. The multiple roles she occupied in these highly concrete and complex places—as housewife, neighbor, friend, expert on raising chickens, churchgoer, farm loan executive, women's club organizer and participant, politician, and farm journalist—all emanated from the opportunities, constraints, expectations, and demands associated with them. Author Louise Erdrich pondered the power that one's sense of place has on a writer. "I've never been able to describe it as well as . . . Isak Dinesen [when she wrote], . . . 'Here I am, where I ought to be.' . . . A writer must have a place where he or she feels this, a place to love and be irritated with," observes Erdrich. "It is difficult to impose a story and a plot on a place. However, truly knowing a place forms the suggestive basis for every kind of linking circumstance. Location, whether it is to abandon it or draw it sharply, is where we start."[7]

Place is where Wilder began with her writing. For almost a decade and a half between 1911 and 1924 and especially after 1915, she drew heavily upon her extensive knowledge of and close relationship with the farming community in and around Rocky Ridge to write her semimonthly columns in the *Missouri Ruralist*. Forty-four years old when she started writing them, in two decades of living there she had absorbed much of Missouri Ozarks culture and felt comfortable writing about its people, customs, and peculiarities. In 1918, the farm newspaper's editor, John F. Case, wrote admiringly of her, "Mrs. Wilder has lived her life upon a farm. She knows farm folks and their problems as few women who write know them. And having sympathy with the folks whom she serves she writes well."[8]

During the early 1930s, however, when she began writing fiction, the setting for her stories would not be her adopted Ozarks but rather the midwestern farming frontier on which she had grown up as a child. This was not the result of a conscious and deliberate plan on her part, for her beginning as a novelist came quite accidentally. But it undoubtedly was to her advantage to be writing about a place she felt emotionally tied to, despite its remoteness in time, rather then a place she may have felt comfortable living in but not entirely connected to. There remained a certain emotional distance between Wilder and the people among whom she was living. There was always a slight hint of superiority, priggishness, stand-offishness—call it what you will—that emanated from her person and which people in Mansfield could detect to the end of her days. Her insistence on dressing up when going into town, her writing for a farm newspaper headquartered in Kansas City and later in Topeka, and her daughter's exploits as a world traveler and member of the national literati all clearly set her apart, to some degree, from the people around her. Perhaps more to the point, she had grown up inside a stream of northern culture, with roots in New England, as reflected in her family's membership in the Congregational Church. Without a local congregation of that denomination available in Mansfield, she and Almanzo had affiliated with the Methodists, not a bad match for them, but still something different from what they had been familiar with. In a broader sense, all down the line she had been forced to adapt to a new environment in Missouri, one dominated by people deriving from Tennessee, Kentucky, Virginia, and North Carolina rather than from the New England stream of migration across the northern Midwest in which she had grown up as a child.[9]

All of this may help explain why writing about her childhood turned out to be a better choice for her as a novelist than writing stories based upon her experiences in southern Missouri as an adult would have been. During the twenties and thirties, Lane churned out short stories and novels about the "hillbilly" culture surrounding them in Mansfield, but while highly marketable and in many ways engaging and entertaining, they were incapable of earning for her the kind of respectful literary reputation for which she so desperately longed. Having grown up in the area and moved away at age seventeen, she was in—but not of—the Ozarks. Unlike her mother, who identified closely with the people in Dakota among whom she had grown up, Lane felt scant connection with most of the Ozarks residents she took as subjects for her literary work.

Lane never felt fully at home anywhere she lived; in some ways she always remained a fish out of water. Spending her last year of high school with relatives in Crowley, Louisiana, and then quickly moving to Kansas City to take up telegraphy, she wound up in California, the quintessential magnet for wanderers. After the Great War, as she entered upon her thirties, she traveled extensively through Europe and the Near East, developing an unusually deep fascination for Albania and a compelling desire to settle there and build a house that she could make her home. Back in Mansfield living with or near her parents for long stretches of time, this world traveler wound up writing fiction largely centered on stories inspired by the local Ozarks residents. Considerable irony attends the fact, therefore, that her mother, who lived contentedly in a fixed location for the last sixty-three years of her life, should have centered her fiction around her family's constant bouncing around on the frontier in search of a better life, while Lane, who had traveled extensively all over the world, spent much of her time writing about people who often had not ventured more than fifty miles from their native counties.

Perhaps just because Wilder felt so comfortably fixed at Rocky Ridge (even though financial worries would dog her and Almanzo until increasing royalties from her books eased their concerns) and because her family's frequent moves during her childhood had represented their unsettled condition and a search for a permanent home, Wilder placed special importance upon the dwellings the family occupied during their travels (or travails). Two of her Little House books (both of the first two written about her family of birth) had "little house" in their titles. *On the Banks of Plum Creek,* about their time in Walnut Grove, Minnesota, starts with their most unusual dwelling, a dugout built into the bank of Plum Creek. *By the Shores of Silver Lake* revolved around the family's stay during their first winter in Dakota Territory in the surveyors' shanty and then Pa's search for a suitable homestead and the building of a claim shanty on the property for the family to live in. Most of *The Long Winter* is about how the family's home (Pa's store building in De Smet) during the terrible blizzards of 1880–1881 literally represented the difference between destruction and survival. In the last two books in the series, the fictional Laura learned about other people's houses; one of them, classmate Ben Woodworth's, was in the second story of the railroad depot. At the end of the final volume, the couple got married and drove off to live in the cozy little house Almanzo had built for them on his tree claim a mile north of town. Ann Romines identifies the Little House series' central motif as "the invention, abandonment, and perpetuation of a series of . . . houses. In large part Wilder tells the autobiographical story of her childhood and adolescence through a plot of housing."[10]

The story of Wilder's childhood provided a ready-made narrative outline for the Little House series that she wrote during her old age.

She relied upon memory for writing her autobiography "Pioneer Girl" in 1930, and then drew upon that source, expanding and elaborating the story to construct her children's novels. The first three books (excluding *Farmer Boy*), about her family's experiences in Wisconsin, Kansas, and Minnesota, centered on their continuous moving around in search of an established home. The last four, set in De Smet, Dakota Territory, increasingly focused upon how community was created through the meeting of difficult challenges and the playing out of a variety of activities in a single place. Inevitably, the locus of the action shifted outward as time went by, progressing from inside the home that the family occupied at the time to engage with the broader community outside the home, as it developed in schools, churches, stores, places of entertainment, ceremonial events, railroad depots, printers' shops, neighbors' homes, and other places. For Wilder and for people living elsewhere on the midwestern prairies and plains, as well as for those who have written about them, place carried importance. Thus it should not be surprising that the subject also figured prominently in her writing. Fred Erisman notes that "the books provide more than autobiography. They provide, in addition, what one critic has called a 'compelling power of place.'"[11]

In putting place at the center of her writing, Wilder resembled other midwestern authors before and after her, as Diane Quantic and others have ably demonstrated.[12] Much of the power of Wilder's work derives from her detailed descriptions of clouds, sunsets, prairie expanses, and other landscape features as well as of the intimate particulars of the contents of people's houses. Beyond the surface features that are mentioned, what draws readers to these stories are the feelings and emotions invoked by the symbolism and meaning that are attached to places. Much of this process is conscious, but a good deal of it also works subconsciously, both in the reader and in the writer. Cultural geographer Yi-Fu Tuan explains the affective bond that exists between people and the places or settings to which they are exposed. Using the term *topophilia* to refer to this connection, he indicates that while varying considerably in intensity, subtlety, and form of expression, it carries considerable force. Also, as Wilder would certainly have been quick to agree, awareness of the past plays an important role in the love of place. The nostalgia her novels stimulated in many readers involved both a sort of homesickness (the original meaning of *nostalgia* derives from the Greek *nostos,* meaning "return to the native land," and *algos,* referring to pain) and a bittersweet yearning for a lost time.[13]

Integral to human perception and understanding of place is the tendency of the brain to break things down into binary oppositions, such as large-small, up-down, inside-outside, good-bad, happy-sad, warm-cold, light-dark, friendly-threatening, and so forth.[14] One of the central organizing themes of the Little House series is the way in which the action takes place either inside or outside the house. Inside connotes warmth, safety, coziness, family togetherness, happiness, and simplicity. Outside suggests coldness, threat, danger, worry, and complexity. Fires, fiddles, stories, conversation, games, visitors, meals, and china shepherdesses are to be found inside; storms, blizzards, grasshoppers, wolves, robbers, and Indians all lurk outside. Inside is the women's and children's world; outside is the province of men. Inside is private; outside is public. Inside is fixed and immobile; outside suggests movement and travel. Houses thus represent far more than a physical presence. They serve to "mediate social relations," Daphne Spain suggests, and provide "the spatial context within which the social order is reproduced."[15]

These dichotomies do not lend themselves to simple attributions of value in terms of good or bad. While the fictional young Laura appreciates and extols the benefits of being inside, safe from the threats and dangers that lurk outside, she also longs for the freedom, the possibilities, and the excitement involved in playing outside in the meadow and the creek, riding on fast horses and in fast buggies, meeting interesting strangers and visiting exciting places, and looking forward to travel and the next sight over the horizon. The boundaries or borders that separate one place from another are not necessarily fixed, and the interpretations placed upon them often are flexible and ambivalent. The house that is one person's refuge can be another person's trap.[16] Happy homes are not universal; witness the knife-wielding Mrs. Brewster, during the time when Laura taught at the Brewster school, and the nasty business that took place in Mr. Clancy's house, where Laura worked sewing shirts.[17]

How people arrange and organize the spaces in which they live and work is hugely important in determining the quality of their lives. More than two millennia ago, Hippocrates connected people's well-being with their surroundings. "Throughout history," Winifred Gallagher writes, "people of all cultures have assumed that environment influences behavior. Now modern science is confirming that our actions, thoughts, and feelings are indeed shaped not just by our genes and neurochemistry, history, and relationships, but also by our surroundings." In *The Experience of Place,* Tony Hiss notes that "the organization of space organizes people's experiences and much of their behavior—including, startlingly, whether they feel that they are allowed to interact with one another and with their surroundings, and whether they will assume responsibility for maintaining some part of the places they use." In their insightful study, *A Pattern Language,* architect Christopher Alexander and his associates identify various spatial and architectural elements that help people feel joyful and alive.[18]

In the little houses in which Laura Ingalls Wilder lived as a child, the close environment necessitated by their diminutive size certainly conduced to togetherness and joyfulness within the family. With no possibility for separate rooms for everyone and no money available for filling them with many consumer goods, the family was forced in upon itself, required to make its own entertainment and much of its own food and clothing, and by necessity constantly getting in each other's way. Performing chores, eating, visiting with friends, singing songs, playing games, and reading and telling stories were the order of the day. For Wilder, both as a child, whose memories provided the basis for her later books, and as an adult, who lived a full and active life at her beloved Rocky Ridge, place was generally a unifying force, binding people together by ties of common perceptions, beliefs, and emotions.

But individual places do not evoke the same emotions and responses in everyone. Eudora Welty reminds us, "There must surely be as many ways of seeing a place as there are pairs of eyes to see it. The impact happens in so many different ways."[19] Rose Wilder Lane had spent her years from seven to eleven on the farm and then lived in town while going to school until moving to Louisiana at age sixteen to complete her senior year of high school. Thus she could claim to be a "Missouri girl" and later added to her experience in the state by living at Rocky Ridge for almost a decade during the 1920s and 1930s. But unlike her parents, who had grown familiar with Missouri customs and mores and loved their farm and home at Rocky Ridge, Lane could not stand the place. She filled diary and journal entries and scores of letters to friends with fervent laments about her inability to fulfill her fondest dream—to remove herself as far away from Mansfield as quickly as possible. Her alienation from the place probably was not conducive to writing great literature about it, although national magazines gobbled up virtually anything she wrote that was set in the region, paying up to $1,200 a story for them and in the case of one serialized novel *(Cindy)* $10,000.[20] Lane never felt fully comfortable living in Mansfield. Ozarkians may have made likely subjects for her fiction or objects for investigation and interpretation, but few of them qualified, in her view, as candidates for real friendship or comradeship on an equal footing. Rose was too much the sophisticated cosmopolitan—traveled, well-read, and worldly-wise—for that.

Lane returned to Rocky Ridge twice out of a feeling of obligation to her aging parents and because they—especially her mother—frequently begged her to come back and live with them there. But in the steady stream of letters she sent to friends in New York, San Francisco, and elsewhere, she frequently complained about the wretchedness of the place, its uninteresting people, the oppressive environment, and her continual boredom. The farmhouse that her parents enjoyed so much and of which they were so proud she referred to, somewhat playfully, as a "peasants' hut" in a letter to her New York friends Berta and Elmer Hader. Another friend and sometime love interest, playwright Guy Moyston, seemed to receive the brunt of her complaints, delivered up in long typewritten letters, postmarked Mansfield: "This is the most awful place to write letters from. I think I've remarked before, somewhere, that nothing happens here?" (April 12, 1925); "I have never been nearer sheer insanity" (January 23, 1926); and so on. With her back on the farm for a second tour of duty in 1930, her diary entries expressed her pain: "This life is really nauseating" (January 30); "I feel as blue as the devil" (February 14); "So horribly blue that dying seems like a relief" (March 30); "I am a failure and a fool. Why was I such a fool as to get into this mess?" (July 29). But most of her diary entries recorded mundane everyday activities, such as playing chess and bridge, going out to dinner, watching movies, witnessing fox hunts, taking her parents on shopping trips, attending court sessions, and visiting friends. Between times, she sometimes could say things like, "Very happily engaged all day making salad and sandwiches for the bridge club meeting" (March 19); and "I feel optimistically ambitious" (May 1).[21] As the economic depression encompassing the country deepened, her despair intensified along with it.

Lane's dream was to get away and build her own house—one that would express herself and allow her to do the kinds of things she had always wanted to do. Writing from Rocky Ridge in May 1925, she let Guy Moyston in on her vision: "Some day, Oh God, I shall have my own house, my own hours, my own selfishly egoistic way about everything. And there shall be a garden, two, six gardens. I love gardening. All of this is in that golden imaginary realm in which I'm not supping and sleeping with poverty. And probably never will happen."[22]

The following year, she was living again in Albania with her friend Helen Boylston, a former nurse who Rose helped get established in her writing career. Living in a rented house in Tirana, she began making plans for building a grandiose villa that would make the farmhouse at Rocky Ridge truly look like a peasant's hut in comparison. She drew sketches of it and went so far as to engage an architect to participate in the planning. Not surprisingly, Lane, who possessed a tendency for grand thinking, romantic imagining, and finding significance where others perceived none, fancied that her house "maybe—just maybe perhaps" was "being born beneath a lucky star." In the beginning, there had been her accidental meeting in 1920 with "Troub" (short for "Troubles," Boylston's nickname) on a train from Paris to Warsaw, occasioned by a French railway clerk's confusing their sleeping berth assignments. In the memorable ensuing conversation with her new friend (not atypically, for Lane, it was said to have lasted "three days and nights, from Paris to Warsaw") she first learned of Albania from an eyewitness, Boylston having just come from there. It was later, in 1922, after visiting Albania and while traveling through Soviet Georgia, Lane recalled, that she had first realized her desire for an Albanian house. High in elevation, "It was like being quite alone on the roof of the world," she wrote her writer friend Clarence Day about her moving experience there. "But here there was only the sky, and a stillness made audible by the brittle grass. Emptiness was so perfect all around me that I felt a part of it, empty myself; there was a moment in which I was nothing at all— *almost* nothing at all. The only thing left in me was Albania. I said, I want to go back to Albania." She got into the car that had brought her there and turned to go back, "thinking that my house would be built on the shore near Durazzo, a house of clay-brick, plastered and whitewashed, its rooms built around courts, and some of the archways leading into walled gardens."[23]

In July 1926 Lane sent to Moyston a sketch of the house as she envisioned it, perched on a high precipice overlooking the Adriatic. The thick, high-walled complex sported a main courtyard sixty feet square and a swimming pool with sides half as long. Constructed in "pure Arab style," it was designed for defense, if necessary, as Lane anticipated war breaking out momentarily in the Balkans.[24] The elaborate, colonnaded living quarters included the main house around an inner courtyard, private apartments, servants' apartments and court, guests' apartments and court, a laundry court, and a large, walled garden. The proposed structure looked as much like a hotel as a house, and one has to wonder who Lane thought would use all the space and how she would ever pay for it. The whole thing smacked of megalomania, or maybe it was just another of her fanciful daydreams. It was all so outlandish as to make one wonder about her state of mind in dreaming it up.[25]

Lane herself seemed to understand the implications of her wild imaginings. In September 1927 she wrote Clarence Day, "Do you know—and this is just between you and me—I am beginning to think that Albania is a mistake. I mean, my living here indefinitely. It isn't that I don't love it as much as ever, because I do. It's the place to be happy in, for me. But I seem to go to pieces in it, to scatter, more than I used to elsewhere. Maybe I would, anyhow. But maybe it is Albania. Maybe the reason I like it is, that it's my natural tendency to disintegrate, and that it's a comfortably disintegrating place." Lane was struggling with a lack of purpose, a sense of emptiness. Perhaps that was what the house idea was all about subconsciously: an attempt to instill in her a sense of purpose and meaning in life. "I keep feeling that I must pull myself together, *collect* my energies, and *do something*. Not that there's anything special I want to do," she wrote.[26] The vacuum that she felt at the center of her being also related to her growing suspicion that the writing she was doing was mere hackwork, not worthy of her true capabilities. Within weeks, Lane was on her way home, back to Missouri, where she would remain living close by her parents for the next seven and a half years. She abandoned the grand plan for her Albanian dream home.

Her dream house's true meaning for her, as Julia Ehrhardt has suggested, consisted in its connection to her longing for personal freedom.[27] To her, the farmhouse at Rocky Ridge, from which she had so eagerly fled in early 1926 and to which, two years later, she was now returning, signified drudgery, boredom, dirt, stink, and, figuratively, prison bars. Yet she felt an obligation to return and assist her parents in their old age. For them, the house they had built up over the years by incredible effort and sacrifice meant something quite different—a place of activity, friendship, joy, and pride, as has already been discussed. The comparison can be extended.

For Laura and Almanzo, the Rocky Ridge farmhouse meant a place for family—for themselves and for their daughter. They wished to have her at home with them, although their ultimate desire was to have her "settle down," marry, and raise a family of her own, just as they had. Rose's dream house in Albania, on the other hand, was for her a personal thing—meant for her and for friends like Troub, who could talk intelligently about books, culture, politics, and world affairs. Lane had long before given up the idea of having a family of her own, determined to maximize her own personal freedom and to avoid marital entanglements.

For her parents, who were quite familiar with moving around, home meant a fixed abode—a refuge, representing stability, predictability, and safety. Among their Ozarks friends, they felt comfortable in being a part of the consensus, willing to break ranks on issues they felt strongly about but generally content to conform to established routines and expectations. Lane, on the other hand, conceived of her imaginary home in Albania as an escape from humdrum routine, making it a statement about her individualistic values and goals. For her, it represented novelty, exoticism, and rebelliousness. It allowed her to be herself and act out some of her fantasies. During the late twenties, moreover, she was feeling increasingly alienated from American culture and expressed a desire to physically escape it.

"I don't like The States because I don't like *The States*," Lane wrote Guy Moyston in February 1927. Perhaps it was a great civilization that people were building there, but they lacked a sense of history, a humane cast of mind, an appreciation for continuity, and a reflective capacity to appreciate quality when they saw it. "It's a civilization of electricity and steel, of movement, of change, a civilization of perception and reflex action in interplay, rapid, chaotic, formless," she commented. None of that appealed to Lane, who said that she did not feel at home in it. Why, she asked herself, should she live her life in what now felt like a foreign country "in a land and among a people with whom I've nothing in common, with whom I can't speak?" The Balkans, she said, provided a refuge in which she could feel comfortable.[28]

References she made to her planned house's "Arab style," along with her interest in Islamic culture, further reflected her inclination to distance herself from convention and received opinion. "The truth is, no doubt, that I must accustom myself to being homesick, wherever I am," she wrote Guy Moyston. "There are so many places that keep so much of me, that there isn't any one of them that can make me feel altogether at home anymore. If only I could make a nice little new world of my own, with only the people I want in it, and all the things I love in every place gathered together into one. . . . I am so greedy, my dear; I want too much. I am the monkey with his hand in the jar of sweetmeats. It isn't a particularly dignified or intelligent position."[29] Here Lane encapsulated succinctly what her projected Albanian house meant to her: a way for her to fabricate "a nice new little world of her own." Virginia Woolf's book *A Room of One's Own* (1929) was rather stridently feminist in its viewpoint, but one suspects that Lane's motives in wanting to design a house of her own were little connected with feminism. She was such an ardent individualist that the question of gender retained minor relevance for her. Her perspective was primarily personal: a wish to achieve maximum freedom for every individual, regardless of sex.

Perhaps the most obvious difference between Lane's ideal house and that of her parents was simply one of scale. Her image was grand and imposing, almost comic in its pretensions; theirs was modest and practical, in keeping with their belief in the virtues of small-scale farming and living, a philosophy Wilder elaborated upon in several of her *Missouri Ruralist* columns. Despite the many rooms, nooks, and crannies contained in its two-story floor plan, for many tourists who walk through the house today the first impression is one of its small scale in comparison to most modern houses, something that the Wilders designed into it.

Beyond outward appearances, however, Laura understood that a house contains a spirit dwelling within it that reflects the attitudes, values, and behaviors of the people who inhabit it. That was a major theme of the novels she would write later on, and it also shone through in some of the articles she published as a farm journalist: "We all know there is a spirit in every home, a sort of composite spirit composed of the thoughts and feelings of the members of the family as a composite photograph is formed of the features of different individuals. This spirit meets us at the door as we enter the home. Sometimes it is a friendly, hospitable spirit and sometimes it is cold and forbidding."[30] If friendliness, cheerfulness, hospitality, and helpfulness were values Wilder hoped to see incorporated in a house, her daughter was more interested in smartness, vitality, novelty, independence, and assertiveness. Most people's homes, to her way of thinking, were boring; to not be boring, the people in them would have had to be different from the ones she normally encountered in southern Missouri.

For Lane's parents, a house was a very mundane and ordinary structure that was designed for efficiency, practicality, and comfort. To be sure, it also was a place of beauty and reflected the owners' sense of who they were, but it need not be large, impressive, or exotic. For Lane, on the other hand, servants would be available to take care of lesser duties like meals, cleaning, and maintenance. Work there would be, but a different kind of work—that of writing great literature—and when that was set aside, conversing on great issues and matters of the day. Leisure, more than work, would be the primary activity of the occupants. Size and splendor, while not advertised overtly, were implicit in the structure itself. Lane's fantasy house was perhaps never meant to be built, but it served as dream work that could occupy Lane's hours when she was not writing. It was all part of her architectural bent, one that compelled her to imagine elaborate structures for living in and large, complicated writing projects that would secure her fame and fortune. "You know, I would be an entirely different woman if it weren't for the pernicious influence of houses," she wrote Fremont Older. "My intelligence sees their perniciousness clearly enough, but I have no character." It was statements like this that prompted Anita Clair Fellman to refer to "Lane's life-long fixation with houses."[31]

Finally, the house at Rocky Ridge was, in the thinking of its creators and owners, simply a place in which to live their lives and interact with neighbors and friends. Lane's imagined house in Albania, in contrast, seemed to be as much about generating material for her writing career as it was about living. A prolific producer of literary copy when she was working on what she considered to be interesting topics and was in good form, she frequently found herself drifting—casting about in search of new subjects to tackle. Although she was able to write a popular book, *Peaks of Shala* (1923), based upon her experiences in Albania, her focus while living in the country remained mostly upon writing "Ozark stories" and longer fiction based upon her experiences back in Missouri. She wrote them "to please the editors and get the checks." Beyond that, however, she looked at Albania as a potential source for story ideas and books that she could market through her agent, Carl Brandt. She hoped to get three books out of her stay in the country: "The Cave of Bulquis," "My Albanian Garden," and what she referred to as "the Scanderbag novel." The second one was directly related to the new house that she kept formulating in her mind, because gardens would form a major part of the complex when it was finished. Until that happened, however, she already had planted a garden at the place that she and Helen Boylston were renting and began keeping a detailed journal of everything she planted and how it was growing, day by day. Motivated by more than simply a wish to publish a book about her gardening experience, she noted another reason for her interest in it in a journal she titled "My Albanian Garden": "It is really the desire to capture something of my days, to hold to it, not to let everything escape, as everything does, and will."[32]

Lane suspected and began to fear that all her ruminations on her house project would come to naught and that her maladjusted cast of mind was ultimately to blame for it. "The world is too big for me to grasp and handle," she wrote in one journal entry. "I don't know anything about the world; about history or geography or philosophy. I don't know anything about any part of life, because I've never lived any of it; I've only muddled about in dreams. Does everyone muddle about in dreams?"[33]

By the end of 1927, Rose was ready to abandon her Albanian experiment and return to the United States, and gradually the dream of building a house on the Adriatic faded in her mind. But determined to show that she was more than a dreamer and compelled by some driving force in her psyche, she spent the better part of her first year back at Rocky Ridge actually building a house that she had decided to give to her parents as a present. The exercise proved therapeutic for her, because she was able to put aside her writing for a time and let her brain focus on nuts and bolts, beams and girders, chimneys and cabinets—something she had a knack for and greatly enjoyed doing. She demonstrated to herself and everyone else that beyond living a life of words and ideas and dreams, she could be very practical when she wanted to.

But her form of practicality was quite different from that of her parents, who were used to pinching pennies and making do with what was available. To outside observers, watching the new house go up on a plot across the hill from the Rocky Ridge farmhouse must have been an interesting experience, for few of them had seen anything like the structure that went up in front of their eyes, except perhaps in picture books. No standard Missouri farmhouse or Sears and Roebuck prefab was like this. Rather, Lane chose to build an English-style rock cottage and to outfit it with all of the latest features and accoutrements. Engaging an architect and a contractor in nearby Springfield and purchasing most of the construction materials from firms in the city, she avoided the route her parents had taken of building with indigenous materials and relying upon local carpenters and their helpers to figure out a workable floor plan and execute the details. The new house would be imported from outside rather than reliant upon local methods and materials. Just as with the Albanian project, it emanated from the dreams of Rose Wilder Lane. Only this time, it went into actual production rather than dying stillborn on the drawing board.

Lane threw herself into the project with gusto, driving back and forth frequently to Springfield; personally selecting materials, appliances, and furnishings; and working with the architect and contractor every step of the way to make sure that everything was done to her specifications.[34] Since she possessed firm ideas about how to proceed and felt flush financially, what with the $10,000 book paycheck she had recently earned and the splendid record of her investments with the Palmer Company, she didn't worry about it when the estimated expense of the project continually escalated as the work proceeded. Originally expected to cost $4,000, the rock cottage eventually wound up costing her approximately $11,000, a huge sum of money at the time. Trying to account for her intense interest in the project and the amount of energy and time she was devoting to it, she explained, "Houses are my vice; I simply can't take 'em or leave 'em alone. But for houses, I know it well, I'd be much more profitable to everyone, including me. This is my 18th habitation, made or re-made, including some apartments. But I can't seem to help it. Every so often my imagination goes off on a house-jag, and there's nothing to be done about it. I can't think in terms of plot and color and character when I'm thinking in terms of plumbing, sheet-metal work, stresses and perspectives."[35]

One thing she apparently failed to do was ask her parents if they actually wanted a new house. It seems obvious now what their answer would have been, since they had built their farmhouse, in part, with their own hands, paid for it with the sweat of their brows, immensely enjoyed living in it, and took enormous pride in it. Nor would they wait long to move back into it once their daughter finally moved away from Missouri for good several years later. But now Lane got it into her head that they needed a new house, that this would be beneficial to them and a gesture of her love and devotion to them, and that she knew what was best for them. Unstated but implicit in this reasoning was one other little fact: that she was planning to take over their old farmhouse once they moved out of it. If there is any record of her presenting her parents with a choice in the matter, none has been found. When her mother discovered what was afoot, she decided to wait until the house was completed before inspecting it or stepping inside it. Undoubtedly, despite Lane's good intentions in seeking to improve the lives of her parents, this was another example of her effort—whether conscious or unconscious—to exert a measure of control over them.

In that, she was ultimately likely to fail, and Wilder's response upon first viewing the new house in December 1928 supports the notion. Lane, who had been expectantly awaiting her mother's reaction, recorded in her diary, "Mama Bess delighted." But a little later, in a letter to Fremont Older, she told the story somewhat differently: "Certainly I should have thrilled all over when my mother walked into the new house. I expected to, and would have done, but for a strange but unexpected turn of events, which I might tell you about, but won't write. The longer I live, the more I am amazed and fascinated by the endless variety of living." What had her mother said or done to indicate her pleasure or displeasure or, perhaps, to indicate her indifference? All we can infer is that she was probably less than enthusiastic about her new house.[36]

The differences between mother and daughter in their values, attitudes, and lifestyles shone through in their different approaches to what an ideal house should be. When Laura and Almanzo moved into their new English-style cottage, Lane and Boylston moved into the old farmhouse. Boylston remained only another year, departing when the Stock Market Crash upset her personal finances. Lane would stay for six and a half years, until a book project took her away to do some research. But in constructing a "little house" for her parents she demonstrated once again that her idea of the good life differed considerably from theirs.

Whereas their prized farmhouse had cost a little more than $2,000 to build, Rose paid about five times that much for the new "cottage" and drew upon an English model for the design. (This may have had something to do with her wild scheme several years earlier to have her parents move to England—or even Albania or New Zealand—and start life anew there.)[37] Her reliance upon local materials reflected an important element of her personal philosophy. In an article in the *Ruralist* in March 1920, echoing the language of architect Frank Lloyd Wright, she wrote, "I have a fancy that the farm home should seem to be a product of the soil where it is reared, a permanent growth as it were, of conditions surrounding it, wherever this is possible, and nothing gives this effect more than a house built of rocks from the fields. Such a house, well built, will last for generations."[38]

Unlike the English model, which was more of a showplace, the indigenous farmhouse was a comfortable working machine to be lived in and enjoyed. Lane implicitly understood this, as was evident in her decision to take over the latter when her parents moved across the ridge. Upstairs in her room, she continued to bang away on her typewriter, turning out reams of copy when in good form.

When in July 1935 Lane drove to Columbia and installed herself in the Tiger Hotel to research a book she had contracted to write on the history of Missouri, she and her parents did not realize that this marked her final break from them and Rocky Ridge. In 1937 she would move into the Grosvenor Hotel in New York City for about a year to write her final novel, *Free Land*. But the dream of discovering and living in the perfect house persisted. In March 1938 she bought a small farmhouse just outside of Danbury, Connecticut, which would make it convenient for her to run into New York whenever she needed to talk to publishers and editors. Although she continued to retain a small apartment in the city for a time, Danbury would remain her home for almost three decades, until she moved to Harlingen, Texas, where she spent the last three years of her life.[39]

No longer driven to imagine or construct grand projects like her Albanian villa or her rock house in Missouri, Lane spent much of her time fixing up, remodeling, and furnishing her new house in Danbury. As her biographer William Holtz notes, "The Albanian house had been a romantic dream, Rocky Ridge a failed experiment, but the house on King Street would at last become a home." Within days of the move she was writing in her diary, "Rooted here more than ever at Rocky Ridge."[40]

Reconciled to her scaled-down ambitions and content in her new surroundings, Lane nevertheless never wavered in her tendency to look for significance and meaning in the places she inhabited. She busied herself with gardening, canning, cooking, and baking. Her young friend Norma Lee Browning wrote a story about her for the *Chicago Tribune* describing friends coming over to her place for tea and hot-from-the-oven cinnamon buns and bread, slathered with homemade cherry jam deriving from trees in her orchard. It sounded like Browning could have been talking about Lane's mother serving up refreshments for a group of clubwomen in the parlor at Rocky Ridge. "There is satisfaction," Lane explained, "in baking your own bread and growing your own food and canning it that cannot be found in writing a novel. More women are finding this out. They are moving out of their jobs and back into the home where they have always belonged." The article went on to note that, in addition to her homemaking activities, Lane could "wield a hammer or saw as expertly as most men. She did much of the 'men's work' in remodeling her farmhouse, including some ditch digging, cement mixing, waterproofing a basement, tearing off a front porch, and revamping a tool shed. She upholsters her own furniture, builds bookshelves, and crochets bedspreads."[41]

In an article that Lane wrote for *Woman's Day* magazine in May 1942, she recalled that upon first visiting and inspecting her new place she quickly felt, "It was not only a house; it was a home." Though she had earlier argued the necessity of employing architects in building and remodeling houses, now she thought it a virtue that her house had no architecture. "It is simply a house, built sensibly for a family to live in." Nothing fancy about it. "These United States are full of such cities as Danbury," she wrote, "and all around them are little houses like mine. Why does anyone, unless he passionately loves work that he can do only in a city, wear his life away at a city job that only keeps him alive to wear his life away at the job? Why do women live monotonously in apartments, and bring up children (half of America's next generation) so ignorant and so helpless that they could not live on this fruitful earth unless somebody brought food to them?"[42] Lane, by this time, had traded in her vision of living in an exotic Albanian villa for a modest, livable, down-to-earth domicile that she lovingly described in every detail, just as she had earlier drawn up plans for her imaginary dream house.

A series of articles Lane wrote for *Woman's Day* between 1940 and

1942 on the subjects of crocheting and needlework provided a different sort of way for her to celebrate her new investment in domesticity. And twenty years later the magazine would run an article of hers entitled "Come into My Kitchen," describing in detail the various cabinets, furnishings, tools, and utensils that she relied on in her daily activities and what they meant to her. By this time, her mother had been gone for three years, but the article's publication thirty-five years after Wilder's "My Ozark Kitchen" had appeared in *Country Gentleman* evokes a sense of déjà vu. For all the differences that existed between mother and daughter over the years, Lane, in her mid-seventies, might have *been* her mother—or so it appeared. Gone were her grand ambitions and perfervid dreams of elegant houses in exotic places; old-shoe comfort and unpretentiousness were her new mantras: "Sometimes my kitchen does look as if it were sitting for its portrait, but oftener it looks like any happy kitchen. You know: clean, except that *already* the windows need washing *again*; and neat, except of course for our teacups and napkins and the cake plate, and the ironing still airing, and the puppies' basket and playthings on the floor; yes, that old shoe is theirs, they like to gnaw on it, and the little imps will sneak paper handkerchiefs from my pocket and tear them to bits all over everything. But they're puppies only once, bless 'em."[43]

Similar to the way in which Wilder made symbolic use of little houses in her fiction, Lane perceived their expressive value, both in her life and in her work. Despite the fact that her story "The Perfect House," written in April 1934, failed to find a publisher, it provided some interesting commentary on her views about houses. In it she may have been partially projecting her own strong yearnings on her protagonist when she began the story,

> In magazines there are pictures and plans of the kind of house that Doris wanted. When the magazines came, alluring with the pristine sheen of untouched pages, she always looked first at A Long Island Country House, or A Small English Cottage, or The Home of the Future. Continued stories waited while she pored over drawingrooms and terraces, breakfast nooks and kitchens. All these pictured houses had a common quality. They were complete and beautiful with an impeccable perfection of neatness.[44]

Too much should not be read into her incorporation of "a small English cottage" into her story, since it makes sense for writers to draw upon images and ideas that come out of their own lives for use in their fiction. But in the story Lane likely was articulating her own strong impulse to create something complete, beautiful, and perfect, and that was significant. Certainly she had a tendency to live in day-dreams, and sometimes she actually was able to achieve her visions. But her story made clear that the house she had perceived as perfect at first glance was, upon further inspection, actually full of imper-fections. Perfection is not usually to be found, and appearances of-ten deceive.

In "A Place in the Country," an article she published in *Country Gentleman* purporting to describe what it was like during the mid-1920s for her to live with her parents in the farmhouse they were so proud of at Rocky Ridge, Lane idealized the situation much as she had when describing her principal character's idealized mental pic-ture of the "perfect house." But in the fiction piece she was trying to demonstrate the irony and folly of such fantasizing, while in the purportedly nonfiction piece she painted a romanticized picture of life on Rocky Ridge:

> Success. The joys of creative work, the joys of recognition. I have written my books. But my father and mother have made their farm; two hundred acres of good land, well fenced, productive.
> They made it, with their hands and brains, from poor acres of thin hillside land, from washed gullies and sassafras patches. They built this house, with its sleeping porches and verandas, its big stone fireplace, its filled bookshelves, its white-enameled kitchen, its modern bathroom. This was a dream of theirs, realized through creative labor, as my books are made. The reward of it to them is the same as mine to me.[45]

Multiple ironies spill out of this passage. A couple of months after the article appeared, she would be saying about her life at Rocky Ridge, "I am so miserable, doing all the cooking and cleaning and everything [her mother was sick at the time]. You never have un-derstood how wretched I am here, and I suppose no one can. . . . I certainly do hate farm-housework, sour milk, splashy cream, bring-ing in wood, walking knee-deep in cats and dogs and trying to do things with no tools." And again, several months later, after having listed for her magazine readers all the reasons why country living superseded that in the city ("It has taken me twenty years to realize that the things I have fought for in the cities all my life have been all that time here on the farm"), she wailed that she was not about to try to make the "best of things" by staying on the farm. "If I'd ever made the best of things, My God, I'd be stuck in Mansfield yet. . . . My whole life has been a series of escapes from that quicksand. . . . A person who starts out as a mal-nutrition child in an Ozark log cabin and gets even as far as I've got, does it by raising hell about things, not by making the best of them."[46] Yet there she was, writing frustrated letters from Rocky Ridge farm, complaining about a situation she felt powerless to control, unable to leave her parents.

The greater irony was that after spending a good part of two years in Albania in 1926 and 1927 she would return a second time to live with her parents. Yet this time she would take that farmhouse, about which she had written so glowingly as the pride and joy of her parents, and essentially invite them to move out of it into a new house that she built for them. Either she must have been disingenuous when she wrote the article describing their deep attachment to it or she must have been coldly calculating in maneuvering their exit from it three years later.

In any case, it seems relatively clear that little houses, while retaining huge meaning for both mother and daughter, signified something quite different for each of them. For Wilder, the houses she lived in possessed great resonance and inspired affection as places where she could do useful work, live a satisfying life, build family attachments, welcome in friends and neighbors, and simply enjoy their pleasures and recompenses. For her daughter, houses meant some of these things, but in a real sense it was not the living that went on inside of them that counted so much as the ways in which they could inspire her dreams and fantasies and the subject matter they might provide for her literary work. Finally, while Lane never fully succeeded in her conscious ambition to convert houses into inspiring subjects for her writing, her mother, who never intended them to become grist for her mill, in fact was able to transform them into elements of some of the most memorable children's literature ever written.

III

Time

What Does History Teach?

Long before—as well as after—the great eighteenth-century German philosopher Immanuel Kant ensconced time and space among the central categories that channel human thought, the two concepts occupied a prominent place in philosophical and historical speculation. From the ancient Greeks to modern epistemologists and metaphysicians, they have served as essential tools for any clear understanding of the way the world works. It is little wonder that Wilder and Lane should find the ideas so congenial.

Time, Ann Lawson Lucas tells us, is one of children's literature's most prominent themes. In imaginatively recapitulating her and her family's saga of wandering and settling down on the midwestern and northern plains frontier during the years after the Civil War, Wilder understood that she was rendering an account of time and place, by capturing a part of the generally understood history of the frontier. Geography and history intermingled seamlessly in her storytelling. Lane, for her part, joined scores of other post–World War I American expatriates who haunted the sidewalks and byways of Europe and the Near East, extending her globe-trotting ways far beyond anything her mother could ever have imagined and visiting places most Americans could only dream of going to. She, too, utilized history as the background and context for some of her writing, but for the most part her work was firmly established in the present. Yet, in collaborating with Wilder on the Little House series and in writing two frontier novels of her own, she would find herself retracing historical journeys. The interpenetration of space and time and their confluent influences in a variety of ways were clearly understood by both writers. "For most of us, *space* is the concrete thing that *time* is like," writes psychologist Daniel Gilbert. "Studies reveal that people all over the world imagine time as though it were a spatial dimension, which is why we say that the past is *behind* us and the future is *in front* of us."[1]

The challenges of writing about people in past time are many. A primary one relates to the problem of identification. Our normal tendency—and this applies with special force to readers of the Little House books—is to attempt to identify too closely with the characters being discussed, especially if we like and admire them. One of the very hardest things to do for students and curiosity-seekers who go roaming through the past is to obtain a true feeling for how different people and conditions often were, despite admitted similarities and connections to their own lives and ways of doing things. In approaching people who lived during the 1930s, Lawrence Levine proposes that we "adopt an anthropological vision and prepare ourselves for the possibility that these people whose lives we are sharing for the moment are not necessarily earlier visions of ourselves whom we can know just by knowing ourselves." We would be on safer ground by assuming they are different from ourselves, he suggests. "To attempt to capture *their* way of doing things, *their* consciousness, *their* worldview, is the stuff of history, the quest that gives historians purpose and meaning."[2]

Beyond this, there is the irreducible complexity of the past. In addition, as Robert Berkhofer reminds us, "Since time is irreversible, the historian knows the past only by the remains left over," thus being unable to "examine his subject's behavior at first hand in all of its complexity." The temptation, David Hackett Fischer warns in his discussion of causal explanations, is to resort to the "reductive fallacy," which he defines as one in which the historian (or biographer) "reduces complexity to simplicity, or diversity to uniformity." Similarly, the "fallacy of essences" holds that "there is one 'essential' inner reality, which can be hunted and found." Fischer contends in opposition to this, "There are many factual patterns—an infinite number of them—which can be superimposed upon past events. A historian's task is to find patterns which are more relevant to his problems, and more accurate and comprehensive than others, but he cannot hope to find that 'essential' pattern, any more than he can hope to know all of history, and to know it objectively."[3]

Historians scarcely need reminding of the difficulties surrounding their task, the multiplicity of interpretations that might be advanced to deal with the facts they unearth, and the tentativeness that often surrounds those very facts. When a scientist such as Stephen Jay Gould pronounces contingency as being "the essence of history," they nod in agreement. With John Lewis Gaddis, they join the chorus of those who reject the notion that "there can be only a single valid explanation of what happened."[4]

In this section I try to open up our discussion of Wilder and Lane by launching three probes into the temporal realm by dealing with their respective approaches to history and with the ways in which we, as retrospective observers, can seek to place them in time. My survey of events and developments that occurred in a single year— in this particular case, 1932—is my effort to deal with the latter challenge. Juxtaposing Wilder with frontier historian Frederick Jackson Turner and Lane with regionalist painter Thomas Hart Benton provides different perspectives on their takes on history, thereby allowing us to see them both in a somewhat different light than is normally advanced. In any case, we can be sure that time was one of the things that frequently occupied the minds of both Wilder and Lane.

4

A Perspective from 1932, the Year Wilder Published Her First Little House Book

History, as it is commonly defined, is the record of the past; biography, it is said, is the record of a life.[1] But these artless declarations encompass a multitude of complexities and surprises. There is nothing simple about either history or biography, as anyone who has the slightest acquaintance with the writing of either will attest. Some authors write "big" and some write "small." One could speculate that some books are extended in length in order to avoid the hard choices entailed if they had fewer pages available to tell their stories. But whatever the length of their treatments, historians and biographers constantly confront decisions about what to put in and what to leave out. "Putter-inners" and "taker-outers" alike can be better understood as creative artists painting a canvas with fixed specifications than as laboratory scientists writing research reports based upon results from controlled experiments. Far from simply relating in clear, transparent fashion all the information gathered from their investigations, historians and biographers must pick and choose, like artists, what to include and what to exclude and what sort of form they will use to present their message as they communicate with their readers.

A book's form, we can safely say, dictates its content to a considerable degree, and the usual compulsion to focus primarily upon what is "relevant" requires the author to leave out many interesting details and points of departure. Freeman Tilden observes, "The 'instinct for compression' is, after all, just another way of describing form. The artist ruthlessly cuts away all the material that is not vital to his story." Biographical treatments of Wilder, no less than the children's novels that she wrote herself, bow to the conventions of their genre and appear to be no more natural in their representation of her life than she was in the stories she chose to tell in her novels. Pierre Nora reminds us that while memory "remains in permanent evolution, open to the dialectic of remembering and forgetting, unconscious of its successive deformations, vulnerable to manipulation and appropriation, susceptible to being long dormant and periodically revived," history "is the reconstruction, always problematic and incomplete, of what is no longer." As countless historians, biographers, philosophers, and literary critics have pointed out, the process of historical reconstruction yields a representation of the past, not the past itself. Nora notes that "history binds itself strictly to temporal continuities, to progressions and to relations between things."[2]

When Laura Ingalls Wilder wrote her Little House manuscripts, based upon her own experiences of growing up on the frontier, the stories that emerged seemed in many ways to be direct, accurate accounts of the lives of typical pioneers. Readers tended to focus more upon the presumed reality and seeming natural qualities of the narratives than upon the artfulness with which they were constructed. Beginning with *Little House in the Big Woods*, continuing with *Little House on the Prairie*, and following through the books set in De Smet, the stories seemed to flow in an effortless, unadulterated progression from simple to complex, as Laura grew older, more mature, and more complicated herself. Wilder's comment at the Detroit Book Fair in 1937 that in telling the story of her and her family's lives she had come to understand that she was also recounting the history of the frontier suggests that in her own mind she thought she was merely reciting a simple, easily understandable narrative about typical frontier experiences.[3]

Scholars who have compared the content of the books to what can be ascertained about the actual historical circumstances and events of Wilder's life have emphasized that the books' story lines heavily modified the facts, omitted many items of importance, reconstructed events, even inventing some out of whole cloth, and, in general, followed the conventions of fiction-writing rather than adhering to the strict demands of historical or biographical research. The stories were, after all, fiction, not history.[4]

"There is a paradox about biographies," literary critic Terry Eagleton observes. "We read them to savor the shape and texture of an individual life, yet few literary forms could be more predictable." Biology, for the most part, he contends, dictates the structure of a biography: a person is born, grows up, gets educated, falls in love, and dies. Biographers and historians who have written about Wilder's adult life, it can fairly be said, have likewise followed the dictates and conventions of those genres, picking and choosing which facts, events, and developments to relate by adhering to what they think such treatments usually demand. Biographers, no less than novelists, face the problem of selection continually, John Batchelor reminds us.[5] While wide latitude exists for deciding what to include, such modes of writing usually put a premium on telling connected stories that progress through time, generally with special emphasis being placed on causal links that explain not only what happened and how it happened but also why it happened.[6] These formulas and guidelines are so well understood and accepted that they are hardly ever consciously thought about, much less discussed or debated.

One of the criteria for inclusion in a text is evidentiary. Historians and biographers, because they desire to tell true stories and not fictional ones, are limited to documents, physical artifacts, and other evidence—traces that remain long after the events occurred. They are not allowed to make their stories up. Generally, biographies include information about individuals, groups, events, social processes, developments, thoughts and feelings, historical contexts, and local environments that impinge on the course of their character's life and which relate to the major themes around which they are building their interpretation. In the case of Laura Ingalls Wilder, these would start with her family relationships, her work, her social interactions, her community activities, and her writing career.

But people don't live their lives only within the confines of the conceptual categories that might interest future biographers. Rather, they live them hour by hour, day by day, week by week, and year by year—one thing following another—everything they do being mixed up with everything else. While some moments and activities stand out in their thinking more than others and whole blocks of time occupied in repetitive or uninteresting tasks may blur in their memories, time unfolds regularly and continuously in their lives, and people's own understanding of their experiences differs considerably from the stories that are constructed about them by writers and biographers.

Understandably, biographers will skip over entire months and even years of their subjects' lives if they fail to uncover evidence about them or if the events they unearth seem of minor importance. Because this situation can have the effect of distorting or omitting significant segments of people's lives, I think it would be of some interest to focus upon a single year in the life of my subject, Laura Ingalls Wilder, to see what kind of picture of her we can derive in the process. Some, if not most, of the things we will look at would likely get left out of ordinary biographies or at least would not be given very much space in the story. Yet at the time they were important, and they reveal something important about Wilder's life.

The difficulty, if not impossibility, of adopting this type of approach in the normal course of writing is immediately apparent. There would not be enough space to accommodate all the information, the material would tend to become redundant, and readers would soon tire of the effort required to read it all (just as many readers fail to make it through James Joyce's novel *Ulysses,* which requires more than seven hundred pages to chronicle a single day in the life of its three main characters). What would be lost to literature by such an exercise would be gained by providing a more thorough and realistic record of human life on earth, for it would give a fuller, more complex, and more experientially accurate account of what people's lives were like than the stripped-down, more focused narration that the typical biographical and historical modes of presentation allow for.

Many things that occur in people's lives, however, do not display continuity, provide no evidence of progress, and do not relate to each other in readily discernable patterns. They are thus unlikely to fulfill the requirements for inclusion in typical histories or biographies. Yet they constitute significant parts of people's lives and can be highly revealing about their characters and personalities. Sometimes the offbeat or seeming unrelated fact is as enlightening as the more obviously "relevant" one that gets cited in books. Certainly its inclusion in the story could make for more interesting or unpredictable treatments.

The year I have chosen to focus upon is 1932, the year of publication of Wilder's first novel, *Little House in the Big Woods*. By April of that year, when Harper and Brothers released the book, the United States was moving into the third year of the worst economic depression in its history. It stands out—along with 1776, 1789, 1861, 1917, 1941, and 1968—as one of the most eventful and significant years in the nation's history. Perhaps the most important single event that year was the nomination and subsequent election of New York governor Franklin D. Roosevelt as president of the United States after four years of a failed Hoover administration. With the ushering in of the New Deal, the public concluded that, indeed, the only thing they had to fear was fear itself, and prosperity gradually reestablished itself during the rest of the decade. While European nations succumbed to fascism and radical left-wing ideologies during the 1930s, the United States pursued a middle-of-the-road path that enabled it to muddle through the depression, placing it in a position to help rescue Europe and Asia from the threats of dictatorship and totalitarianism during World War II.

Among the more notable developments punctuating the news in 1932 were the continuing slide of the country into the trough of economic depression; the landslide victory of the Democrats during the fall elections; Amelia Earhart's transatlantic flight; the kidnapping of the golden-locked baby son and only child of Anne Morrow and Charles Lindbergh, who just five years earlier had stunned the world with the first solo flight across the Atlantic; the expansion of road-building in the United States; growing concern about the chain-store phenomenon; the death of historian Frederick Jackson Turner, popularizer of the frontier interpretation of American history; Babe Ruth's "called shot" that fall in the World Series; and the publication of Frederic C. Bartlett's pathbreaking book on the workings of memory. All of these events had a direct or indirect connection with the life of the sixty-five-year-old Wilder, who that year began publishing her Little House books about life on the late-nineteenth-century frontier.

Certainly the most important thing on Americans' minds day by day throughout the year was the economic disaster that gradually set in after the Stock Market Crash of October 1929. Like most of their neighbors and friends, Laura and Almanzo Wilder were slow to grasp the implications of what at first appeared to be just another periodic correction in stock prices. But by 1932 the evidence was compelling and worrisome everywhere they looked; in the throes of economic disaster, the country confronted its most difficult challenge since the Civil War. The question at hand was not merely when the economy would revive but, more ominously, whether the republic would survive. Missouri farm prices dropped 55 percent between 1929 and 1932. Farmland values fell proportionately. Added to farmers' woes were drought, beginning in 1930, and infestations of locusts and other pests. Heat waves drained people of energy and even the will to live. Value added by manufacturing in the state declined by over 50 percent, a loss somewhat smaller than the national average. Average unemployment in the state increased to 16 percent in 1930, 27 percent the following year, and 38 percent in 1932 and 1933.[7]

For families that had never accumulated very much in the way of material possessions, the Great Depression was less traumatic than it was for those who had never known want. For the Wilders, over the years, eking out a living on Rocky Ridge farm just outside of Mansfield, and living for a time in town on the income from Almanzo's draying business and Laura's cooking, had not been easy. What modest prosperity the couple had come to enjoy by the late 1920s, as Laura entered her sixties and Almanzo his seventies, was due largely to the concern and solicitude of their daughter, Rose, who provided them with an annual income subsidy of five hundred dollars. The Great Depression pinched the family's finances. Earlier hopes that their money worries could be put behind them evaporated. The strain showed itself more in their daughter than in her parents. Unlike them, she had acquired extravagant spending habits, chafing under the poverty-stricken circumstances in which she had grown up. Her approach to money assumed that it was easier to earn more of it than it was to try to save it. Rather than attempting to cut back on expenditures, she pushed herself to churn out ever more material for book publishers and magazine editors, frantically trying to keep her head above financial water.

The depression forced Rose to become more realistic about her expectations. There were limits, she began to realize, to what she could do and accomplish. Having built up a substantial nest egg in a New York brokerage account, she received the devastating news in November 1931 that the entire investment had become worthless.[8] During the next several years, while her mother's writing career began to blossom, thanks in large part to the work that she herself put into editing and revising Wilder's handwritten manuscripts, her own writing career sputtered. In a journal entry on May 28, 1932, she wrote, "Nothing has changed in my circumstances. I am still deep in debt, held here where I hate to be, grown old, losing my teeth, all that—and never anyone knowing I am here, so that I feel forgotten in a living grave." Lane's biographer William Holtz notes that she recognized a connection between her own mental depression during the 1930s and the economic depression that the country was suffering through.[9]

If Lane came to better understand her limits as a result of the Great Depression, her mother was just beginning to recognize her potential as an author. After much encouragement and cajoling, Lane had finally gotten her to sit down in 1930 and write her autobiographical account, "Pioneer Girl," which added up to about two hundred double-spaced pages when Lane ran it through her typewriter. Although nobody was willing to publish the manuscript in that form, the first part of it became the basis for a fictionalized story that Wilder wrote about her childhood in the Chippewa River logging region of western Wisconsin after the Civil War. After several fits and starts, a children's book under the title of *Little House in the Big Woods* came out under the imprint of the New York firm of Harper and Brothers in early 1932.

As the depression continued, it certainly had some negative impacts on Wilder's writing career: it depressed sales of her books, reduced the royalties she received, and forced the cancellation of her original contract with Alfred A. Knopf, leading to her later long-term relationship with Harper's. But the depression also provided the psychological and intellectual backdrop for the books that she wrote about the frontier, emphasizing the individualistic virtues of hard work, perseverance, initiative, and industry, as well as the communal values of patience, cooperation, sacrifice, and tolerance. For Wilder, as well as for her daughter, the same sorts of habits and values that had conquered the frontier were capable of pulling the country out of the Great Depression. They both worried that excessive government paternalism, which they associated with Roosevelt's New Deal, would undermine the sense of sturdy individualism that had made the country strong and successful in the past. The depression, thus, was a test, and both of them feared that the New Dealers were increasing the likelihood that the country would fail it.

The causes for the emergence—as well as the persistence—of the Great Depression during the 1930s invited a great deal of speculation at the time and has continued to perplex historians and economists ever since. Among liberals and New Dealers, a large part of the explanation could be found in the disappearance of the frontier, which they connected with a decline in effective demand for the nation's agricultural and industrial products. They linked this to University of Wisconsin historian Frederick Jackson Turner's frontier thesis of American history, which argued that American historical development could best be explained by the constantly receding frontier line marking the edge of settlement in the West.

New York governor Franklin D. Roosevelt, like many other progressive-minded politicians in 1932, took it for granted that the closing of the frontier had played a major role in bringing on the economic catastrophe the country was going through.[10] Although the frontier phase had passed four decades earlier, the country was still experiencing, he concluded, the long-term consequences of that phenomenon in the form of reduced demand, overbuilt factories, excess production, and inadequate consumption. In a famous speech at the Commonwealth Club of San Francisco on September 23, six weeks before the election, Roosevelt expressed his belief that economic growth in the United States had largely come to a halt. "Our industrial plant is built," he asserted; "the problem just now is whether under existing conditions it is not overbuilt. Our last frontier has long since been reached, and there is practically no more free land." The conclusion to be drawn from this seemed obvious to the Democratic candidate: "Our task now is not discovery or exploitation of natural resources, or necessarily producing more goods. It is the soberer, less dramatic business of administering resources and plants already in hand, of seeking to reestablish foreign markets for our surplus production, of meeting the problem of underconsumption, of adjusting production to consumption, of distributing wealth and products more equitably, of adapting existing economic organization to the service of the people."[11]

This statement set the tone for the "scarcity economics" approach of the "First New Deal" of 1933 and 1934. Roosevelt and his team would later repudiate the pessimistic assumptions of the Commonwealth Club speech and opt instead for economic growth.[12] If the Wilders and their daughter read Roosevelt's remarks in San Francisco, it would have reinforced their suspicion that he and his advisors were on the wrong track. It did not take long for both generations of the family to start warning darkly about the wrong direction in which FDR was leading the country.

While Wilder may not have been directly acquainted with Turner's writings, Lane, who was a prodigious reader of history, politics, current events, and other subjects, must have been aware of Turner and his thesis. She shared in the assumption of the frontier's central importance in American history and in the validity and significance of the attributes the Wisconsin historian associated with the frontier, such as democracy, individualism, self-reliance, initiative, and industry. Indirectly, at least, Turner's views wove their way through the books both women wrote during the 1930s. His death in March 1932 marked the end of an era, and his frontier thesis of American history would come under increasingly sharp criticism from scholars during the 1940s and 1950s. But average Americans, who were more interested in figures like Davy Crockett and Daniel Boone and who found Turner's sanguine interpretation of frontier influences to their liking, demonstrated a continued interest in and admiration for frontier heroes whom they could identify with and look up to. That pervasive fascination with frontier adventurers and heroes fed into the popularity Wilder achieved in writing her novels.[13]

By the end of the thirties, foreign policy issues began to trump domestic ones, and both Wilder and her daughter, not surprisingly, found themselves at odds once again with the man in the White House. They backed the America First Committee when it emerged in 1940 to organize isolationists against the interventionist foreign policy of the administration. One of the most publicized and influential isolationists of the period was Charles Lindbergh. The year 1932, which had been such a good year for Franklin Roosevelt, struck tragically at the family of the famous aviator, who later became a leading America Firster. His nineteen-month-old son was kidnapped from the family's home near Hopewell, New Jersey, on March 1, launching a round-the-clock media watch that almost eclipsed the coverage that had been given to the photogenic pilot after his brave and dangerous flight across the Atlantic in 1927.

In the late 1930s, Lindbergh, risking—but at the same time utilizing—the popularity that had come to him from his transoceanic adventure, emerged as the most popular spokesman in America for the isolationist cause. After visiting Germany more than half a dozen times during the decade, he concluded that Hitler was unstoppable and that the United States should not waste its precious resources in bailing out what he considered to be the feeble and doomed democracies of Western Europe. In his insistence that we stay out of the political cockpit of Europe and in his denunciations of the drift of the administration's foreign policy, Lindbergh was expressing Wilder and Lane's opinions exactly.[14] In this instance, foreign-policy views reinforced domestic-policy positions, increasing their opposition to the man in the White House. Wilder spent considerable energy in late 1938 campaigning for the Ludlow Amendment, a proposed constitutional change that would have required a national referendum before war could be declared on another nation, except in the case of a direct attack on American soil. The effort failed, but the episode illustrated the continuing strength of isolationism at the time.[15]

The issues of the local weekly newspaper, the *Mansfield Mirror*, consisted of only four pages in 1932. With local government, railroad, and church notices, many ads, and a number of filler stories from other papers and sources taking up space, not much room was left for straight news. Most of the local information consisted of short personal items or paragraphs like those that pervaded every newspaper of its type. One kind of story that got fairly frequent mention was news of the progress of area road-building programs. Considerable improvements had been made on the highways during the 1920s, but much work remained to be done. Town boosters pushed hard for increased state funding for roads, believing that increased mobility would mean more cars on Main Street and more customers in their stores. That was true, but only to a point. They could have detected a clue to the future in some of the paragraph items in the *Mansfield Mirror* under the heading "Terse and Not So Terse." There, one could read about who had had a baby shower, who was entertaining whom in their homes, which young people were attending college in Columbia and Springfield, and how the latest revival meetings were going. Increasingly, however, residents were going golfing or shopping or attending to business in Springfield, fifty miles to the west on Highway 60. A lot of the items mentioned visits to or visitors from nearby towns such as Ava, Hartville (the country seat), Cedar Gap, and Mountain Grove, and more distant places such as Seymour, West Plains, Monett, and Joplin. Sometimes people even drove to or rode the train as far as Kansas City, St. Louis, and Memphis. The long-range outcome of all of this mobility became apparent later on: the same cars that brought people in from the country and nearby towns to shop and go to movies in Mansfield could also take Mansfield's residents to shop and entertain themselves in Springfield and elsewhere. That was the long-term trend, but the portents were there already by 1932 for those able to read them.

Federal Highway 60 ran east and west through Mansfield, while Route 5 ran north and south through town. The federal numbering system had been put in place in 1926. Three years later, the Highway 60 Association emerged to organize efforts of businessmen and other supporters in towns along the route to advertise it, promote it, and put pressure on government officials to increase funding for it. Nearly one hundred members gathered in Mountain Grove in April 1932 to attend a meeting of the Missouri Highway 60 Association, reelecting W. S. Candler of that city as president of the organization. In September, the group celebrated the opening of a twenty-mile section of concrete surfacing from Springfield east to Rogersville, and plans were in the offing for extending the concrete slab further east through Mansfield and on to the eastern boundary of Wright County.[16]

In November, the *Mirror* ran for its readers a short word of advice, similar to thousands of similar items published in small-town newspapers all over America during the twenties and thirties and later:

> If you want to keep your town going there is no better argument in the world than to trade at home. It is the hometown merchant who helps to keep the schools, the churches, the streets and parks in condition for the enjoyment of all. We've heard of people right in our town, business men if you please, who buy out of our town, when the identical goods at just as good a price can be bought here. We do not deny the fact that persons can spend money where they please but by exercising that right to our mind displays poor business policy. Of course some will take the attitude that the other fellow does not buy from him. Perhaps if you try him first you both will profit.[17]

"Buy at home" became the battle cry of small-town businessmen and newspapers in the decades after automobiles and better roads began to increase the range of American shoppers. The early 1930s witnessed a growing reaction against the chain-store "invasion" of small-town America, and it saw efforts by some state legislatures to tax them out of business or at least to make them compete fairly with locally owned stores. In 1930, thirty-three-year-old Philip La Follette made his attack on chain stores and chain banks the central theme of his successful bid for the governorship of Wisconsin. The Great

Depression heightened concerns of Main Street store owners that the unfair competition of the chains would put them out of business. In 1936, Congress passed the Robinson-Patman Act, making it illegal for manufacturers or wholesalers to give preferential discounts or rebates to chain stores or other large buyers.[18] Just twenty-six years later, a University of Missouri graduate named Sam Walton, whose family roots were in adjoining Webster County, would open his first Wal-Mart discount outlet not too far away in northwest Arkansas, helping take the chain-store phenomenon into a whole new dimension. Southwest Missouri would be in the heart of "Wal-Mart country."

If the full implications for small towns like Mansfield of industrial change, improved highways, and the chain-store "menace" still lay several decades in the future, the rise of a media culture was making itself felt with increasing insistence by the early 1930s. Commercial radio, sound movies, and mass-circulation print media had already begun to colonize people's minds, diverting attention from traditional local subjects and concerns. Increasingly, people would spend their time on and turn their thoughts to movies at the local theater, programs on the radio, and stories in the popular press, which created a whole new reality for them, different from what they had been familiar with in the past.[19] In addition to the Lindbergh kidnapping, the year 1932 saw the publication of Erskine Caldwell's *Tobacco Road*, the introduction of the *Buck Rogers* program on CBS Radio, the opening of Radio City Music Hall, and Amelia Earhart's crowning as the first woman to fly solo across the Atlantic. Lindbergh, Earhart, FDR—all were part of a new celebrity culture that was emerging around the burgeoning mass media. Radio programming, *Time* magazine, movie newsreels, and other media outlets were transforming celebrityhood into something larger, more pervasive, and more influential than it had ever been before.[20]

By the end of the decade, despite the fact that she was writing about her own and her family's personal experiences on the prairie frontier—an obscure family whose only distinction was that its story was being read by thousands of eager readers—Laura Ingalls Wilder had become something of a celebrity herself. Unlike her daughter, who didn't mind the limelight being directed at her, Wilder felt uncomfortable away from home and familiar surroundings and seldom traveled very far from Mansfield. Except for several visits back to De Smet (one by way of California) with her husband, the only major exception to this was her trip to Detroit in 1937, when she was one of several speakers spotlighted by the J. L. Hudson Department Store during a book fair it was sponsoring.

Lane, on the other hand, felt much more comfortable with and was much more facile in connecting to the newly emerging celebrity culture of the twenties and thirties. The former decade witnessed the flowering of a remarkable batch of writers: F. Scott Fitzgerald, Ernest Hemingway, Gertrude Stein, William Faulkner, Sinclair Lewis, Willa Cather, H. L. Mencken, John Dos Passos, T. S. Eliot, and others. Their celebrity status carried over into canonic renown in the literary firmament in subsequent years. Lane later would recount hobnobbing with the likes of John Reed, Floyd Dell, and Max and Crystal Eastman in New York. She ghosted books for Lowell Thomas, attended a party hosted by Sherwood Anderson and became a minor character in one of his books, and wrote lives of celebrities like Henry Ford, Herbert Hoover, and Jack London. With Dorothy Thompson she walked the Loire Valley and drove the primitive roads of Albania in a Model T Ford. In 1931, when Thompson traveled with her husband, Sinclair Lewis, to pick up his Nobel Prize for Literature in Stockholm, Lane babysat the couple's infant child in Connecticut.[21]

Laura Ingalls Wilder had little opportunity to cross paths with the kinds of celebrities or would-be celebrities that her daughter did. Strangely enough, significantly enough, however, she did have a tenuous geographical connection to one of the most famed stars of the great Age of Ballyhoo—New York Yankees slugging outfielder Babe Ruth. Entering the 1932 season, the thirty-seven-year-old "Sultan of Swat" had pounded out 611 home runs, far more than any other player who had ever played the game. The forty-one that he tallied that year marked his lowest number in seven years (he had led the league in round-trippers the previous six years and had set a new major league record with sixty in 1927), but it was still a considerable feat for an aging player. The Yankee slugger saved the best for last that year, however, adding luster to his legend in the Fall Classic when he allegedly "called his shot" against Chicago Cubs pitcher Charlie Root in game three of the World Series.

The 1932 Yankees were one of the greatest teams of all time, winning 107 games against only 47 losses and finishing 13 games ahead of the Philadelphia Athletics in the American League pennant race. Their National League rivals were no slouches themselves, having won 90 games during the regular season, but the Yankees juggernaut swept all four games of the World Series by a combined score of 37 to 19. No love was lost between the two teams, and the bench jockeying was ferocious throughout the series. For the third game, in Chicago's Wrigley Field, with the Cubs down two games to none, an overflow crowd of almost fifty thousand mostly partisan fans jammed into every part of the ballpark, yelling epithets at the pinstriped invaders from the East and especially at their great, but now fat and aging, left fielder.

After blasting a three-run homer into the right-field bleachers in the first inning and later sending a long fly ball to the right-center-field fence in the third, Ruth approached the batter's box in the fifth inning to a chorus of boos and catcalls. Taking two pitches across the plate, he raised first one, then two, fingers to acknowledge the number of strikes against him. Ruth told the Cubs catcher that it only took one pitch to hit it, then yelled out to Root on the mound something like, "I'm going to knock the next pitch down your blankety-blank throat." He also, according to many in attendance at the game, made a grand gesture before stepping back in to face the next pitch. Some people swore that he pointed to the center-field bleachers, suggesting that he would park the next pitch there, and then he proceeded to do exactly that. Other observers believed he was simply signaling that he knew there were two strikes against him (the count was two balls and two strikes). In baseball lore the moment goes down as the time that Babe Ruth "called his shot" against the hapless Charlie Root—one of the greatest moments in baseball.[22]

There is no evidence to indicate that Babe Ruth ever played an inning of baseball in Mansfield, Missouri, although he frequently went on barnstorming tours around the country after the regular season ended. But there is a connection between him and the town: he played on two different teams with Carl Mays, a hard-throwing right-handed pitcher who compiled a 207–126 lifetime record, making him one of the most effective pitchers in the majors during the late teens and early twenties. Along with Babe Ruth and several other hurlers on the Boston Red Sox during the late teens, he was part of one of the best mound staffs of the era. Then, just one year before Ruth was traded over to New York, Mays was sent there himself, and from 1920 through 1923 the two helped convert the so-so Yankees into one of the best teams in baseball.

Mays, tragically, is most remembered as the only major leaguer ever to kill another player in a game. In August 1920, with twilight descending, Mays hit the Indians' Ray Chapman in the left temple with one of his deceptive underhanded curve balls, which were difficult enough for batters to pick up in broad daylight. Mays, a tough, hard-nosed competitor who intimidated batters by brushing them back with pitches in on their chin, was not well-liked around the league by either the players or the fans. Babe Ruth, although he was a teammate with Mays for the better part of a decade, had a very different personality and never much cared for him.[23]

But in Mansfield, Missouri, Mays retained the status of a hero, being the only local player playing in the major leagues. He frequently returned home during the off-season to hunt and to fish, and he built a lodge where he could bring some of his teammates and friends to relax. He won special notice in the community when he brought some used Yankee uniforms that were worn by the Mansfield town team the following summer.[24] Before Laura Ingalls Wilder emerged as Mansfield's most famous personage, its best-known personalities were her daughter, Rose, and Carl Mays. No one in the Wilder family seems to have paid much attention to baseball or other sports, and Mays probably never had the pleasure of meeting Laura Ingalls Wilder, but he knew and understood the pressures of celebrityhood and could have told how quickly one's fame can come undone once the spotlight of publicity shifts away to someone else.

A baseball player, who has to depend upon a strong arm or a sharp batting eye to break into the lineup, can have his day in the sun come and go overnight. Carl Mays threw his last big league pitch in 1929 at the age of thirty-seven. Laura Ingalls Wilder hadn't even begun her writing career at that age; she wasn't even "Laura Ingalls Wilder," for that matter. Rather she would have been known as "Laura," "Bess," "Bessie," or "Mrs. A. J. Wilder" to friends, neighbors, and acquaintances. Laura Ingalls Wilder was the pen name she began to use when she started writing magazine articles and books.

There is one more angle of illumination we might take advantage of in this rather eclectic survey of events and developments that surrounded and shaped Wilder's life during the single year of 1932. It relates to the functions and characteristics of memory, for that faculty was crucial to Wilder's ability to write the children's novels that would bring her so much success and acclaim. Again, it is coincidental that a landmark book on the subject of memory should be published during that particular year, but by choosing to focus our attention upon it, we obtain the luxury of pondering the role that memory might play in a writer's life.

By the time that she started writing her autobiography in 1930 and then mined it to fashion her autobiographical novels between 1932 and 1943, Wilder had to rely almost entirely upon her memory of events that had occurred half a century earlier to tell the story. While her ability to recall things that had happened so far in the past was better than average, Wilder frequently grew frustrated over her inability to bring back to consciousness events that could serve as grist for her stories. In 1938, while working on her sixth book, *The Long Winter,* she complained in a letter to Lane, "Strange how my memory fails me on all but the high lights."[25]

What becomes obvious in comparing Wilder's description of the life she led as a child and young adult with what we are able to ascertain about what actually happened at the time is that her books, while drawing upon actual experience, were highly selective and creative in treatment and emphasis and frequently deviated from actual events.[26] When we read between the lines of her original manuscripts, successive drafts (which Lane also had a lot of input into), and the final versions in book form, we are able to infer much about the process that took place in the production of the books. We can also make some conclusions about how memory operates when a person in her sixties and seventies sets out to recall her life as a child fifty or sixty years earlier.

Research on memory has greatly advanced our knowledge about its workings. Memory, we can postulate, is selective, creative, purposeful, and functional. Rather than operating like a mirror or a photographic film, it is active and creative, often distorting, omitting, combining, or reorganizing past events as it posits an interpretive screen on which our past experiences vaguely and fuzzily march before us. As Edmund Blair Bolles notes, "Emotions, perceptions, and reminders all stir the imagination, and imagination, not storage, is the basis of memory."[27]

The year 1932, interestingly enough, marked the publication of a trailblazing book in the scientific investigation of memory. *Remembering: A Study in Experimental and Social Psychology,* by Sir Frederic C. Bartlett of Cambridge University, was not the first study to suggest the heavily constructive nature of memory's operation, but it was much more systematic than previous works and placed scientific investigation of the problem on a new level of sophistication.

Bartlett took direct aim at the view that memory consisted simply of a process of calling up "traces" that are "made and stored up in the organism in the mind." Utilizing instead the concept of "schema," which refers to "an active organization of past reactions, or of past experiences, which must always be supposed to be operating in any well-adapted organic response," he disputed the notion that memory was primarily or literally some kind of duplication or reproduction of the experiences of a person. He argued rather that construction played much more of a role in memory than reproduction. In sum, "Remembering is not the re-excitation of innumerable fixed, lifeless and fragmentary traces. It is an imaginative reconstruction, or construction, built out of the relation of our attitude towards a whole active mass of organized past reactions or experience, and to a little outstanding detail which commonly appears in image or in language form. It is thus hardly ever really exact, even in the most rudimentary case of rote recapitulation, and it is not at all important that it should be so."[28]

Readers who take this insight into account when dealing with Wilder's novels will be less likely to get concerned about questions regarding the literal accuracy of her work. Too much effort gets expended in trying to trace the real people, places, and events that are mentioned in the books. In the first place, Wilder intentionally modified many facts to make a better story; she was, after all, writing fiction. Beyond that, however, even if she had been trying to reduplicate the past, the workings of memory—as theorized by Bartlett and his followers—made it impossible to accomplish the task. As he wrote in 1932, "our studies have shown us that all manner of changes in detail constantly occur in instances which every normal person would admit to be genuine instances of remembering. There are changes in order of sequence, changes of direction, of complexity of structure, of significance, which are not only consistent with subjectively satisfactory recall, but are also perfectly able to meet the objective demands of the immediate situation."[29]

Those evocative and emotionally charged Little House stories that readers love so well and that Wilder began to publish in 1932, in other words, need to be understood in light of what scholars like Frederic Bartlett that same year were revealing in scientific studies like *Remembering*. The world that Wilder depicted in her novels was a relatively simple one. The world she actually lived in, on the other hand, was increasingly complex and problematical. It is ironic that the books that her readers enjoyed reading in large part denied the complexity of that world and offered compensations for the anxieties and tensions produced by it.

This little excursion into the year 1932 has taken us down some paths not frequently traveled in biographical treatments of Laura Ingalls Wilder. Veering from the usual narrative emphasis of biographical writing to focus more closely on the happenings of a single year allows us to gain a somewhat different perspective on Wilder's life. Rather than organizing our inquiry in strict chronological fashion or around a small set of tightly focused themes, I have chosen to digress for a moment to take in some of the serendipitous happenings and developments that occurred during the year of publication of Wilder's first book. Authors often invite criticism when they succumb to the temptation to digress in their writing. But I identify with J. D. Salinger's red-capped Holden Caulfield, who flunked Oral Expression for digressing too much in his class assignments: "I like somebody to stick to the point and all. But I don't like them to stick *too* much to the point." As the Pencey Prep scholar noted, things often get more interesting when we stray far enough from the particular subject at hand to ponder surrounding contexts and circumstances. Science fiction writer Ray Bradbury, in his 2003 coda to *Fahrenheit 451,* a novel that originally appeared two years after *The Catcher in the Rye,* affirms the point. "For, let's face it, digression is the soul of wit," he writes, approvingly quoting Laurence Sterne: "Digressions, incontestably, are the sunshine, the life, the soul of reading!" Thus, we can say that just as a star in the heavens may be perceived more clearly by peering slightly to the side of it, rather than directly at it, so a person's life may sometimes be comprehended more fully by departing from the kind of tight narrative structure that usually imposes itself upon the writing of biographies. Maurice Mandelbaum's advice on the writing of history relates as well to the genre of biography when he suggests that the task at hand is one not so much of "tracing a series of links in a temporal chain" as it is "to analyze a complex pattern of change into the factors which served to make it precisely what it was."[30]

No one wants "all the facts," Jacques Barzun reminds us, advising fellow writers to be selective and to work their facts into an "intelligible pattern." But one person's pattern makes for another one's exclusion. Thomas Babington Macaulay asked what it means to say that an event in the past is important or insignificant. "No past event has any intrinsic significance," he contended. Significance needs to be ascertained by its relation to other events and by how it will affect the future.[31] My approach in this chapter has been to break the usual pattern of linear biography and to hone in on a single year in Wilder's life and to look for significance where it might not otherwise be found. Some of the points no doubt would have found their way into many biographical treatments—the impact of the depression and Roosevelt's election, for instance. Others—the World Series exploits of Babe Ruth, the hometown connection with Carl Mays, the Highway 60 Association road conference, and the Lindbergh baby kidnapping—probably would not have. But I think we know a little more about Wilder as a result.

One final point needs to be stated. Until 1932, when Wilder published her first book, her life, like those of most of her female contemporaries, had largely revolved around household responsibilities and chores and had been filled with daily routine, drudgery, and mundane happenings. Like that of Wilder's, women's lives tended to be more private than men's, which were more often conducted in the public realm. According to Linda Wagner-Martin, where men's lives focused mainly outward, women's tended to focus inward.[32]

But that changed measurably for Wilder once her books began to roll off the presses and acclaim knocked on her door. While Wilder had been involved in local community organizations and activities for decades and the daily routines of the household did not change all that much in many ways, her life took on more of a public face than had earlier been the case. Now her biography assumed more of a linear cast, resembling that of male celebrities in a way it never had before. From our vantage point today, we can trace the progression of the publication of her books, appearing at regular intervals between 1932 and 1943, and take note of the awards and recognition that she received. The year 1932 marks the fulcrum of Wilder's life. From then on, she would have a new role to play, that of the children's author Laura Ingalls Wilder.

5

Laura Ingalls Wilder, Frederick Jackson Turner, and the Enduring Myth of the Frontier

The frontier, an integral part of American history as well as one of its central myths, has inspired countless novels, short stories, poems, movies, television programs, monuments, works of art, and books of history. Becoming well established in the national psyche, both in the popular mind and in critical circles, it has always appealed more to the imagination and fantasies of observers than to their critical and empirical faculties.[1]

Attempting to connect children's author Laura Ingalls Wilder with one of the United States' most prominent academic historians, Frederick Jackson Turner, may seem incongruous at first glance. Juxtaposing the two, however, provides opportunities for viewing both of them in clearer fashion, for both were mythologists of the American frontier. They each grew up on the Wisconsin frontier during and right after the Civil War, and they focused their writing energies on the perceived realities as well as the mythological implications of the frontier experience. In the process, they emerged as two of America's most celebrated and influential authors within their respective fields. Considering their two careers in tandem allows us to broaden our views and enhance our understanding of the United States' foremost historian of the frontier and the person who recast the entire field of American history in the process, on the one hand, and one of America's most popular children's authors, who made the frontier the context for her fiction.

In the process of making the comparison it will become evident that while the ideas and attitudes of both authors were heavily influenced by similar cultural imperatives to glorify, celebrate, mythologize, and partly misrepresent the frontier, they also demonstrated their own particular takes on it, picking and choosing which elements to emphasize, heavily influenced by their own backgrounds and personalities. If they both tended to draw selectively from their own native Midwest, gender drove them apart in their visions. Turner self-consciously portrayed a midwestern garden as a way of escaping from eastern domination of historical scholarship, while Wilder simply took for granted that the heartland frontier in which she grew up was somehow central to the meaning of American life. Turner relied on training, intellect, and professionalism in writing his version of the frontier, while Wilder drew upon memory, experience, and family lore, but both applied hefty doses of imagination and creativity to their works.

A number of writers have already made this connection between Turner and Wilder. Fred Erisman, for example, suggests that treating the Little House books as a part of American Western literature "provides perhaps the most satisfying approach to the works." Anita Clair Fellman notes that "it is Wilder's evocation of [the] parallel myths of frontier and family to which reviewers and critics have responded enthusiastically decade after decade, even as they praised the stories for their authenticity." Gail Schmunk Murray observes that "recent scholarship has found Wilder's construction of frontier life skewed to conform to the 'frontier myth' that historian Frederick Jackson Turner used to hypothesize the American spirit of conquest, adventure, and individualism at the end of the nineteenth century."[2]

Although I have come across no direct evidence to indicate that Wilder actually read Turner or was aware of his writings, she certainly was a Turnerian in the sense that she had imbibed many of his ideas from the culture around her and agreed with him on the central importance of the frontier in American life. To the degree that Wilder was a Turnerian, a mystifying paradox arises: she constructed a fictional frontier full of women's (as well as men's) activities and participation while Turner almost entirely excluded women from his analyses and discussions of the region. Elizabeth Jameson points out that the only woman mentioned in Turner's famous frontier essay of 1893 was Kit Carson's mother. In all his books and essays they seldom had more than an implicit presence.[3] The contrast between Turner's and Wilder's treatments of the frontier could hardly be starker. He focuses upon male conquest, individualism, lawlessness, and the search for autonomy, while Wilder depicts a dual West, where men's actions are set off against women's interests in making gardens, building homes, and sustaining community, thereby providing an alternative vision of what the West was and could be.[4] Thus, in the Little House books a continual tension existed between Pa's impulse to keep going west into an ever-expanding frontier, and Ma's desire to stay put—to cultivate home and community in a settled place.

Frederick Jackson Turner was a thirty-one-year-old history professor at the University of Wisconsin when he delivered a paper in 1893 during the Chicago World's Fair on "The Significance of the Frontier in American History." Though initial reaction remained somewhat muted, enthusiasm built quickly, and Turner's professional trajectory was swift and steep. His paper today is considered the most influential one ever written by an American historian. The frontier thesis that he enunciated in it dominated historical interpretation in the United States for a generation, and Turner himself emerged as one of the half dozen most important American historians of all time, and, in the minds of some, the greatest of them all.[5]

Turner managed to produce only one real book in his lifetime, *Rise of the New West, 1819–1829*, published in 1906. A collection of his essays on the frontier appeared in 1920, and a compendium of his pieces on the subject of sectionalism in American history came out in 1933, a year after his death, capturing a posthumous Pulitzer Prize. The "big book" that he had been working on for a quarter of a century, *The United States, 1830–1850: The Nation and Its Sections*, finally was published in 1935 in unfinished form, with editorial assistance from a couple of Turner's devoted protégés. Unlike Laura Ingalls Wilder, who turned out books with assembly-line regularity every year or two after 1932, Turner, for various reasons, found it almost impossible to produce book-length publications. But he was prolific in other ways, churning out dozens of essays and articles as well as numerous reviews, speeches, reports, and other writings over the course of a career that lasted four decades. His was serious research, based upon countless hours spent in archives poring over documents and manuscripts and consulting thousands of books and articles written by his fellow historical investigators. Turner was so enamored of the quest for historical truth that he found it difficult to actually sit down and write up his findings.[6]

Wilder's procedure in writing about her own frontier experience was much simpler and faster. Sitting at her desk or in a chair near a window overlooking the Missouri countryside, she would pull out a pencil and a five-cent tablet and fill its lines with memories of her childhood and young adult years, turning out page after page of draft copy. Occasionally, she would do a little research to pin down a date or a fact. Though she was writing fiction and was willing to alter facts and circumstances to make for a better story, she was also dedicated to recapturing the essential truth of the past as she envisioned it just as much as Turner was in his bid to recreate history for a general readership.

Turner's father had arrived in Portage, Wisconsin, at the confluence of the Fox and Wisconsin rivers, in 1855, only a year after the town's founding. More so than Charles Ingalls, who gained some esteem in De Smet as a founder of the town's Congregational church and in a variety of official positions, including justice of the peace, town clerk, and street commissioner, Andrew Jackson Turner was influential statewide as a civic and political leader, serving as editor of the weekly *Wisconsin State Register* and participating actively in Republican party politics, serving three terms as mayor of Portage and four terms in the state legislature, attending four Republican national conventions as a delegate, and filling a number of other positions.[7]

Growing up as a curious, energetic lad, young Frederick Turner was able to observe the remnants of the fur trade as well as Indians in their tepees while on hiking and fishing expeditions in the area around Portage. It was a bustling little town. Its population jumped quickly to 2,870 by 1860, then gradually expanded to around 4,300 during the time Turner spent there, before enrolling at the University of Wisconsin in 1878. Portage was a much larger and more progressive little town than the ones that Wilder grew up in, as her family bounced around from place to place and finally settled permanently in Dakota Territory in 1879. While the frontier experiences of Wilder and Turner were by no means identical, the rural environments they intimately came to know impressed themselves mightily upon their memories and imaginations, serving as vital backdrop to as well as compelling motivation for their writings as adults.

At a Detroit Book Week celebration in October 1937, Wilder reflected upon the outpouring of readers' responses to the publication of her first book five years earlier, when children had begged her to write more stories:

> I began to think what a wonderful childhood I had had. How I had seen the whole frontier, the woods, the Indian country of the great plains, the frontier towns, the building of railroads in wild, unsettled country, homesteading and farmers coming in to take possession. I realized that I had seen and lived it all—all the successive phases of the frontier, first the frontiersmen, then the pioneer, then the farmers and the towns. Then I understood that in my own life I represented a whole period of American history.[8]

Wilder's frontier history emerged in the form of autobiographical memory of her own life on the prairie, converted into fiction through minor modifications of fact and chronology, the blending or amending of some characters, a few name changes, and a fair amount of invention, much of it springing from the fertile imagination of her daughter. Rose Wilder Lane's initial role as editor of her mother's volumes was transformed by the second volume into one of true collaborator.

In writing about the frontier, Turner, like Wilder, remained heavily influenced by his childhood environment. Having been attracted to historical study and thereby diverted from a journalistic career by Professor William F. Allen at the University of Wisconsin, he was able to engage in original research on local frontier history as an undergraduate student, following that with a master's thesis on the Wisconsin fur trade. By the time he returned to Madison to settle into a job with Allen in the history department, after a single year of working on a Ph.D. degree at Johns Hopkins University, he had already decided upon a bold career move—to focus his scholarly research upon the history of the American West, a topic almost entirely neglected up to that time. Conversations in Baltimore with visiting professor Woodrow Wilson, who, like him, believed that his native section (in his particular case, the South) had been slighted by historians from the Northeast, reinforced his belief that the West and, more particularly, the Midwest deserved more attention from American historians. Three decades after delivering his 1893 essay, Turner confided, "The Frontier paper was a programme, and in some degree a protest against eastern neglect, at the time, of institutional study of the West, and against western antiquarian spirit in dealing with their own history." He went on to build a hugely successful career, first at Wisconsin and then at Harvard, around western themes—initially the frontier, later sectionalism—always heavily emphasizing his own native Middle West.[9]

Laura Ingalls Wilder also focused her attention on the frontier, the West, and, more particularly, her own Midwest. But it was not a program, a research agenda, or a historical thesis that drove her writing. Rather, she took her own life as her primary subject, and in endeavoring to chronicle it simply and straightforwardly she set the parameters of her inquiry. In the process, as she noted in her Detroit speech, she also became involved in the writing of frontier history. Beginning in 1911 at the age of forty-four, she had frequently injected stories about her and her family's frontier experiences in her biweekly columns for the *Missouri Ruralist*.

Running like a red thread through all of her novels was the theme of persistence and triumph against all odds and setbacks while struggling for survival on the western frontier. While Wilder avoided confronting the harsh realities of frontier economics and the frontier environment during the 1890s, Turner began his analysis with the report of the director of the U.S. Census indicating that drawing a frontier line in the West was no longer possible. The frontier, in effect, was over. On this pessimistic note he began his work.

Though the Wisconsin historian and many of his readers fretted about the implications of the end of the frontier, Turner also celebrated the progress that the nation had achieved thus far and remained generally optimistic about its future prospects. In this, his thinking was right in line with Wilder's. "Up to our own day," Turner wrote, "American history has been in a large degree the history of the colonization of the Great West. The existence of an area of free land, its continuous recession, and the advance of American settlement westward, explain American development."[10] Integral to the frontier thesis was Turner's stage theory of development. Although he stated them somewhat differently in a variety of publications, these stages included the progressive appearances of Indians, hunters and woodsmen, fur traders, cattle drovers, miners, pioneer farmers, mechanized farmers, manufacturing classes, and town and city dwellers. The continually westward-moving frontier denoted the division between "savagery and civilization," in Turner's terminology. Though highly aware of the Indian presence on the land before the arrival of European immigrants, Turner seldom paid them the attention they deserved and largely viewed them as obstacles to progress rather than as peoples worthy in their own right and deserving of equal historical treatment.

The popularity of Turner's frontier thesis depended heavily upon the positive images he projected of the frontiersmen (to the almost complete exclusion of their female counterparts). The characteristics he variously ascribed to them included, in the first place, nationalism, individualism, and democracy. They also possessed, in his view, coarseness and strength, acuteness and inquisitiveness, practicality, inventiveness, exuberance, restlessness, and nervous energy. Additionally, they were egalitarian, optimistic, idealistic, visionary, courageous, aggressive, ambitious, volatile, energetic, hardworking, quick to lead, devoted to the notion of the self-made man, rough, wasteful, less cultured, careless of niceties, and resistant to outside control.[11]

While Wilder would undoubtedly have agreed with many of those characterizations, her whole outlook was colored by the fact that she was a woman. Unlike Turner, she had a lot to say about the opposite sex. She viewed the frontier from inside out, focusing on the family, while her scholarly counterpart, who professed to seek objectivity and comprehensiveness in his dissection of frontier society in all of its complexity, approached it from the outside in. Over against Turner, who sought to achieve a balanced integration of social, economic, and political history, Wilder viewed everything through her own eyes as a girl and young woman undergoing socialization and maturation within a specific family.[12]

Turner largely denied individual agency, seeing people not so much as self-directed agents but rather as exemplars of tendencies and trends linked to broader social forces. For him, the group counted more than the individual. Even his heroes—most prominently, Andrew Jackson—stood out more as representatives of historical tendencies (in his case, frontier democracy) than as individual actors in their own right. Absorbing the evolutionary theories of teachers such as William F. Allen, Herbert Baxter Adams, and Edward A. Ross and discerning further reinforcement for their ideas in his wide reading, Turner made his major units of analysis social structures, political developments, and broad social, economic, and environmental forces rather than the caprices of individual biography and personal relationships and interactions. Starting from a perspective of environmental determinism, he developed over time an increasingly complex model of historical explanation, but always in his thinking the individual gave precedence to the group.[13]

Wilder, in contrast, maintained her steady focus on individuals, beginning with herself and her family and broadening the circle to include neighbors, friends, community members, and those outside it. Hers was a moral vision as much as a descriptive one. Her historical actors were less buffeted by social and economic forces than constantly forced to choose between moral alternatives and given opportunities to redeem themselves or fall into error. Turner's histories did not lack moral content and they generally expressed an approving—even celebratory—attitude toward the frontier developments he was describing, but they remained primarily works of scholarship, implicitly committed to objectivity, empiricism, logical argument, and fair-mindedness. Wilder's treatments, on the other hand, were sentimental, dramatic, high-minded, and replete with moral lessons for their readers. Her stories sometimes seemed as if they had been written as much for the moral principles they embodied as for the content they contained.

Both authors identified emotionally with the frontier environments they were describing, and their writings were colored by remembered experiences from their childhoods. "Is it strange that I saw the frontier as a real thing and experienced its changes," Turner asked rhetorically. "My father was named Andrew Jackson Turner at his birth in 1832 by my Democratic grandfather, and I still rise and go to bed to the striking of the old clock that was brought into the house the day that he was born, at the edge of the Adirondack forest. My mother's ancestors were preachers! Is it strange that I preached of the frontier?"[14] Wilder's ancestors, like Turner's, traced back to early New England, and both partook of the strong Puritan belief in the power of education. Their common Yankee backgrounds inclined them both to striving, seeking, and contributing to the welfare of the community.

The inherent tension existing between individual autonomy and group participation also manifested itself in both of their lives. The Ingallses and the Wilders had not risen as high on the social scale nor had they climbed as high on the educational ladder as the Turners. The financial situation of Laura and Almanzo Wilder remained precarious until both were past retirement age, while the Turner family enjoyed a comfortable middle-class lifestyle, replete with servants, trips to Europe and the coasts, and a summer home. That the finances of the Turners were generally in disarray traced more to their undisciplined spending habits than to any deficiency in their annual income, which put them near the top of the academic pyramid.

In Mansfield, Missouri, the Wilders participated actively in the Methodist church, the Masonic and Eastern Star lodges, the county agricultural society, bridge and card groups, women's study clubs, and partisan political activities. While she was living in De Smet, Laura's parents had provided a model, on a more modest scale, for civic participation with their leadership in the Congregational church and her father's activities as justice of the peace and in a variety of other positions. Turner likewise took a page from his father's book by involving himself in a variety of civic and educational organizations, both in Madison and in Boston. Both families exemplified the observation of historian Robert V. Hine that on the frontier, community, not isolation, generally prevailed. What Alexis de Tocqueville had first observed during the 1830s—a high degree of group activity and civic participation—carried through in the lives of both Wilder and Turner, whether they happened to live in the country, in small towns, or in the city.[15]

Wilder's and Turner's writings won both of them the highest accolades from their respective peers as well as from the general public. Although somewhat embarrassed by his own lack of productivity in producing books of history, Turner did obtain wide acclaim for his articles and essays in historical journals as well as in popular periodicals, ranging from the *Atlantic Monthly* and the *Nation* to *World's Work* and *Yale Review*.[16] In 1910, the year he moved from Wisconsin to Harvard, he served a term as president of the American Historical Association, the premier historical organization in the country. No historian outranked him in prestige and influence during the first three decades of the twentieth century. Wilder's reputation likewise rose quickly after she emerged on the literary scene during the early 1930s. She won many awards on her way to becoming one of the most beloved children's authors of the century. Five of her volumes were selected as Newbery Honor Books. Her titles sold hundreds of thousands of copies and grew further in popularity later on when they inspired television and movie spin-offs. Wilder's magnetic persona, so friendly and approachable, only added to her appeal.

For all their fame and popularity, however, neither author managed to stave off criticism. Turner expressed surprise in a 1922 letter to Professor Arthur Schlesinger that he had not received more criticism than he had. After his death, the scattered sallies that had earlier been directed against him increased significantly. Accusations of vagueness, contradictions, exaggeration, insufficient evidence, and a variety of other sins gathered steam during the fifties and sixties. During the seventies and later, his theories became a virtual punching bag for revisionist historians pioneering the "New Western History." They went far beyond their predecessors in accusing Turner and his followers of provincialism, triumphalism, racism, patriarchy, ethnocentrism, misdirected emphasis, and a variety of other sins. Turnerians were accused, in many cases quite rightly, of underestimating or leaving out of their stories altogether Indians, women, blacks, Latinos, and Asians. The story of the frontier, in the eyes of Patricia Limerick, had been one characterized less by discovery and progress than by conquest and treachery. She and her colleagues insisted on a much broader, more inclusive, and more complex story of the western past. The New Western Historians put their emphasis on the West as a place rather than on the frontier as a process. To them, Turner was not a god but a mortal with feet of clay who had misled students of the West far too long.[17]

Wilder, too, took her lumps from a variety of angles. Lacking Turner's status as the founder of a reigning school of scholarship and not involved in producing any overarching theories of American historical development, she posed a much more elusive target than Turner, but that did not immunize her from criticism. Though her works were fictionalized accounts aimed at a children's audience, historians, literature scholars, and other academics have mined her books for evidence on the social history of the West. Since her books are so widely read and have had such a great influence upon their readers, some critics have taken her to task for slighting Native Americans and other minorities, for accepting assumptions of nineteenth-century Manifest Destiny, and for describing the landscape as empty of human beings—virgin territory available for the taking by European settlers. Some have also criticized her for the conservative political messages contained in her books.

The criticisms and attacks directed at Turner and Wilder, however, were not enough to dislodge them from their exalted positions in the opinions of both average readers and professional scholars and critics. Both benefited from decades of tradition, from the magic wielded by their own glittering personalities, and from their association with an iconic element in the American psyche—the frontier. Wilder's image both as the sprightly, undaunted, slightly rebellious subject of her novels and as the kindly, lovable, older woman who wrote the books provides a magic combination, rendering it difficult to attack. Turner's image both as master teacher and as appealing writer likewise has made it difficult for critics to permanently debunk him.

Those who knew Turner well unanimously testified to his charm, personal integrity, sincerity, humility, and eager intellectual curiosity. His warm manner, vibrant voice, and approachableness made him almost impossible to dislike.[18] Preferring not to label himself primarily as a teacher, he liked to think of himself rather as a fellow seeker along with his students in the eternal quest for historical truth. "We were somehow made to feel that we are all prospectors together," was the way one of his former students affectionately described the process.[19] Professor William Cronon, a leader in the New Western History, has noted the "remarkable persistence of the Turner thesis in the face of so much criticism," observing that "we have not yet figured out a way to escape him. His work remains the foundation not only for the history of the West, but also for much of the rest of American history as well."[20]

If historians such as Richard Hofstadter could view Turner's western history as a case of "arrested development" and other critics could consign Wilder to the dustbin of naive ethnocentrism, one could also make a case for him as a model of historical scholarship and for her as a sensitive and empathetic storyteller. Turner himself was among the first to recognize the inadequacy of his frontier thesis as a single, all-embracing explanation for American historical development, despite the uncompromising assertions he set forth in his original 1893 paper. Realizing that the moving frontier had left a series of different sections in its wake—the Old Northwest (or Middle West), the Southwest, the Rocky Mountains, and the Pacific Coast, among others—starting in the early 1900s he devoted the rest of his career to understanding and explaining the influence of sectionalism on American life. His monograph for the American Nation series, *The Rise of the New West, 1819–1829,* was a pathbreaking case study that attempted to illustrate the variety of ways in which sectional diversity influenced American society and politics.[21] His difficulty in bringing to completion *The United States, 1830–1850* illustrated the grandness of his ambition as well as his personal difficulty in finishing a book.

Turner was a man ahead of his time. Many of the ideas espoused by James Harvey Robinson in his groundbreaking book *The New History* in 1912 had earlier been put forward by Turner, some of them prior to his 1893 essay. His present-mindedness, interest in quantification, calls for interdisciplinary scholarship, attention to the social history of ordinary people, and emphasis on the complexity of history placed him in the vanguard of innovative thinking about historical methodology.[22] In "The Significance of History," a remarkably prescient essay published in 1891 when he was only thirty years old, Turner observed, "Each age writes the history of the past anew with reference to the conditions uppermost in its own time." The wide scope of his vision and the catholic sweep of his approach shone through in the discussion. History, he insisted,

> is to be taken in no narrow sense. It is more than past literature, more than past politics, more than past economics. It is the self-consciousness of humanity—humanity's effort to understand itself through the study of its past. Therefore it is not confined to books; the *subject* is to be studied, not books simply. History has a unity and a continuity; the present needs the past to explain it; and local history must be read as a part of world history. The study has a utility as a mental discipline, and as expanding our ideas regarding the dignity of the present. But perhaps its most practical utility to us, as public school teachers, is its service in fostering good citizenship.[23]

Turner was largely misunderstood, not only by many of his most outspoken critics, but also by some of his friends and admirers. His ambitions as a historian far exceeded his ability to achieve them, but in his expansive vision of the historian's task and in his ambitious research agenda he set worthy goals and an inspirational standard of achievement. He constantly emphasized the complexity of historical forces and the difficulty of comprehending them. How to wade through the mass of evidence on any particular subject or, conversely, how to cope with the lack of evidence; the multiple biases of witnesses, society, and oneself; the lack of distance one suffers from in dealing with contemporary events—these and other obstacles always had to be taken into account.[24] Turner was nothing if not humble and open-minded in approaching these kinds of problems.

Wilder's view of history was much simpler, unsophisticated, and straightforward than Turner's. Though her books were set within a historical context and provided interesting cultural details for future historians of the period, she was at a far extreme from being a professional historian, and she was not writing history. Her métier, instead, was fiction—historical fiction, if you will. She had her own challenges to face.

Writing about events that had occurred five or six decades earlier posed difficult problems of reconstruction for her.[25] It shouldn't have seemed so strange that a woman in her sixties and seventies could not recall specific details of her life as a child, knowing what we know now about the vagaries and constructedness of people's memories. But Wilder confronted challenges that made her task different from Turner's. Not obligated to present a factually accurate story, she faced the necessity of molding one that would keep young readers interested and would also remain true to the essential nature of the frontier experience. That required careful attention to plot, structure, language, and characterization. In addition, she tried to aim her writing at readers who were approximately the same age that Laura had been in the action being described in the books, so the point of view had to keep changing and maturing, book by book. Wilder could not have done it by herself, although she had twenty years of experience of writing a farm newspaper column. While much of her prose was evocative and compelling and required little revision, in many places her daughter wielded a heavy editor's pen, and in some cases she did major rewriting and even inserted considerable segments of her own material. "Your writing is really lovely," Lane told her mother while working on revising the manuscript of *By the Shores of Silver Lake.* "The only thing I would change at all is some of the structure. Learning how to handle material structurally is a hell of a job, I guess it's never done."[26]

Structure was a particular forte of Frederick Jackson Turner. As a historian, he was inclined to think in structural terms. Much of his life was spent reading books and articles and working in archives amassing facts that he categorized and classified in burgeoning files that continued to accumulate right up to the end of his life. Since he was a compulsive collector and saver, most of his incredibly volu-minous notes and jottings are available for researchers at the Hunt-ington Library in San Marino, California. Working through those files, one can almost see the wheels of Turner's mind spinning as he continued to collect facts and statistics and filed them away in fold-ers, boxes, and file drawers. If he succeeded only partially in trans-lating his vision into words on a page, it was not for lack of trying. And, it must be remembered, he was a pioneer in establishing con-ceptual categories and building up an architectonic structure that could help inform his fellow social scientists and historical col-leagues, including Edward A. Ross, Thorstein Veblen, John Dewey, Josiah Royce, Charles A. Beard, Vernon L. Parrington, and a grow-ing army of other scholars.

If the kinds of truth that Turner and Wilder aimed at were quite different in some ways, both of them were trying to illuminate the nature of society and individuals within it in a humane and em-pathetic way. Both approached their work in an honest and well-meaning fashion. If evidence of their political biases sometimes seeped into the stories they related (Wilder was staunchly conser-vative by the 1930s; Turner, temperamentally inclined toward pro-gressive or liberal views, followed a vacillating course in his personal politics, early on supporting Theodore Roosevelt and Woodrow Wil-son while later becoming enamored of Herbert Hoover),[27] they sel-dom consciously fashioned their narratives or utilized language specifically designed to promote their respective causes. Both were humble and realistic about their own capabilities but also proud and determined to make a mark on society, being careful about their own reputations. Both reflected the biases and general assumptions of their contemporaries, but they also sought, as best they could, to transcend those biases and seek a higher truth. Both failed in now obvious and fairly significant ways, but both attempted in their own ways to overcome their limitations, to the degree that they could.

Standing out strikingly about them is their creativity. Wilder broke out of the role expectations associated with being a Missouri Ozarks farmwife to write for an agricultural newspaper and then for other regional and national periodicals. After failing to publish a serialized memoir of her life in a magazine, she extracted material from the manuscript to write, with help from her daughter, eight semiautobi-ographical children's novels that won wide popularity during the thirties and forties. Unbeknownst to most of her multitudinous fans, some of her most interesting and creative ideas had been expressed earlier in her biweekly articles in the *Missouri Ruralist* during the teens and twenties.[28]

Turner, like Wilder, was a highly creative writer. Unlike the Missourian, whose education had ended partway through high school, he accumulated the highest scholarly credentials, boasting a Ph.D. from the most prestigious graduate school in the United States at the time and teaching for three decades in two of the country's finest institutions of higher learning. That he would promulgate what became the dominant thesis of historical causation in the profession for more than three decades was enough to establish him in the pantheon of historians. That he would have followed that with another pathbreaking (though less influential) thesis, on sectionalism, added to his luster. But, as I have tried to suggest, it was Turner's vision of the historical process, as expressed in a variety of articles and in his own practices as a researcher and teacher, that remains his most important legacy.

An unusual tie connecting Wilder and Turner, and an illuminating factor in helping to explain them, is their common interest in poetry. Both, in their separate ways, were artists. Ultimately, they were romantics. Wilder herself wrote some poetry and liked to quote it in her articles and books.[29] Though apparently not a writer of poetry himself, Turner possessed a poetic bent that shone through in frequently evocative and picturesque language. To some degree in his writings and frequently in his classes, he included poems, often from favorite authors such as Ralph Waldo Emerson and Rudyard Kipling. One poem that he copied out and filed away and used in his classes was Tennyson's "Ulysses." He had underlined the last line of the poem in red:

> 'Tis not too late to seek a newer world.
> Push off, and sitting well in order smite
> The sounding furrows; for my purpose holds
> To sail beyond the sunset, and the baths
> Of all the western stars, until I die. . . .
> *To strive, to seek, to find, and not to yield.*[30]

Wilder, for her part, ended her last book with a fragment of a poem, no less dreamy and romantic, from a song her father had enjoyed playing on his fiddle:

Golden years are passing by,
These happy, golden years.[31]

Coinciding with swelling criticism in recent years of Turner's historical views and his famous frontier thesis has been a tendency among many critics to interpret Wilder's writings through the lens of Turner and the frontier and to take her to task for it. This has especially been true among critics influenced by the New Western Historians, who have taken Turner and others to task for their complacency in accepting the expropriation of Indian land by European settlers and the devastating impact the process had on Indian society and culture. While it certainly makes sense to relate her treatment of frontier life to his and to detect shortcomings in both of their works, placing too much weight on the connection between the two can obscure as much as it illuminates. The two were working in different genres, aiming at different audiences, relying upon different kinds of evidence and investigation, and operating in different historical eras. Since Wilder likely never read Turner, his influence on her was probably indirect. Intelligent and creative as both of them were, they reflected many of the assumptions, views, and intellectual proclivities of their respective zeitgeists. Mindful of their failures of or deficiencies of imagination, which leaves their writings vulnerable to critics today, we can still appropriately recognize them as giants in their own time, and that merits applause.

Would they write the same works today that they did decades ago? It is not likely. Should we uncritically accept everything they wrote and not expose it to careful scrutiny? Certainly not. But more than most of their contemporaries, they were capable of learning and growth, and I doubt whether they would have been content to remain stolidly set in their ways while the world changed around them. Turner, especially, was aware of and encouraged his fellow historians to respond to cultural shifts with creative adaptations of their own. A sympathetic understanding of their output as authors requires us to weigh their contributions and insights against their deficiencies and failures and to remember that we all are influenced by—if not totally captured by—the times in which we live. They likely will continue to be read long after most of their critics and defenders have been forgotten, remaining cultural icons and (flawed) models for future generations of readers and interpreters.

6

Rose Wilder Lane and Thomas Hart Benton

A Turn toward History during the 1930s

The 1930s, a decade of crisis and challenge surpassing almost any other in American history, provided the setting for many profound changes and transformations in the United States. At the same time, many Americans also grasped at history, partly for reassurance during a time of stress and anxiety, partly in order to search for solutions and alternatives that might relieve at least some of that strain and hardship. Congressional funding for Mount Rushmore, the opening of Greenfield Village, the restoration of colonial Williamsburg, and the construction of the National Archives during the late 1920s and early 1930s all testified to a growing sense among many Americans that history could provide guidance, that it could motivate people to higher achievement, and that it could point a way out of the many dilemmas then confronting American society. The pervasive turn toward history in the thirties manifested itself in a variety of ways, including W.P.A. murals in public buildings, historical novels ranging from Margaret Mitchell's *Gone with the Wind* to John Dos Passos's *U.S.A.* trilogy, the writings of the Southern Agrarians centered at Vanderbilt University, and the concerted effort of researchers like Constance Rourke to collect folklore and folk art.[1]

Laura Ingalls Wilder and her daughter, Rose Wilder Lane, participated in this turn toward history as, beginning in 1932, they both published novels set in Dakota and on the western frontier, based upon the stories of the former's experience and that of her husband and parents. Both saw the frontier theme as one containing rich materials for narrative development as well as for appeal for potential readers. They also viewed in it an opportunity to comment upon contemporary dilemmas confronting American society and to champion the kinds of values and traditions that they believed essential for national recovery from the economic disaster brought on by the Great Depression. For them history was not simply a dispassionate, academic exercise in ferreting out facts and weaving plausible, objective interpretations of the past. Rather, it was an engaged and often passionate commentary on the human condition, containing clear and positive lessons about how to live one's life and transform the surrounding society.

Wilder's Little House series of children's novels and Lane's adult novels *Let the Hurricane Roar* and *Free Land* clearly reflected the cultural assumptions and values of their authors and were intended, in part, to serve as cautionary tales meant to inspire their readers, who could derive from them shared history lessons about industry, self-reliance, and freedom from government interference. In this chapter, however, I would like to take a somewhat different tack by looking at a nonfiction book that Lane wrote about the history of Missouri, which is not well known, because she was unable to come to an agreement with the publisher who had commissioned the book about what it should contain. The manuscript remains now—seventy years later—unpublished, having been read by only a few curious researchers who have located it in the stacks of the Herbert Hoover Presidential Library in West Branch, Iowa. Although the book has never been made available to the general public, it provides an interesting read, and a close analysis of it reveals its author inserting nuggets of her personal political philosophy at various points. By taking account of Lane's ideological stance in this manuscript we can enhance our understanding of how she used her and her mother's fiction during the period as a vehicle for promoting their shared right-wing conservative political views. Adding interest to the discussion was the simultaneous production of a historical depiction of Missouri by the celebrated and often controversial painter Thomas Hart Benton.

Benton's 1936 mural *A Social History of the State of Missouri,* which covers all four walls of the House Lounge in the Missouri State Capitol, quickly gained attention as one of the best-known examples of the depression decade's historical turn. Instantly famous, his bold and energetic artistic rendering of Missouri's historical development elicited both extravagant praise and vitriolic scorn, polarizing viewers along political and aesthetic lines. Benton himself came to consider it his masterpiece, and art critics and historians, while hardly unanimous in their estimates, have generally concurred that it ranks among the significant works of twentieth-century American art.[2]

While Benton's progress on his mural was bathed in the spotlight of publicity, Lane toiled quietly on her book, operating out of her room in the Tiger Hotel in Columbia. Working only thirty-five miles apart from each other, Benton and Lane shared common assumptions and goals in aiming their works at lay audiences and focusing upon social history.[3] Lane had no direct connection with Benton, and their simultaneous efforts to interpret the history of the Show-Me State might have amounted to nothing more than an interesting coincidence were it not that each of them reflected a deeply felt impetus, encouraged by the thirties environment, to call upon history for inspiration, morale, models of behavior, and ideological underpinning.

Examining the resulting works in juxtaposition can help to illuminate the historical impulse that flourished during the depression decade, including the way in which it was manifested in the writings of Lane's mother, Laura Ingalls Wilder. Benton, Lane, and Wilder all provide excellent examples of the historical mentality at work during the depression, and by comparing Benton's and Lane's motives, assumptions, techniques, and ideologies, we might better understand why Benton's masterpiece established itself as a work of permanent significance while Lane's manuscript failed even to find a publisher. In the process, we might come to see Wilder's work, which was also being done at the same time, in a different light, too, because she also—sometimes consciously, sometimes subconsciously—injected ideological assumptions and values into her art.

The contrasting receptions received by Benton's and Lane's works should not obscure the fundamental similarities that tied them together. Close in age (Lane had been born three years earlier) and connected by geography (Benton grew up in Neosho, Missouri, 125 miles southwest of Mansfield), the two emerged as highly energetic, opinionated, ambitious, and creative artists during the early twentieth century. Both of them, though working in different mediums, spent considerable time researching their subjects, focused their attention on social developments, aimed at popular audiences, presented their ideas in simple, easy-to-understand terms, and brought well-thought-out—though contrasting—ideological assumptions to their work. Both had earlier departed Missouri for more cosmopolitan climes, then returned when they were in their forties to establish a regional setting for their art. For both, history functioned as a form of myth, embodying deeply felt and fundamental assumptions and values.[4] Benton brought a populist vision to his art, casting ordinary people as heroic pioneers and community-builders, often in opposition to the forces of bigotry, provincialism, economic exploitation, and extreme right-wing political philosophy. Lane's version of the myth projected different villains—tyrannical government restrictions on individual freedom and socialistic and left-wing political philosophies—while glorifying the individual rather than the community.

Benton was fresh from three other major mural projects completed during the previous five years (done for the New School for Social Research and the Whitney Museum of Art in New York City in 1930 and 1932 and for the Indiana building at the Chicago Century of Progress Exposition in 1933) when he was invited by the Missouri state legislature in 1935 to paint a mural depicting the history of the state. His innovative style of work was bound to offend many people and certain to generate controversy.[5]

The staid, conventional, ancestor-worshipping depictions so common among mural painters were not for him! Both content and form stretched the limits of convention. His subjects included prostitutes, night riders, and hooded Klansmen, along with farmers, workers, and politicians. They were rendered in bold—even garish—color, in unusual perspectives, and in strange juxtapositions. The Missouri legislators knew they would get something brash and challenging for the sixteen thousand dollars they offered to pay him, but they seemed willing to take the risk. For Benton, it would provide another platform from which to express his ideas about the true function of art and the role of the artist in modern, twentieth-century American society. More than that, the assignment entailed an opportunity to further his career and put some money in the bank (although in the end, two-thirds of the money went for materials).[6]

Like Thomas Hart Benton, Rose Wilder Lane also hoped that her historical labors would boost her career, improve her finances, and say something useful about history. Her career, unlike his, was on a descending trajectory by 1935, though probably not as precipitously as she herself feared that it was. Strapped for money and feeling like she needed a change of scenery if she was to pull her life together and get her career back on track, Lane responded quickly when notified by her agent, George Bye, that the McBride Publishing Company was offering a fifteen-hundred-dollar cash advance for her to write a volume about Missouri for a series of state books that it was doing. She snapped up the offer immediately and quickly went to work.[7] For more than seven years she had been living near her parents on Rocky Ridge farm. By this time, her mother was beginning to acquire greater financial security from the sales of her first three novels.[8] In fact, her mother's career was taking off just as her own seemed to be on the downswing.

Lane had earlier dreamed up a grandiose history project that might bring her wealth and recognition—a huge novel in ten volumes chronicling the westward movement of the United States from the Atlantic seaboard to the Pacific coast. The effort would require "an enormous canvas, covering horizontally a continent, vertically all classes." In it, Lane's gaze would be as much on the present as on the past; she hoped to explain the current situation in America by going back to its historical roots. "American history," she noted in her journal, "therefore our life now, is a swirl of currents across the landscape. Cultural currents deflected, altered, by economic (based on geographic?) and geographic conditions."[9]

Receiving the invitation to do the Missouri book, then, naturally complemented Lane's growing interest in history. She had read Charles and Mary Beard's *Rise of American Civilization* in January 1933 and five months later was reading Spengler's *Decline of the West* at the same time that she hammered out a prospective outline for her grand novel.[10] Although she never got properly started on the project, the work she did on her mother's Little House novels served as a partial substitute for it, as they chronicled life on the late-nineteenth-century agricultural frontier.

After two months of researching state history at Rocky Ridge, Lane decided that to do her assignment right she would need access to a large research library. That led her in July 1935 to drive from Mansfield to Columbia, setting up operations downtown in a room in the Tiger Hotel. It was a short walk from there to the State Historical Society on the University of Missouri campus. She started reading county history books, personal memoirs, specialized monographs, and anything else that might feed into the scheme developing in her mind.[11]

Before getting fairly started at the task, however, she accepted an invitation from her writer friend Garet Garrett to accompany him on a trip through Illinois, Iowa, Kansas, and Nebraska to collect material for a *Saturday Evening Post* assignment he had been given on New Deal farm policy.[12] Lane, whose antipathy to Roosevelt and the New Deal had grown steadily since the inauguration, not surprisingly managed to unearth considerable evidence to support her own jaundiced view of the New Deal while she traveled around the Midwest with Garrett. People's tax dollars were disappearing down a rat hole of misconceived government bureaucracies, in her estimation, and her direct observations seemed to confirm that.

Back in Columbia, more than ever convinced of the bankruptcy of Roosevelt's programs, she wrote an article entitled "Credo," an impassioned polemic against the direction that the "crowd" in Washington was taking the country. "I'd like you to understand why I'm a Jeffersonian Democrat," she wrote George Bye, "and will vote for anybody—Hoover, Harding, Al Capone—who will stop the New Deal."[13] After being rejected initially by the *Saturday Evening Post,* the article was given the lead position in the *Post*'s March 7, 1936, issue, generating some of the most intense reader response ever experienced by the magazine's editors.[14] Lane's intensifying conservatism also vented itself in her Missouri manuscript. Researching the book in 1935 and early 1936 afforded her a time for escape and reflection— escape from the dullness of Mansfield and a welcome relief from her mother's constant and sometimes suffocating presence, reflection on the state of the nation and her own political views and on what her future course should be.

Parallels between what Lane was undergoing and what was happening to Thomas Hart Benton, working away in Jefferson City, were almost uncanny. He, too, was in the process of escape and re-examination. While remaining politically left-of-center and firmly pro–New Deal, his general orientation, like Lane's, had shifted rightward. In their twenties, Benton and Lane had both gone through radical phases, though his commitment to the kinds of socialistic and communistic ideas that were being preached in Greenwich Village had been more intense and longer lasting than hers.

Both Benton and Lane had spent time in Paris and traveled in Europe after leaving home. But living in New York City for more than twenty years, until his well-publicized departure in 1935, had brought him into closer contact and association with left-wing radical politics during the teens and twenties. Lane's intellectual transformation from left to right was much more thorough than Benton's, leaving her by 1935 a rabid anti–New Dealer on the way to an extreme right-wing conservatism that would surface prominently by the 1940s. Benton's rightward shift stopped somewhere to the left of Roosevelt and the New Deal, as he rejected his former Communist friends and assumptions but retained a firm belief in the efficacy of state action to remedy social and political injustices. Thus, when Benton called himself a disciple of Thomas Jefferson, for him it meant something far different from Rose Wilder Lane's application of the term "Jeffersonian" to herself. Whereas Benton's painted interpretation of the state's social history reflected his faith in New Deal–type liberal reforms, Lane's written version of state history repudiated those very beliefs and values.[15]

Parallels between Lane and Benton, however, do not end there. Both displayed similar personality traits, being self-styled independent thinkers, willing to offend people and stir up controversy, if necessary or if it drew attention to themselves. Words like *cantankerous, controversial,* and *outrageous* easily fit Benton; he seemed to enjoy the publicity that his outspoken statements generated. Severing his ties with former colleagues, he departed New York City in 1935, terming it "provincial," denouncing the Marxists there as "dogmatic, self-righteous, and humorless," and asserting that its artistic community had been invaded by homosexuals. "The great cities are dead," he pronounced. "They offer nothing but coffins for living and thinking." Making her points with similar force in "Credo," Lane included left-wingers—a classification that would have included Benton himself—among her targets. Like him, she was also in the process of burning her intellectual bridges behind her as she began identifying with a small coterie of extreme conservative thinkers. Both Benton and Lane also came to see the Midwest as a nurturing environment for their respective arts, Benton calling it "the least provincial area of America. It is the least affected, that is, by ideas which are dependent on intellectual dogmas."[16]

Their research procedures also linked Benton and Lane. Both omnivorous readers, they boned up on Missouri history.[17] They also rec-

ognized the importance of physically venturing out and actually seeing the state. Benton, who had reacquainted himself with Missouri
when he came back home at the time of his father's death in 1924,
now spent weeks traveling from place to place, sketching people and
scenes that he later incorporated in his mural design. In the Thomas
Hart Benton Trust in Kansas City there survives a notebook that he
used to jot down ideas for organizing the mural and to list themes
and subjects to be included and connections to be made.[18] Most of
the planning for the mural, however, probably went on in his head
and never got put down on paper.

Lane also hit the road, purchasing a secondhand Ford and em-
barking on a three-week motor tour of the state with her Mansfield
friend Corinne Murray, before returning to Columbia for further
work in the archives of the State Historical Society. There she spent
week after week, filling notebooks with minutiae of Missouri history, including names, dates, anecdotes, statistics, topographical descriptions, and factual details about the counties. She also took notes
on the heroics of early Spanish and French exploration, the fur trade
traffic on the Missouri River, episodes in St. Louis, St. Charles, and
Ste. Genevieve, Civil War battles, and the rise of industry.[19]

Lane's notebooks indicate that her self-defined task differed considerably from and posed more difficulties than Benton's. This explains, in part, why her efforts turned out to be less successful. Employing words for a narrative history dictated different strategies
and considerations than did the assignment to do a wall mural depicting that same history. Detailed and complex as it was, Benton's
painted history could contain, by the nature of the medium, only
a small fraction of the information entailed in Lane's narrative account. The multitude of anecdotes, facts, and background information she collected apparently were intended to be integrated into her
story. What her publisher was apparently looking for, however, was
more of a contemporary travelogue of Missouri, making fewer
references to history than the heavily detailed historical narrative
that Lane eventually produced. Topography—not chronology—
was McBride's major concern. Ultimately, Lane's manuscript turned
out as good as it did because she largely ignored most of her volu-
minous notes, focusing instead on stories that lent themselves to her
considerable dramatic skills. She fashioned a kind of geographical
history of the state, lingering at various points along the journey to
recount the history of the area. Much of the resulting manuscript was

intriguing and highly readable. Yet there was nothing especially striking or unique about her treatment that was unobtainable in other standard sources. Eventually the manuscript was rejected by two different publishers.

After the McBride company turned it down as out of keeping with its series' intent, Lane's agent offered it to Longmans, Green and Company. Maxwell Aley of that press wrote Lane an encouraging letter in August 1936, assuring her that while he thought she had placed too much emphasis on the early French and Spanish periods, this defect could be rectified in a revised draft. "But this book brought back to me the fact that, By God, Madam, you can write!" he exclaimed. "There are passages in the book that are extraordinarily beautiful and carry a thrill that I seldom get from any contemporary work." In the end, however, Longmans also rejected the manuscript, and, after making desultory efforts to induce several other authors to join with her in launching a series of state books along the lines of the one that she had done, Lane abandoned the project as a wasted effort.[20]

Despite the failure of the Missouri history to find its way into print, it is worth paying attention to, for it stood out as one of many depression-era efforts to call on history for guidance and support in addressing contemporary problems and dilemmas. As an abortive effort of a popular and successful writer, it raises the question of why it failed. In part, at least, Lane's failure and Benton's success can be attributed to the changing political tenor of the times. Experimenting in a genre that was unfamiliar to her—unlike Benton, who was working in a well-practiced medium—certainly put Lane at a disadvantage. And Lane's right-wing ideology, while attractive to a major segment of the public, appealed less to the general populace than did Benton's progressive, pro–New Deal political stance.

Both artists depicted Missouri and its history in their works, but their descriptions partook as much of myth as of "scientific" or unbiased observation.[21] In a note attached to the manuscript, she informed her readers, "It is not my intention to make this a guide-book nor a story of any definite journey in Missouri. Rather," she wrote, "I would take the reader's imagination along the outlined route, dropping back into the historical events of the past when the present scene suggests them." Good journalist that she was, Lane effectively chose scenes and historical anecdotes for their ability to attract her readers' attention and served them up in a colorful and sometimes exaggerated prose style. A description of the Missouri River in an early version of the manuscript revealed her approach:

> The river that flows through this land is unlike any other river of America. On earth only the Yang-tse resembles it, a yellow river that seems less like water flowing than like a living serpentine thing. It is not possible to be indifferent to the Missouri river; one loves it or hates it, and to look at it long is to be fascinated, loving or hating, ever after. The fascination of this sluggish, muddy, powerful and monstrous river is not imagined. All men who know this river hate it, love it, fear it, and can not leave it. Look for one hour at the Missouri river, and forget it if you can.[22]

This is not the language of "objective" history, journalism, or science; rather, it is the province of myth. Lane herself suggested as much. "This is not a history of Missouri," she informed her readers. "We speak a language here too rich in memories and meanings to explain to those who do not know it. The land itself speaks with a thousand tongues. The hill, the spring, the tiniest stream, is a word and a volume." Everything about Missouri was different, strange, and unique, as Lane described it. "The charm of these hills and valleys that rise above the continent's great plains is a mysterious charm, reticent, subtle," she wrote. Missouri stood at the center of everything—a place "to which men come and from which their children go to come back again."[23] While the notion that the state displayed more of this and exhibited more of that than its neighbors was part of the myth that Lane expounded, the central myth in her narrative was the theme of freedom. If she could not develop it in a ten-volume novel about the entire American frontier, she could at least use a single state—her own Missouri—as a case study of how human liberty evolved and triumphed as the dominant value here in America.

"All Americans are born to personal freedom, an individual independence, unknown to other peoples," Lane observed in the section on the Missouri Compromise, but the independence and loyalty of Missourians possessed a special quality. Again, in describing the new American government, she happily observed that the "mad radicals" at the Constitutional convention of 1787 had formed a polity based on the principle of "All power to the individual." What excited her about historical figures like Moses Austin was the way in which they exemplified the principles of freedom and individual autonomy: "Here was action, release, freedom. A man could do any-thing legal, and much that wasn't, without asking anyone's per-mission.[24] The myth at the center of her narrative, then, was one re-garding individualism and freedom from all constraint, especially governmental.

Lane was drawn to her historical subject matter as a means of de-scribing and interpreting her contemporary midwestern milieu. Ben-ton in his native Missouri and his fellow regionalists Grant Wood in Iowa and John Steuart Curry in Kansas and Wisconsin also turned to historical themes as they tried to evince a sense of place that would stand against, in a way, the forces of industrialism and urbanization that were evidently undermining traditional values and ways of liv-ing in the Midwest.[25] Lane also turned to history as a logical outcome of her interest in the region in which she lived—Dakota as a young child and Missouri as a maturing child and adult. After having writ-ten serialized biographies of major figures such as Herbert Hoover, Henry Ford, and Jack London and having drawn upon her experi-ences in Paris, Albania, and elsewhere for story themes, Lane had turned increasingly to local Ozarks material as the basis for her pop-ular magazine fiction during the late 1920s and early 1930s. Her wide reading habits had always included a heavy smattering of history, but now her historical inclinations were reinforced by the work she did on her mother's autobiographical children's novels and by her own desire to write a big historical novel of the frontier. Reading Spengler and the Beards was just one small indicator of her serious interest in history. Unlike some pessimistic Europeans, however, she clung to much more optimistic notions about history's direction, be-lieving that if people were allowed to live up to their true potential, without excessive government intervention, they could better them-selves and improve society in the process.

Unfortunately, the state history format that she had to work with did not afford her the scope she needed to develop her grand themes of opportunity, personal initiative, self-improvement, and creativity. The book, to be sure, contained interesting and eloquently written passages, but in many ways it lacked balance and perspective. Lane devoted so much time to describing the early French and Spanish settlements that little space was left for later developments; most of the important transformations occurring after the Civil War were left out. There were interesting vignettes of lead mining at Potosi, French culture in Ste. Geneviève, and the wanderings of artist George Caleb

Bingham, but they could not compensate for the omission of large social and economic developments.

Lane's treatment of the state's geography likewise suffered from a lack of balance. She managed to get almost two-thirds of the way through the text before moving outside of a fifty-mile radius encircling Portage des Sioux, St. Louis, Ste. Genevieve, and the Potosi mines. She apparently originally intended a more comprehensive approach, but in the final manuscript it was not until the fifth of seven sections that she got to "The Boone's Lick Trail" (roughly the same route taken later by U.S. Highway 40), leading to Columbia, Jefferson City, and Boonville (near Old Franklin). The last two sections about the Santa Fe Trail and the Ozarks finally brought her home to the area she had grown up in around Mansfield.[26]

Lane relied upon several methods for telling her story: direct reporting of places and scenes that she had observed during her travels; biographies about leading figures of the type that filled textbooks; autobiography (the introductory section recounts the story of her coming, at the age of six, with her parents from South Dakota to Missouri in 1894); historical accounts of events and developments like the rise of the fur trade, the persecution of the Mormons, and the New Madrid earthquake; social history of a sort (confined primarily to descriptions of the Osage Indians and the French aristocrats who lived along the Missouri River); and even something resembling anthropology in her final observations about dances and "frolics" in the Ozarks region near her parents' place. But while parts of it worked well, as a whole the manuscript fell flat. It was too idiosyncratic, lacking any easily recognizable logic of inclusion and exclusion. It suffered from a wild imbalance of subject matter and chronology, and it failed to develop a central historical theme that could tie it all together. The one feature that lent it a certain continuity was the ideological gloss that Lane frequently imposed on events. In her interpretations, certain episodes served as lessons pointing to the need to protect individual freedom and to restrict government activity. Ultimately the effort failed as history, however, because it lacked a framework encompassing its frequently absorbing scenes and vignettes within some sort of coherent whole.

Lane's work was weak exactly where Benton's was strong. No matter how observers reacted to particular features of his mural, most would have agreed that the artist had put them all together with consummate skill. Its mirrored composition, narrative progression, juggling of three different modes of presentation (social history, episodic history, and mythological history), and symmetry of overall design impressed celebrants and detractors of the work alike. They might disagree about its robust colors, its exaggerated features, its unorthodox subject matter, its interpretive principles, or its political implications. But Benton's skill in putting it all together was never in doubt.

The architectonic greatness of the Missouri mural resulted from the extreme care that Benton exercised in preparing for and planning it, as well as from the experience he had gained while doing his three previous major mural assignments. The Indiana mural, especially, which had been on display at the Chicago Century of Progress Exposition in 1933, had taught him what he should avoid and what he should concentrate his energies upon. Not the least of his tricks was the skill he had acquired in handling people whose politics differed from his own and irate critics who questioned the accuracy of his judgment or his motives. His most difficult encounter during the painting of the mural occurred when a black politician took offense at Benton's depiction of the maltreatment of a group of slaves working in Missouri's lead mines before the Civil War. Not desiring a confrontation, Benton informed the man that he had been searching for a model for a black onlooker at a political rally in another scene and that he appeared to be perfect for the task. Would he allow his face to be incorporated in the mural? Quickly mollified, the aggrieved politician agreed to pose, and soon his likeness was up on the wall. His protest died aborning.[27]

Benton carefully planned which subjects to include in the mural. This was a daunting task. It was not difficult to find enough stories or historical developments to depict. The challenge lay in finding a way to incorporate as many themes as possible in the relatively small space that was available. Benton later acknowledged that "it was a considerable technical problem to get them all in there."[28] Except for four panels on the west wall, separated by windows (which he devoted largely to depictions of oil derricks and cornstalks), Benton had available on the north and south walls of the room spaces twenty-five feet long and sixteen feet high. The long east wall extended fifty-five feet. Complicating the assignment was the presence in the middle of each of these walls of large double doors, reaching about halfway up to the ceiling, that he had to work around.

Benton decided to divide each wall into three different types of space: above each door he painted a legendary scene (Huckleberry Finn and Jim on the Mississippi River, Jesse James and his gang staging a holdup, and the legend of Frankie and Johnnie); flanking each door were two small panels depicting some episode or historical situation (for example, slave labor in the lead mines, the Pony Express, and entertainment in a twenties speakeasy); the main wall space pictured broad social developments that had transformed Missouri between the days of early European settlement and modern urban-industrial civilization. The south wall, for example, featured mirror images of St. Louis and Kansas City and the changes that had gone on in those places.

For Benton, the true challenge of the mural lay in discovering how to encompass this multiplicity of subjects in a coherent, meaningful framework. He succeeded better than Rose Wilder Lane did in her endeavor for several reasons: he provided a more balanced temporal and spatial image of the state's history; he covered a wider range of subjects and time periods; he managed to depict both the energies and accomplishments of ordinary Missourians while also providing a critical commentary on social evils such as slavery, political corruption, and violence; and he presented his material in a distinctive artistic style that was immediately recognizable to those who were familiar with his earlier mural commissions.[29]

Lane's ideological commitment was more to freedom and individualism, abstractly considered, than it was to real people in all their varied tints of humanity. Benton, on the contrary, despite his sophistication and experience, was able viscerally to identify with the types of ordinary people he painted, and this came through convincingly in his mural. Authentic subject matter fused with a vigorous style to produce a powerful aesthetic statement. Benton's leftist New Deal predilections shone through in a number of places, from the positive portrayals of hardworking farmers and laborers to the negative depictions of Ku Klux Klanners and corrupt politicians and businessmen. For him, as for Lane, history fused with myth, but his version differed considerably from hers. Progress consisted not simply in lifting the weight of authority from individuals and granting them absolute liberty but in forming stronger bonds of community in which "the people" collectively could strive to progress to higher levels of production and a better quality of life, aided, if necessary, by political institutions.

Benton devoted much time and thought to what subjects to include in his composition and how to arrange them in such a way that they would tell a meaningful story about the state. The result was a masterpiece of American art that stood the test of time and ranks as one of the most important murals done by a twentieth-century artist.[30] Flawed as the painting may have been in some of its details, it stood out on the walls as a coherent whole, accomplishing what Benton had intended. That intent had been made very clear from the outset, and had, in fact, been written into his contract with the state legislature. This was to be a *social* history of Missouri. That largely determined the kinds of subjects to be depicted, although it certainly did not solve the whole task of inclusion and exclusion. "I wasn't so much interested in famous characters," Benton later recalled, "as I was in Missouri and the ordinary run of Missourians that I'd known in my life. The better part of that mural is stuff that I had actually experienced myself."[31]

Like Lane's, his work was in part autobiographical, and his political views influenced his methodology. Concerned about and committed to the betterment of the "common man," it was this type of ordinary American that he was bent on depicting. When critics objected to the exclusion of such figures as General John J. Pershing and namesake Senator Thomas Hart Benton, he shot back that "in the social history of Missouri, General Pershing was no more important than an ordinary bucksaw, and my grand-uncle, Senator Benton, was of far less importance than a common Missouri mule."[32] His midwestern brand of populism, learned at his congressman father's feet, led him to this position along with his commitment to an art that would be understood by and that would accurately depict "the people." Referring to French philosopher and critic Hippolyte Taine's theories about the social motivation of art, Benton made the Missouri mural the crowning achievement of his midwestern regionalist approach.[33]

Subject in hand, Benton went one step further before rendering his design on the wall. He modeled his conception in little clay figures and then painted them before projecting the desired image onto the walls. This process, too, involved several steps, requiring an outline drawing or "cartoon" of the mural on a smaller canvas and then the transferring of that image to the walls before finally painting them while standing or sitting on scaffolding.[34]

The social history of Missouri, as Benton conceived it, included the early settlement period (on the north wall); the nineteenth-century transformation of the state from a rural, agrarian society to an urban, industrial one (on the east wall); and the emergence of a modern, technological society dominated by big business and large institutions, as exemplified by Kansas City and St. Louis (on the south wall). In its large configurations, this narrative approach turned out to be more satisfactory than the one presented by Rose Wilder Lane in her book manuscript, because it was more inclusive and because it better explained how modern industry and agriculture in the state had come into existence. But the compelling interest—and the major source of controversy—of the mural lay in its details. It included scenes of fur traders plying Indians with whiskey, steamboats on the rivers and trains riding the rails, a baptism by a river and a political speech in front of a courthouse, loggers fashioning boards and miners drilling ore, farmers in the field and housewives in the kitchen, a jury in a courtroom, butchers in a meat plant, typists in an office, printers at their trade, schoolchildren and society matrons at a museum, and patrons in a nightclub.

Generating considerable criticism at the time were depictions of a bare-bottomed baby having its diaper changed at a picnic, a lynching, a Jesse James holdup, Frankie getting her revenge on Johnny, and Kansas City political boss Tom Pendergast nonchalantly listening to a speaker drone on at a dinner. Many observers also objected to the alleged inaccuracy of some of the portrayals, including scenes of a cow being milked and a mule pulling a plow. Real cows and mules did not look that way at all, some critics complained. Other observers did not appreciate what they deemed to be "modernist" distortions generated by Benton's style, although art critics generally viewed him, as a leading regionalist during the 1930s, as a realist in opposition to the trends of high modernism.[35]

What many viewers missed at the time were the deeper meanings that Benton encoded in his painting. Boss Pendergast's presence at the dinner was hardly as important as the sinking of political discourse to a much lower level than it had been at the time that Benton's father (depicted in the scene in front of the courthouse) had been active. The posture of Colonel M. E. Benton in delivering his extemporaneous (or memorized) speech to a rapt group of listeners was exactly the same as that of the businessman reading his speech at the Kansas City luncheon attended by Pendergast (who, one might infer, had dictated the contents of the speech). The audience of the latter is deeply bored and obviously not partaking of the same spirit of Jeffersonian democracy as is the first one.

The art that a society produces constitutes a telling commentary on its deepest values and ideas. During the depression decade, social and intellectual fissures deepened to crisis proportions in the United States. The historical works of Thomas Hart Benton and Rose Wilder Lane—joined in time and space by experience and history—provide an unusual window through which we can look three-quarters of a century later to trace some of the intellectual history of the period, especially its turn toward the past to locate values and principles that could sustain them and guide them on their journey into the future.

Like many other artists during the period, Benton and Lane looked to the past for insight into the future, but the lessons they derived were at a far remove from each other. Benton sought neither an idealized past nor a return to a Jeffersonian agrarian society but rather hoped for a reinvigorated democratic community, helped along by New Deal–type reforms.[36] Lane drew exactly the opposite conclusions from her historical musings, calling for the establishment of a laissez-faire individualism untainted by the "communistic" schemes of New Deal liberalism. She took her stand with rugged individualists who could stand alone in either a rural or an urban setting. Ultimately, however, the former succeeded and the latter failed in their Missouri history efforts, not so much because of the ideologies they espoused but rather because of the artistic approaches they took. In their own separate ways, both contributed to one of the major phenomena of that tumultuous decade in American life: a turn toward history.

In the months and years after Benton completed his mural, Lane would write her second historical novel, *Free Land,* and work on the last four of her mother's Little House books. In both cases she would follow the practice she had established in *Let the Hurricane Roar* and her Missouri book—injecting doses of conservative political ideology (more in her own book than in her mother's) for the benefit of her readers. Thus, she provides an excellent example of how thirties culture in America raised up historical consciousness as well as conservative political thinking as a counterweight to the dominant liberal ideology that temporarily ruled the roost.

Laura Ingalls Wilder had this formal portrait taken at age seventy, in 1937, when she was invited to speak at a book fair in Detroit. *Laura Ingalls Wilder Memorial Society, De Smet, South Dakota.*

Rose Wilder Lane in 1942 in her middle fifties.
Collection of William Anderson.

Laura Ingalls Wilder and her daughter, Rose Wilder Lane, hiking through the woods at Rocky Ridge farm around 1910. *Herbert Hoover Presidential Library.*

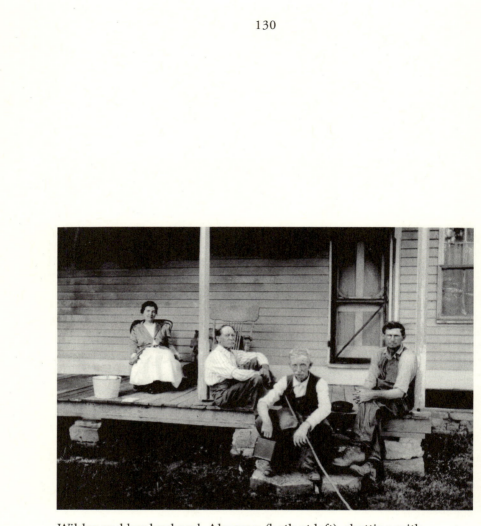

Wilder and her husband, Almanzo (both at left), chatting with neighbors during the late 1920s. *Herbert Hoover Presidential Library.*

The Wilders' Rocky Ridge farmhouse, which they built and expanded over a period of almost two decades. *Photo by John Miller, June 2007.*

The English-style rock house Rose Wilder Lane constructed for her parents in 1928. *Photo by John Miller, June 2007.*

Lane in the living room of her parents' farmhouse, which she took over from them between 1928 to 1935, after they moved into the rock house she had built for them. *Laura Ingalls Wilder Home and Museum, Mansfield, Missouri.*

Sketched in 1926, this was the Albanian dream house that Rose
Wilder Lane hoped to build on the shore of the Adriatic Sea. *Herbert
Hoover Presidential Library, with permission from Abbie MacBride Allen.*

Thomas Hart Benton used his father, Congressman Maecenus E. Benton, as the model for the political speaker featured on the east wall of his mural *A Social History of the State of Missouri*, which decorates the House Lounge in the state capitol at Jefferson City. *Missouri State Museum; art © T. H. Benton and R. P. Benton Testamentary Trusts/UMB Bank Trustee/Licensed by VAGA, New York, N.Y.*

Benton's controversial mural featured legendary scenes, such as Huck Finn and the slave Jim; social history, such as fur traders dickering with Indians; and specific historical episodes, such as the expulsion of the Mormons from Missouri (lower right panel). *Missouri State Museum; art © T. H. Benton and R. P. Benton Testamentary Trusts/UMB Bank Trustee/ Licensed by VAGA, New York, N.Y.*

IV

Culture

How Should People Live, and How Should Society Function?

A primary function of children's literature is to instruct its young readers in correct behavior and to reproduce the culture by passing down the wisdom of the elders. Part of the unstated agenda of Laura Ingalls Wilder's novels, according to Claudia Mills, is to trace the moral development and awareness of its protagonist, the fictional Laura Ingalls. "Laura's moral maturation is rich and multilayered," writes Mills, "but at the heart of the Little House books, and shaping their progression as one multivolumed novel, is the theme of obedience giving way to autonomy, literally moral self-rule." The process described in the books coincides with psychologist Jean Piaget's theory of moral evolution in the child as well as to Lawrence Kohlberg's well-known six-stage scheme of moral development. Laura "grows from stage-one heteronomous morality, where she follows externally imposed rules to avoid externally imposed sanctions, to stage-six morality, where she recognizes that moral rules are binding on her because she legislates them for herself," Mills observes.[1]

The Little House books, whatever else they may be, are primers in values and prescriptions for right living. Wilder's primary motivations in writing them were to make money, garner a little prestige, and preserve some of the stories she had heard as a child and ones she herself had related over the years about her family's wanderings on the frontier. But she was incapable of thinking without casting moral judgments and making social commentaries on the characters she placed in the center of her stories. That she was a judgmental person is clear from the comments her daughter made about her in the voluminous letters that she wrote. That Wilder also harbored some interesting and perceptive thoughts about people's moral choices, obligations, and behaviors is apparent from reading her novels and, prior to that, her columns published in the *Missouri Ruralist* during the teens and twenties.

For Laura Ingalls Wilder, meditating on individual morality morphed naturally into translating the principles she favored in the personal realm into the sociopolitical arena. Ethics and politics meshed seamlessly in her thinking. Adherents of traditional values of hard work, personal freedom and responsibility, individual effort, kindness, and decency can choose to be progressive or liberal in their political views, but in Wilder's case devotion to these types of values evolved by the 1930s into an outspoken and emotional opposition to New Deal policies and staunch conservatism in politics.

Her daughter, Rose Wilder Lane, possessed a more sophisticated knowledge of philosophy and ethics while displaying greater inconsistency in her thinking about personal morality. She agreed with her mother about the follies of the Roosevelt administration, but her commitment to an uncompromising brand of personal liberty led her by the thirties to an extreme right-wing version of politics, taking her considerably beyond the more conventional position taken by Wilder. Today she is viewed as one of the early inspirations for modern libertarian thought in the United States.

This section addresses three of the most important aspects of the sociopolitical thinking of Wilder and Lane: the values Wilder championed in her farm journalism, the increasingly controversial debate that has occurred in recent years over the stance taken by Wilder (and Lane) toward American Indians in the Little House books, and the mutual antipathy of Wilder and Lane toward Franklin Roosevelt and the New Deal and the ways in which their shared conservative political values may or may not have entered into their writings. Literature has always been a point of contestation over morality and culture. That controversy attaches to the writings of Wilder and Lane should not surprise us, nor should we be taken aback if in the future those controversies persist and multiply.

Some readers, upon hearing that Wilder's and Lane's writings are colored with a particular political branding, remain skeptical and are reluctant to admit the truth of it. This is a reminder that literature, while always being informed by some sorts of political and moral perspectives, tends to disguise those preferences or even to deny them. It also needs to be observed that writers may not be aware themselves of the implicit moral and political messages contained in their works, but this does not obviate their presence there.

Two words of caution are in order. In the first place, all the work that has been done on reader-response theory should remind us that literary works can be read in many different ways and that their authors often have little control over the varying interpretations that may be given to their works. This observation necessarily implies that at any given time a text will inspire more than one competing interpretation and that over time the received meanings of texts will evolve under the influence of shifting cultural determinants. In the second place, trying to trace the influence of works of literature on their audiences poses particularly hazardous challenges. Scholars are much better able to probe inputs than outputs in this regard. We have the words of the authors, after all. In many cases we have considerable evidence concerning what authors intended. But seldom do we possess concrete or convincing information about how texts actually affected or influenced their readers. In other words, caution and a bit of humility are strongly advised in this area.

7

Wilder's Apprenticeship as a Farm Journalist

The publication of Laura Ingalls Wilder's first book, *Little House in the Big Woods*, in April 1932 generated enthusiastic responses from readers and reviewers alike. *Atlantic Bookshelf* recommended it as a "delightful and absorbing true story," and the *New York Times* lauded it for its "refreshingly genuine and lifelike quality." *Books* noted, "Too few, nowadays, can tell as real and treasurable a story. Moreover, this story is delightfully told." The reviewer went on to praise the "gentle cadence" of its "simple sentences" and urged all children of the region and "many others" to read it.[1]

Delighted readers of the children's novel were surprised and intrigued to discover that the book's author was a sixty-five-year-old farmwife from southern Missouri with no previous experience in the genre. Its stories and depictions of family life on the post–Civil War Wisconsin frontier were so engagingly told and so seemingly authentic that people assumed that their author had simply sat down one day to put her earliest childhood memories on paper and had succeeded brilliantly in capturing them whole. Apparently here was an untutored genius whose transparently real descriptions of her childhood possessed the power to evoke warm feelings and to call up nostalgic reminiscences in her audience.

The remarkable success of Wilder's Little House series over time, reflecting both the immediate acclaim for the books as they appeared and their continued staying power, has been a cause of considerable wonderment to many observers. To what can we ascribe the high degree of skill with which this woman in her sixties, with no previous experience as a fiction writer, turned out in rapid order—one every year or two—a series of children's books that transformed her into a twentieth-century literary icon?

In the eyes of her fans and admirers, Laura Ingalls Wilder was the literary equivalent of Grandma Moses, a painter of homespun rural scenes who finally displayed her latent artistic talent in her late seventies. According to this view, Wilder's potential had always been present; it merely required an opportunity to unleash it. With the discovery of her daughter Rose Wilder Lane's significant role in the production of the books, another explanation suggested itself: that Wilder herself never amounted to more than a "determined but amateurish writer to the end" and that "[a]lmost everything we admire" about the books resulted from her daughter's "fine touch" in editing and rewriting them. This is the conclusion reached by William Holtz in his biography of Lane, *The Ghost in the Little House: A Life of Rose Wilder Lane.*[2]

While Lane certainly deserves substantial credit for her contributions to her mother's success, a more satisfactory explanation exists for the seemingly remarkable emergence of Wilder's children's novels between 1932 and 1943, books exhibiting stylistic qualities that attracted large numbers of readers and containing moral insights that continue to provoke our interest. It is necessary to look at Laura Ingalls Wilder's writing career in its full context to adequately understand it. This was not a woman initially launching a new career at an age when most people are retiring. Rather, her decision to turn her hand to children's novels was the culmination of a long period of practice and development that provided her with the kind of experience and confidence she needed to set words down in a way that would keep her readers turning the pages. Pamela Smith Hill provides the most comprehensive discussion of Wilder's development as a writer in her excellent biography *Laura Ingalls Wilder: A Writer's Life.*[3]

Little attention was paid at the time to the fact that for the better part of two decades Wilder had been honing her craft as a writer, mainly authoring columns for farm journals. By the time she accepted her daughter's challenge to get the story of her life down on paper, she was already experienced at putting words on a page. She was no neophyte taking a wild stab at something totally new to her. If relating stories in extended fictional form that would appeal to a broad readership and win the approval of New York publishing firms *was* indeed a new experience for her, the basic process of stringing words on a page in meaningful form in such a way as to appeal to the average reader was *not*. What was different and had to be learned—and what *was* learned, through experience and the helpful assistance and skillful tutoring of Lane—was establishing a voice that would be understandable and appealing to children. These, after all, were to be children's books, not adult ones, and so Wilder had to learn a whole new way of writing.

Since her days as a schoolgirl in Dakota Territory, Wilder had enjoyed expressing her creative urge through writing. William Anderson has brought to light a number of poems that she wrote, beginning in her teens, on subjects ranging from the assassination of President James Garfield and the prairie winds that blew across the landscape to the evils of lying and admiration for her sister Mary. The poetic muse also beckoned to Wilder periodically as an adult. In 1915, while visiting her daughter in San Francisco, she wrote several poems—mostly about faeries—that Rose was able to get published in the *San Francisco Bulletin*. In 1930, when her old hometown in South Dakota was celebrating the fiftieth anniversary of its founding, she sent a rather pedestrian poem about life on the prairie as she remembered it to editor Aubrey Sherwood, who published it in the big golden anniversary edition of the *De Smet News*.[4]

Wilder's primary training ground and testing place as a writer was the work that she did between 1911 and 1924 for Arthur Capper's semimonthly farm newspaper, the *Missouri Ruralist*.[5] At first only sporadically, but regularly beginning in 1916, she used her column to explore a variety of subjects, from raising poultry and making housework more efficient to promoting rural community and commenting on the virtues and foibles of human nature.

Having established a reputation by 1910 for her expertise in raising chickens, Wilder was frequently called upon to speak on the subject at agricultural fairs and meetings. On one of these occasions when she was too busy to attend the event, she sent her talk along to be read to the audience. Among the listeners that day and impressed by what he heard was the editor of the *Missouri Ruralist*, who invited Wilder to send in some of her material for publication in the newspaper. Her first article, an address prepared for Farmers' Week, appeared on February 18, 1911, as "Favors the Small Farm Home." Like many of her later pieces, it praised rural living and the progress that had been made up to that time, while urging her readers to continue their work to improve cultural, social, and intellectual life in the countryside.[6]

Wilder's baptism as a farm journalist coincided with a major transformation of the publication, which had been known simply as the *Ruralist* from its origin in 1902 until its purchase by Arthur Capper in July 1910. The hugely successful Kansas publisher, who later served two terms as the state's governor between 1915 and 1919 and then spent three decades in the U.S. Senate, built an empire of a dozen papers—including the *Topeka Daily Capital, Capper's Farmer, Capper's Weekly,* and farm papers in Kansas, Nebraska, Oklahoma, Missouri, Michigan, Ohio, and Pennsylvania—with a combined circulation of more than four million readers.

Even before he began to devote most of his time to politics, he left the daily management of his publications largely to his editors. Having gone through three different editors after purchasing the *Missouri Ruralist,* Capper in 1913 had the good fortune to be introduced to John F. Case, a remarkably bright and energetic thirty-seven-year-old small-town Missouri newspaper editor and local postmaster, who would go on to edit the paper for most of the next four decades.[7]

By the time Case took the job, Capper had already made extensive changes in the publication, adding "Missouri" to the title, transforming it from a weekly to a semimonthly (thereby reducing its cost from one dollar to fifty cents a year), dressing it up with more pictures, and transferring its printing facilities from Kansas City to Topeka. Circulation, which had stood at 10,500 in 1910, jumped to 52,600 by 1913 and continued upward, reaching 90,000 in 1920, and, after merging with the *Journal of Agriculture,* 151,000 in 1924. Writers generally earned fifteen to twenty-five cents per column inch for their work. During Wilder's tenure with the paper, the *Missouri Ruralist* had no serious competition in its field. Usually coming in at twenty or twenty-four pages, about half of them given over to advertisements, the paper ran one or more feature articles in each issue, serving up most of its material through approximately a dozen departments, including ones devoted to poultry, livestock, dairying, horticulture, farm crops, farm management, legal matters, children, and home. Stories appealing to farm women appeared on the "home" page, which ran in every issue, focusing its attention on cooking, child care, sewing, gardening, and fashions. Wilder expanded the purview of this section during the time that she wrote for it and edited it.

With an audience consisting primarily of dirt farmers and their families, the *Missouri Ruralist* preached the virtues of rural life and called for better roads and farming methods, purebred livestock, more practical agricultural education, use of silos and commercial fertilizer, farmers' short courses, extension of rural free delivery, state fruit inspection, and a variety of other advances designed to improve rural life. Although it frequently ran Arthur Capper's editorials and reprints of his speeches, it remained nonpartisan and largely nonpolitical in tenor. In sum, it provided an ideal forum for Laura Ingalls Wilder to reach a wide audience for her ideas and to develop her writing talent over the course of approximately a decade.

Until the publication in 1991 of a collection of Wilder's early farm journal writings, edited by Stephen W. Hines, these writings were difficult to locate, and few people paid much attention to the pieces. Since then, several other volumes have also reprinted some of the columns, and in 2007 Hines came out with an expanded edition of all of the *Missouri Ruralist* columns in their original format.[8] Reading these articles in the perspective of the novels that came later helps to clarify and extend our understanding of Wilder as an author. In the first place, they constitute evidence of her authorial competence before she began collaborating with her daughter in writing the Little House books. Second, they provide a picture of the furnishings of her mind—the themes, concerns, and subjects she was interested in and paid attention to as a mature woman. Third, in calling up the stories of her childhood, they expose some of the contents of her memory and provide a sort of preview of the novels that would come later. Finally, they allow us to observe the mechanisms of her thought processes—illuminating her assumptions and worldview, her didacticism, her powers of description, and her inclination to attribute meaning to everything she encountered.

A reading of Wilder's farm journalism demonstrates that Wilder, while not yet a skilled novelist at the time, was a competent and often eloquent stylist as a nonfiction writer. She understood language and how to communicate with readers. Later, it was possible for large sections of *Little House in the Big Woods* to go directly from Laura's penciled manuscript to Harper's hardbound edition almost verbatim.[9] If Lane considered it necessary or desirable to make whole-sale revisions in her mother's manuscripts as the series progressed, at least it can be said that, early on, Wilder displayed considerable competence both as a nonfiction and as a fiction writer.[10]

Her ability to put words on a page in interesting and compelling fashion should not have been a surprise to those who had followed her progress as a farm newspaper columnist. Her columns in the *Missouri Ruralist* reached a wide audience around the state. For five years after the publication of the original article in February 1911 only occasional articles appeared, between one and three a year. But after Wilder visited her daughter in San Francisco in late 1915, she was featured regularly, twice a month, in the farm newspaper. The pieces' frequency declined to around fifteen a year during 1921 and 1922, and her output fell by another third in 1923 and 1924 before they disappeared altogether. Through April 1919 and sometimes af-ter that the articles were individually titled, but between then and December 1920 they generally ran under the heading of "The Farm Home," and from June 1921 through the end of 1924 they were called "As a Farm Woman Thinks." Unpretentious in tone, but in a voice that established its authority through a blend of ordinary common sense and uncommon psychological insight, these columns exhibit-ed an intelligence that had been honed by years of experience, ob-servation, and reflection. Almost always, Wilder moved beyond pure description to seek the meaning and significance of what she was describing, and usually there was some kind of lesson or moral to be derived from it. Her columns were almost always instructive—providing practical advice on farming, gardening, and homemak-ing, suggesting ways to make everyday life more livable and enjoy-able, and urging people to get along amiably with their neighbors, promote the betterment of the community, and always do the right thing.

An excerpt from her May 15, 1923, column provides a sample of her writing style:

> "The days are just filled with little things and I am so tired of do-ing them," wailed a friend recently. Since then I have been think-ing about little things, or these things we are in habit of thinking small, altho I am sure our judgment is often at fault when we do so. . . .
>
> Doing up cut fingers, kissing hurt places and singing bedtime songs are small things by themselves but they will inculcate a love

for home and family that will last thru life and help to keep America a land of homes.

· Putting up the school lunch for the children or cooking a good
meal for the family may seem a very insignificant task as compared with giving a lecture, writing a book or doing other things
that have a larger audience, but I doubt very much if in the ultimate reckoning they will count as much. . . .

It belittles us to think of our daily tasks as small things and, if we
continue to do so, it will in time make us small. It will narrow our
horizon and make of our work just drudgery.

There are so many little things that are really very great and
when we learn to look beyond the insignificant appearing acts
themselves to their far reaching consequences we will, "despise
not the day of small things." We will feel an added dignity and
poise from the fact that our everyday round of duties is as important as any other part of the work of the world.

And just as a little thread of gold, running thru a fabric, brightens the whole garment, so women's work at home, while only the
doing of little things, like the golden gleam of sunlight runs thru
and brightens all the fabric of civilization.[11]

Written in clear, straightforward prose and aimed at ordinary,
literate Missouri farm women, the columns combined description,
narration, information, advice, encouragement, humor, and general
observations about the world of rural Missouri in brief, pithy fashion. Generally taking off from her own experiences living in and
around Rocky Ridge and the town of Mansfield, Wilder also discovered inspiration for her writing in newspaper stories, magazine articles, government reports, academic conferences, and memories
conjured up from her childhood. Frequently they were stimulated
by something her husband (referred to in the articles as "The Man of
the Place") said or did and sometimes by her daughter.

Always readable, frequently charming, and sometimes profound
in the insights they rendered, these columns collectively established
Wilder as a voice worth listening to and provided a platform from
which she was able later to transform herself into a writer of fiction.
Except apparently for one article appearing in 1925, Wilder finished
her association with the *Ruralist* toward the end of 1924, later attempting sporadically to place articles in national magazines before
turning her attention to her autobiography at the end of the decade.

Another thing we can learn from reading Wilder's farm newspaper columns is something about the subjects she was interested in

and concerned about as a resident and citizen of a small farm and small town in southern Missouri. Even better than the novels, which necessarily operated under a variety of narrative constraints and which could only indirectly reflect her thoughts and feelings, Wilder's early nonfiction writings indicate the way in which her mind was furnished. In usually five hundred to a thousand words, she focused upon happenings and themes that attracted her interest in the ordinary rounds of daily living and ones that she thought her readers might find interesting and useful or be able to identify with. The themes she chose to write about revealed many of her own predilections, interests, and anxieties. They included nature, the centrality of the family, devotion to work, technological progress, societal trends, the need for love and neighborliness, evolving women's roles, balance as an ideal, and the positive and negative effects of talk and gossip.

While often commenting on her and her husband's experiences at Rocky Ridge farm, which lay a mile east of Mansfield, she rarely cast the town itself as her subject. Beyond an article describing her own Wright County, the county seat of Hartville, and Mansfield, its largest town, she made the townspeople of Mansfield and their activities her subject only infrequently.[12] She did mention the annual county fair in Mansfield but not its origins or its leading promoters and growth over time. She noted that Mansfield had a public square with a park, but she failed to describe all of the many activities that went on there. Unlike her later novels about De Smet, which were full of recognizable town dwellers, her newspaper columns spent little time discussing the inhabitants of Mansfield, whether prominent or humble. In one column she mentioned local celebrities Congressman Cleveland Newton, author William Hamby, baseball pitcher Carl Mays, and her daughter, Rose, but this was an exception that proved the rule.[13]

Generally her attention fixed on farm life and rural happenings or on people in general. The vicissitudes of human nature fascinated her, just as they would later in her novels. She was attracted to the ironies and contradictions of people's behavior, pointing, for instance, to "those who persistently disobey the laws of health, which being nature's laws are also God's laws, and then when ill health comes, wonder why they should be compelled to suffer." People pay for their deeds, she believed. "We begin to pay the dentist when our teeth first need attention whether they have that attention or not," she observed. People possess choices, and the choices they make determine their destiny.[14] Always the ultimate goal is balance. Lives are not meant to grow "lopsided and crippled!" Instead, "They should be well developed and balanced, strong and symmetrical, like a tree that grows by itself in the open, able to stand safely against the storms from whatever direction they may come—a thing of beauty and satisfaction."[15] Wise in her observations about human nature in her farm columns, Wilder carried those insights into her children's novels when she started writing them.

Her experiences at Rocky Ridge also made her a protoconservationist and an advocate of the "small is beautiful" ideal.[16] She believed that the manner in which she and her husband lived pointed the way to "a freer, healthier, happier life." No one needed a large farm, in her view. "In a settlement of small farms the social life can be much pleasanter than on large farms where the distance to the nearest neighbor is so great," she wrote. A strong sense of community was her ideal: "Fifteen or twenty families on five acre farms will be near enough together to have pleasant social gatherings in the evenings. The women can have their embroidery clubs, their reading club and even the children can have their little parties without much trouble or loss of time. This could not be done if each family lived on a 100 or 200-acre farm."[17]

Along with visiting neighbors, Wilder's social life during the 1920s largely took place within a variety of women's groups, including bridge and embroidery clubs. She took special interest in self-improvement study groups such as the Friday Afternoon Club, the Justamere Club, the Interesting Hour Club, and the Athenian Club, the last of which she helped organize along with some women from Hartville.[18] Friendship, community, and cooperation all occupied high places in her pantheon of values. It is well to keep this in mind, since she is sometimes asserted to have been an advocate of unrestrained individualism. It is true that she distrusted government and sought a maximum of individual freedom, but these values must be measured against her enthusiasm for community and collective activity. "To work for the good of the community without full reward in money but because we love our fellows and long for the common betterment is work with a big 'W,' work that will keep our souls alive," she advised.[19]

"It used to be that only the women in town could have the advantages of women's clubs," Wilder observed, "but now the woman in the country can be just as cultured a club woman as though she lived in town. The Neighborhood club can take up any line of work or study the members wish." She provided advice on how to organize new clubs and where to obtain information and materials to carry them on. She spoke for women who wanted to do more than merely take care of their families and manage the household and who wanted to go beyond socializing and finding enjoyment in social clubs by endeavoring to "cultivate their minds and increase their knowledge."[20] To this degree, at least, she found herself participating in the feminist yearnings that her daughter was involved in at a much deeper level.

Like Secretary of Commerce Herbert Hoover, who was the subject of one of Lane's biographies and whose little book *American Individualism* came out in 1922, Wilder believed strongly in the utility and desirability of voluntary cooperation. In a column in March of that year, she wrote about a neighbor crippled with rheumatism who was not able to put up his wood for the winter. Responding to this, his neighbors organized a "working" to do it for him, acting out "a blessed, old-fashioned way of helping out a neighbor" and in the process enjoying "a regular old-fashioned good time."[21] So long as people behaved neighborly to each other like this, the long hand of government could be restrained.

Politics played a minor role in Wilder's columns. She was not as antagonistic to the notion of governmental activity and intervention as she would later become. In November 1918, after a year and a half's participation in a world war that saw President Woodrow Wilson expanding the power of the federal government enormously, she lauded the preparation and training he had brought to the job and the energy with which he applied himself to the task. The wartime challenge catalyzed Wilder to urge her fellow citizens to do their patriotic duty to support their nation. At a time when soldiers were risking their lives overseas for democracy, she asked her readers if they were "fighting bravely for these things all down the line." The necessity of supporting the government's objectives in the circumstances seemed incontestable to her. She urged people to participate in collective action through buying Liberty Bonds and War Savings Stamps, raising food, and giving to the Red Cross. "By the sacrifice we make in giving we show our love for humanity," she wrote, "our pity for the helpless and our generosity toward those less fortunate than ourselves." She urged people to support their governmental leaders and not become impatient and too critical of them: "Friendly, constructive criticism is one thing and unkind, nagging fault-finding is another quite different." Government was a worthy activity and deserved people's respect and support, in Wilder's view: "Let's talk to each other about the ideals of life and government that President Wilson is putting before the world! If we, the people hold fast to and live by these beautiful ideals, they are bound to be enacted by our government for, in a republic the ideas of the people reach upward to the top instead of being handed down from someone at the top to the people who must accept them whether they like it or not."[22]

Addressing the problem of inflation a year after the armistice, she struck a balance between collective action and individual responsibility, writing, "There are problems that should be handled for us all collectively but as in so many other things of our national life, it is also a matter for each of us to attend to. If each one of a crowd acting independently does the same things, it produces a mass action that is powerful, and we can handle this problem of high costs for ourselves much better than we have been doing if we try."[23]

Wilder acknowledged devoting some of her time to politics, along with club work and lodge work.[24] Her activities in local Democratic party politics, running (unsuccessfully) for office, and serving as secretary-treasurer of the local branch of the National Farm Loan Association all distinguished her from the vast majority of her female cohorts. She thought women had something to contribute in ways that men, who dominated the political scene, did not easily understand. As nationwide women's suffrage loomed on the horizon with the passage of the Nineteenth Amendment, Wilder wrote, "If women, with their entrance into a free discussion of politics, can do away with the 'hot air' and insults, with 'making the Eagle scream,' and 'twisting the Lion's tail,' and 'shaking the bloody shirt,' and all the rest of the smoke screen, bringing politics into the open air of sane, sensible discussion—a discussion of facts and conditions, not personal discussions of leaders, they will have rendered the country a great service."[25] The calm and reasonable tone of political discussion that Wilder urged upon the readers of her *Missouri Ruralist* columns and her willingness to accept a major role for government in people's lives were largely forgotten—or abandoned—a decade and a half later when she found herself frustrated and enraged by the actions of Franklin Roosevelt and the New Deal.

The impact of movies, the automobile, and other modern technologies also drew Wilder's attention, inspiring her to exclaim, "Glory! What Days in Which to Live!"[26] The east-west road running through Mansfield, which became Federal Highway 60 in 1926, sliced through the hill in front of the Wilder's house. The expanding activities of the good roads movement during the early part of the decade won her admiration. "We were told that motor cars could never be used in our hills; now nearly every farmer owns and runs one," she wrote in December 1923. "We were told that we never could have good roads, but there are now fifty-three miles of state roads in good condition and more building. The very best materials for permanent roads lie all along the highways and are being used in the construction of these roads."[27] The words echoed the ardent patter of Chamber of Commerce spokesmen and local boosters of the time. Wilder had no hesitation in joining with them.

In the very first article that she wrote for the *Missouri Ruralist* on February 18, 1911, Wilder enthusiastically described some of the beneficial changes wrought by new technologies. People's workloads decreased and life became pleasanter with oil stoves, electricity, cream separators, pumps, running water, Rural Free Delivery, washing machines, sewing machines, telephones, circulating libraries, and even interurban trolleys. Wilder, however, was no unrestrained advocate of technological innovation and modern ways of doing things. She recognized the negative consequences that often attended such changes. There were times when she became nostalgic for the old human-powered butter churn. "Sometimes I wonder if telephones and motor cars are altogether blessings for country people," she mused in January 1919, implying that indeed they were not. "When my neighbor can call me up for a short visit over the phone, she is not so likely to make the necessary effort to come and spend the afternoon, and I get hungry for the sight of her face as well as the sound of her voice." And again, she wondered, "What became of the time the motor car saved us?" Now people seemed more hurried than ever. No one seemed to have time for anything.[28]

Ambivalence also marked her reaction to growing emphasis on women's rights. Though welcoming new opportunities and choices that were opening up for women, she explicitly refused to identify with "feminism," because she believed that farm women had always been capable of and had often demonstrated a strong sense of individualism and independence.[29] But Wilder also perceived new possibilities opening up for women as society underwent rapid change. During World War I, for example, she noted, "All over the world women are bravely taking their part in the conflict and doing what they can to defend those things they hold most sacred, their homes, their children and their honor. In all the allied countries women are filling places of responsibility and danger, doing hard, unpleasant work to help in the struggle to 'make the world save for women.'"[30]

In addition to providing evidence of her competence as a writer and reflecting the interests and concerns of a fairly "with-it" woman in the teens and twenties, Wilder's farm journalism also stimulated memories in her of childhood and life on the midwestern agricultural frontier. Many of the stories dredged up in memory for inclusion in her columns got recycled later in her fiction. Some of these reminiscences were general, as when she recalled picking wildflowers, driving cows to and from the pasture, and experiencing heavy drought years in the Dakotas during the 1880s.[31]

But sometimes Wilder's columns described specific episodes from her childhood that later appeared in modified form in her Little House books, such as the story of her cousin Charley crying wolf, quarrelling with her sister Mary over what kind of dressing to prepare for Thanksgiving dinner, grinding wheat in a coffee mill during the hard winter of 1880–1881, and riding home with Almanzo from her first schoolteaching assignment when it was allegedly forty degrees below zero.[32] In January 1919, almost four decades after the remembered events had occurred, she recalled the fun she and others had experienced while attending Friday night "literaries" in the De Smet schoolhouse. "At early candle light, parents and pupils from all over the district gathered at the schoolhouse, bringing lanterns and candles and sometimes a glass lamp to give an added touch of dignity to the teacher's desk," she wrote, noting the pride the schoolchildren took in reciting their pieces and dialogues. And then came the debate, the memory of which stimulated her to comment, "I have been thinking lately what a forum for discussing the questions of the day, political and others, the old-fashioned debate would be. I think that farmers do not discuss these things enough, among themselves, these days."[33]

As many as twenty years before she started writing her novels, Wilder was mulling over in her mind the episodes and activities of her youth that later got dramatically reshaped in fictional form. In writing the Little House books, her stories were guided, just as her writing in the *Missouri Ruralist* had been, by the conviction, stated in a July 1917 piece, that "it is the sweet, simple things of life which are the real ones after all." Wilder was quick to admit that "Distance lends enchantment to the view" and that "older persons think things were better when they were young."[34] In part because of this, some of the kinds of subjects that she avoided writing about in her children's stories she willingly addressed in her farm journalism. There, the darker sides of life sometimes drew her attention—things like child abuse, teenage suicide, illiteracy, corruption, idle and malicious gossip, and night-riding violence.[35]

Finally, a reading of Wilder's farm journalism throws new light upon some of her thought processes, further enabling us better to understand her later fiction. The assumptions upon which she operated and her entire worldview were permeated by the conviction that people lived in an orderly universe, ruled over by God and subject to his will. What evils existed in the world derived primarily from a lack of true Christianity (to be distinguished from mere adherence to church structures or religious forms).[36] Social problems, in other words, were fundamentally the result of individual failure rather than issues that could be easily solved by social reform or governmental intervention. Wilder's views were deeply felt and carefully considered positions, reflecting years of experience and contemplation. While not unanimously popular in her time or in ours, these opinions were hard-won, having been subjected to more than a little critical examination. "What we see is always affected by the light in which we look at it so that no two persons see people and things alike," she cautioned. "What we see and how we see depends upon the nature of our light."[37]

Wilder devoted considerable energy to preaching the lessons she had learned, which she thought any intelligent person would agree with, given the proper training and circumstances. Didacticism rang out both in her fiction and in her nonfiction writing. Many commentators have noted that Wilder's books drip with values.[38] The lessons she taught and preached were numerous, some of them being: it is a crime to ruin the land; we should not waste timber; we need to strive to translate our dreams into reality; money does not bring happiness; people should accentuate the positive; honesty is the best policy; we should always keep on building; gossip and idle chatter should not be indulged in; and people should eliminate the word *can't* from their vocabularies.[39]

Wilder often sounded like an ethicist or a preacher with her penchant for dispensing moral advice and ethical commentary, just like the schoolteacher that she had briefly been during her teens. The values she encouraged and strove to elicit in people were the mainstream conservative values of midwestern piety and social relations: friendship, neighborliness, hospitality, cooperation, helpfulness, fair dealing, cheerfulness, honesty, charity, and hopefulness. "Not all of us can become famous," Wilder wrote, "but nowhere are there better neighbors or truer friends. If misfortune, sickness or sorrow comes to one, the neighbors rally to help, with a whole-hearted good fellowship that makes living worthwhile and dying easier."[40]

Stressing the power of love to cement personal relationships and undergird social institutions, Wilder emphasized the importance of developing good character in people. Values, she asserted, were permanent, and the basic place they were learned and developed was in the home. Much depended upon children's getting the right training. People needed to dream and to develop a vision of the good life; then they needed to act upon it. Idealism in this way fused with practicality.[41] This was no bigoted, narrow-minded, parochial vision; rather, it was in the American grain, a philosophy of practical idealism, one emphasizing growth for the diligent and redemption for the delinquent. "We are either broader minded, more tolerant and sympathetic now than we used to be or the reverse is true," Wilder wrote in February 1917. "The person who is selfish, or mean or miserly— does he not grow more so as the years pass, unless he makes a special effort to go in the other direction?"[42] Self-control was a primary virtue in her scheme, as was illustrated in a column written during World War I. "We must fight our appetites, overcome our inclinations and conquer our selfishness," she admonished her readers. "The work for those who cannot go and fight is to so govern themselves that they may not cast discredit upon a free country."[43] Many of the same values that she extolled in her columns later found their way into the Little House books.

Similarly, Wilder's practice of reciting maxims or proverbs carried over later in her novels. As a farm writer she constantly reiterated them: "There is no great loss without some small gain"; "Sweet are the uses of adversity"; "To thine own self be true"; "We never miss the water 'till the well runs dry'"; "To appreciate Heaven well, a man must have some 15 minutes of Hell"; "The moment that growth stops decay sets in"; "It is so much easier to plan than to accomplish"; "A soft answer turneth away wrath"; "Practice makes perfect"; "If we would win success in anything, when we come to a wall that bars our way, we must throw our hearts over and then follow confidently."[44]

The ambiguities and contradictions sometimes contained in such advice did not escape Wilder. She noted, for instance, the frequent discrepancies that exist among proverbs, as between "A stitch in time saves nine" and "It is never too late to mend." Or again, "All work and no play makes Jack a dull boy," but on the other hand, "all play and no work would make hoboes of us."[45] Pushing things to extremes was always a dangerous proposition. Wilder constantly urged the necessity of balance in people's lives. Any virtue carried to excess might transform itself into a vice. Wilder got to wondering "whether perhaps it is not as great a fault to be too energetic as it is to be too idle." This caused her to reflect, "Vices are simply overworked virtues anyway. Economy and frugality are to be commended, but follow them on in an increasing ratio and what do we find at the end? A miser!" Likewise, while work was necessary and right, it was also true that "giving all our time and thought and effort to personal gain will cause us to become selfish and small and mean."[46]

Women had special roles to play in insuring that matters be kept in proper perspective. Being too single-minded in the pursuit of any goal, whatever its merits, threatened to distort one's priorities. It came down to a matter of priorities, being able to distinguish the significant from the insignificant. People needed to recognize that "we cannot possibly accomplish everything. We must continually be weighing and judging and discarding things that are presented to us if we would save ourselves and spend our time and strength only on those that are important."[47]

Not everything to be observed suggested simple lessons or rules of behavior. Much of Wilder's material in her farm journalism columns consisted of simple, straightforward description, as with her discussions of cultivating apple orchards, tending gardens, and working out systems to transport springwater to a farmhouse.[48] Her graphic and often highly detailed descriptions skillfully created visual images of her subjects in readers' minds. She passed on to her readers, for instance, observations about the all-too-common dysfunctional design of furniture, the unnecessary ugliness of country roads, the festering problem of illiteracy in the United States, and the innate sense of justice to be found in children.[49] To view things rightly required that one look clear-eyed at them and not be blinded by one's cultural assumptions and socially mandated rules about what was correct and proper. "Our inability to see things that are right before our eyes, until they are pointed out to us, would be amusing if it were not at times so serious," she cautioned. "We are coming, I think, to depend too much on being told and shown and taught instead of using our own eyes and brains and inventive faculties, which are likely to be just as good as any other person's."[50] Wilder's sense of curiosity, fairness, and pragmatism thus contributed to an openness that sometimes led her to question and reject ingrained values and assumptions that had earlier limited her ability to see.

Beyond that, her attraction to wonder and fantasy likewise sometimes took her beyond humdrum, predictable ways of viewing life and society around her. The faerie poems that she wrote for *San Francisco Bulletin* in 1915 illustrated Wilder's romantic side. "I have a feeling that childhood has been robbed of a great deal of its joys by taking away its belief in wonderful, mystic things, in faeries and all their kin," Wilder wrote in one of her columns not long after returning home.[51] Wilder's attraction to fantasy and faeries and her sense of hope and optimism, on the one hand, and her impulse to carefully describe and comment upon the routine, mundane details of ordinary life, on the other, combined to create in her a spirit of practical idealism that shone through continually in her work—both fiction and nonfiction.

Finally, it must be remembered that Wilder always searched for the wider meaning and significance of everything she observed and wrote about. Objects were not simply inert, nor were actions accidental and unconnected. Rather, everything possessed its proper place in a universe superintended by a higher presence. Thus she had an impulse to find meaning everywhere she looked and to articulate for her readers what that meaning was. This proclivity, observable in the Little House novels, derived directly from habits of thought that had been nourished through years of writing for farm journals. The values that permeated her thinking guaranteed that she would find meaning in the ordinary things of life. Love, beauty, joy, neighborliness, a sense of community, balance—these and other such goods-to-be-aimed-at heavily shaped Wilder's thinking. If in her own life she did not always live up to her highest ideals, at least they served to light her way and to discipline her along the path. The assumptions, values, and ideas that Wilder expressed in her farm journal writing during the decade and a half after 1911 provided a strong foundation for her later, more famous fictional achievements and also do much to illuminate those writings for us.

8

"They Should Know When They're Licked"

American Indians in Wilder's Fiction

None of Laura Ingalls Wilder's books have proved more contro-versial or generated more scholarly debate than *Little House on the Prairie,* and none of the subjects she wrote about have been as sensi-tive as the relationship between Native Americans and white settlers on the post–Civil War frontier. As the Little House books rolled off the presses and for several decades thereafter, little controversy at-tached to Wilder's treatment of Indians in her books, and her third book, set in Indian Territory in Kansas, quickly emerged as one of her readers' favorites and was likely their number-one choice over all the others.

The burgeoning of cultural change and critical attitudes during the turbulent 1960s—with the rise of the civil rights movement, anti-war protests, organized feminism, and a general concern for differ-ent cultural groups and minorities—changed all that. By the 1970s, a rising group of historians practicing what earned the label of New Western History increasingly called into question the dominant pos-itive view of the process of frontier settlement that had been associ-ated with the writings of historian Frederick Jackson Turner. In their classes and in books, articles, and conference papers they began to describe a frontier laced with violence, greed, oppression, sexism, and racism. In addition to the dominant whites, males, Europeans, entrepreneurs, shopkeepers, and farmers who had dominated Turner's narrative, the New Western Historians depicted a frontier populated by Indians, blacks, Asians, and other racial and ethnic minorities, women, transients, wage laborers, and other previously neglected groups.[1]

A subject that rose to special prominence in the new historical outlook was American Indians. Operating upon similar interests and impulses, literary historians and critics began to criticize Laura Ingalls Wilder for her treatment of or failure to include Native Americans in her fictional narratives. She was deemed guilty of the same kinds of faults and weaknesses that they associated with other writers: ignorance, misinterpretation, blatant racism, derogatory depictions, falsification, failure to include in her stories important aspects of the Native American experience, complicity in the expropriation of Indian lands, and other deficiencies.

Wilder came to be associated in many minds with the persistent tendency of children's authors to denigrate and misunderstand American Indian culture. In her 1993 book *Teaching Multicultural Literature in Grades K–8,* Violet J. Harris noted, "False assumptions about Amerind culture are presented in the most recent novels, as well as in those from the past." In *How Much Truth Do We Tell the Children?* Magda Lewis isolated four major types of cultural bias against North American Native peoples as depicted in picture books for young children: tending to depict them as warlike and aggressive; portraying white men, in contrast, as "superheroes"; locating Native peoples in the distant past rather than as part of current reality (the "vanishing Indian" syndrome); and associating them with animals, which implies that they are inferior, incapable, and invisible. I would suggest that all of these stereotypes apply, to one degree or other, to the way Indians are depicted in *Little House on the Prairie.* Nowhere in most of the books that she read, writes Lewis, "does one get a sense of the validity of the Native culture, the invasion of this culture by the white settlers or that physical retaliation is not an unusual or unprecedented response to such invasion."[2]

It is difficult for anyone embedded in a culture to transcend the assumptions, beliefs, and values holding sway in it. Two fundamental, but contradictory conceptions dominated white thinking about Indian culture from the very beginning of European settlement, according to historian Robert Berkhofer. These boiled down to the stereotypes of the "good Indian," who was peaceful most of the time but brave in battle, handsome in appearance, calm and dignified in bearing, solicitous of family, and friendly and hospitable to strangers, on the one hand, and the "bad Indian," who was combative, treacherous and brutal in battle, indolent, superstitious, naked and lecherous, filthy, deceitful, and tyrannical with women, on the other. Beyond these images, sometimes a third one raised its head—that of the degraded, often drunken, degenerate, and poverty-stricken Indian with no redeeming characteristics. "Under these conceptions," Berkhofer writes, "civilization was destined to triumph over savagery, and so the Indian was to disappear either through death or through assimilation into the larger, more progressive White society. For White Americans during this long period of time, the only good Indian was indeed a dead Indian—whether through warfare or through assimilation." Tracing the lineage and pervasive repetition of the hideous proverb "The only good Indian is a dead Indian," anthropologist Wolfgang Mieder notes its ubiquity and powerful continuing influence, observing just how difficult it was for anyone to resist it and to think or speak otherwise. The scabrous statement not only permeated speech and inspired countless "jokes" but also found written expression in everything from scholarly books and novels to newspaper stories, magazine articles, and cartoons.[3]

In recent years, the bar for writing about indigenous peoples has risen significantly.[4] Melissa Kay Thompson observes that children's book authors as well as critics have typically stereotyped Indians, whether intentionally or not, thereby perpetuating false images and prejudice in their readers. Even authors with good intentions experience difficulty trying to transcend long-established assumptions and mind-sets, unable to place themselves inside the cultures they are writing about.[5]

Operating within the context of these kinds of understandings of the tremendous influence of such powerful cultural stereotypes and assumptions, scholars since the 1990s have increasingly trained their guns at Laura Ingalls Wilder and what they understand to be her retrograde attitudes and beliefs about Native Americans. Sharon Smulders contends that "despite its seeming authenticity, *Little House on the Prairie* ultimately denies the real experience of aboriginal Americans in order to validate the assimilation of the American landscape to the civilizing project of frontier settlement." Frances W. Kaye states things more bluntly. She finds it impossible to "read *Little House on the Prairie* as other than apology for the 'ethnic cleansing' of the Great Plains. That Wilder's thought was unremarkable, perhaps even progressive, for the time in which she lived and wrote should not exempt her books from sending up red flags for contemporary critics who believe in diversity, multiculturalism, and human rights." For Kaye, balanced critique does not suffice; it is necessary to go beyond that to denounce attitudes that may once have seemed defensible but in present circumstances are poisonous.[6]

Other scholars have demurred at such single-minded critique and attempted more evenhanded accounts. Keeping in mind the climate of the times in which Wilder lived and wrote and wishing to establish her firmly within her historical context, they have expressed greater sympathy for her treatment of Native Americans in her books. Donna Campbell, for example, argues that dismissing *Little House on the Prairie* "as though Wilder's vision of other races represents a monolithic whole is to deny the ways in which the novel raises questions about racial identity even as it affirms some negative stereotypes." She perceives multiple voices in the book, suggesting disturbing possibilities, which force readers to question their own assumptions and values. Virginia Wolf, while not exonerating Wilder from charges of racism, also notes the tensions and contending viewpoints inherent in the narrative, which require careful thought and analysis to sort out and interpret. One thing is fairly certain: Wilder was more enlightened in her thinking on the issues than her daughter, who referred to Indians as "barbarians" who lived a "communist" lifestyle in an article in the *Saturday Evening Post* in 1939.[7]

To sort out the issues involved, it is necessary to understand the circumstances in which Wilder was writing, the nature of her audience, the knowledge she possessed, and the climate of opinion at the time. We also need to distinguish between how the books were intended and received at the time and how they fit into our contemporary culture today.

A statement she made to *Missouri Ruralist* editor John F. Case in 1918, despite its brevity, suggests that her thinking on the subject at that time was basically naive, conventional, and permeated by images generated by the popular culture. "My childish memories hold the sound of the war whoop and I see pictures of painted Indians," she wrote in response to a request for information about her, thinking about the brief time her family spent in Kansas.[8] Far from being either an Indian hater or ignorant about their importance in the region's history, however, Wilder came to harbor an appreciation for Indians as persons, a fascination with their way of life, and an awareness of the pressures that were forcing them into more and more constricted circumstances. While the author did not treat Indians in a comprehensive way in her books, her aim was not to write history but children's fiction. In that, she was true to her genre, giving readers a sense of the complexities of frontier life, including relations between Indians and settlers. As history of Indian culture or of Native-white relations, the books are not very useful, but as children's novels they provide a basis for better understanding of interactions between Indians and non-Indians if they are read and taught with sensitivity and placed in proper context and if an effort is made to understand the changes that have occurred during the time since the books were written.

Contemporary critics have taken Wilder to task for the first words of her first book. "Once upon a time, sixty years ago, a little girl lived in the Big Woods of Wisconsin, in a little gray house made of logs," Wilder wrote in *Little House in the Big Woods*. "The great, dark trees of the Big Woods stood all around the house. . . . As far as a man could go to the north in a day, or a week, or a whole month, there was nothing but woods. There were no houses. There were no roads. There were no people. There were only trees and the wild animals who had their homes among them." This passage prompted Michael Dorris, who was part Modoc Indian himself and who had read Wilder's books to his part-Chippewa daughters, to respond: "Say what? Excuse me, but weren't we forgetting the Chippewa branch of my daughters' immediate ancestry, not to mention the thousands of resident Menominees, Potawatomis, Sauks, Foxes, Winnebagos, Ottawas who inhabited mid-nineteenth-century Wisconsin, as they had for many hundreds of years[?]" Indeed, the land that the Ingallses and their fellow European "invaders"—to borrow a term from historians James Axtell and Francis Jennings—took over in western Wisconsin was Indian country, and in order to appropriate it non-Indians resorted to every trick and crime in the book. "This cozy, fun-filled world of extended Ingallses was curiously empty," Dorris observed, "a pristine wilderness in which only white folks toiled and cavorted, ate and harvested, celebrated and were kind to each other."[9]

If Wilder's slighting of American Indians upset Dorris, her books' omissions downright infuriated Dennis McAuliffe Jr. Writing about his family's Osage background, McAuliffe criticizes Wilder's third book, which chronicles the Ingallses' move to the Osage Diminished Reserve in Kansas in 1869 and 1870. "Little Laura Ingalls, her sisters and their beloved Ma and Pa were illegal squatters on Osage land," he charges. "She left that detail out of her 1935 children's book, *Little House on the Prairie*, as well as any mention of ongoing outrages— including killings, burnings, beatings, horse thefts and grave rob- beries—committed by white settlers, such as Charles Ingalls, against Osages living in villages not more than a mile or two away from the Ingallses' little house." McAuliffe finds Charles Ingalls, with his "two-foot-long vinery of beard" and his "dark, narrow, hard, glassy, chilly, creepy eyes," to be so repulsive that he compares him to Charles Manson, the Hollywood murderer. "Pa's résumé," he con- tends, "reads like that of a surfer bum in search of the perfect amber wave of grain. He couldn't stay in one place or hold down a home- stead." McAuliffe goes on to note the negative characterizations of the Osages contained in Wilder's novel, which he finds "replete with anti-Indian ethnic slurs." His indictment could not be more pas- sionate.[10]

Only two and a half years old when her family moved to Kansas and around four when they moved away, Wilder was most likely too young to have understood or remembered much of what transpired there, helping to explain why what she wrote about this period was less than perfectly accurate and comprehensive by today's standards of historical interpretation. Similarly, Wilder would have remem- bered nothing of her first two years of life on a farm near Pepin, Wis- consin, on the edge of the "Big Woods." The material she used later for *Little House in the Big Woods* was based upon the stories of her par- ents and relatives and her own memories dating from the family's *second* stay in the area, *after* they had journeyed to Kansas and re- turned.[11] In her novels, Wilder wrote from the viewpoint of a girl the same age that she herself had been at the time most of the action was taking place. Her narratives develop through the eyes of a young girl, not through the sophisticated mind-set of a well-informed, highly trained, and politically astute observer.

In point of fact, Wilder did not refer specifically in her novels to the Chippewa and other tribes in Wisconsin. Nor, in writing about her family's stays in and near Walnut Grove, Minnesota, did she mention by name the Santee Dakota, whom settlers had pushed out of the eastern part of the state and onto a reservation along the Minnesota River. Her description in her unpublished autobiography, "Pioneer Girl," of the family's stay in Burr Oak, Iowa, failed to talk about the Winnebagos, Sauks, and Foxes who had recently inhabited that region. Nor did she mention the branches of Dakota Indians who had been pushed from eastern Dakota Territory after the Civil War as the vast influx of settlers, including the Ingalls family, arrived with the Great Dakota Boom. There were no references in Wilder's books to George Armstrong Custer or to the Battle of the Little Bighorn, which had occurred in eastern Montana Territory just three years before her family's arrival in De Smet. Finally, *The First Four Years,* the posthumously published account of her first years of married life with Almanzo Wilder from 1885 to 1889, made no mention of the Ghost Dance religion, which grew to tremendous proportions in 1889 and culminated in the tragic Wounded Knee massacre on December 29, 1890.[12] These historical omissions and the vagueness of reference to Indian culture and behavior reflect that she was writing stories for children and not accurate or detailed historical interpretations, although her fictionalized accounts indeed did operate within the limits of the historical conventions that she shared with her contemporaries.

Questions arise regarding just what obligations children's authors assume for providing accurate and thorough depictions of history, taking into account the age and relative incomprehension of their young readers and how far they should go in presenting conflicting voices and contending points of view in their narratives. Considering the fairly stringent limitations that are usually imposed on them with regard to word counts and the strong imperative to keep stories interesting and enjoyable, the obligation to remain true to the past continually vies with the literary desire to keep the reader turning the pages.

Although Wilder failed to chronicle many specific people or events that were likely to be included in history textbooks, her autobiography covers many of her own and her family's personal encounters with Indians, and many of these and others would later be included in the eight-volume Little House series as well as in the posthumously published *First Four Years.* In beginning "Pioneer Girl" with her family's stay of more than a year in Indian Territory in southeastern Kansas, Wilder placed the Osage Indians at the start of her own story. The author later made this episode the basis for her third novel, *Little House on the Prairie,* which revolved around the issue of forcing Indians off the land so that non-Indians like the Ingallses could appropriate it for farming. The early pages of "Pioneer Girl" depict Indians, smelling awful because of the skunk skins they wore, entering the Ingalls cabin to ask for food and tobacco. Wilder also writes in her autobiography of accompanying her father to an abandoned Indian camp, where she and Mary picked up some beads, and of begging her parents to get an Indian baby for her to play with. The Indians, however, remain an incidental presence in the manuscript, and the fundamental nature of Indian-white conflict over control of the land in Kansas never gets addressed in the brief account.

The most prominent treatment of American Indians in the autobiographical "Pioneer Girl" is its sympathetic references to the French-Indian horseman and gambler the family meets later in the Dakota Territory, who impresses Charles Ingalls as "a darned good fellow." This story is retold in *By the Shores of Silver Lake.* Wilder also incorporates into her autobiography the prediction of an old Indian that the winter of 1880–1881 would be an especially hard one, a forecast that becomes the central theme of *The Long Winter.* In addition, "Pioneer Girl" mentions episodes that do not make it into the novels, such as a story of a doctor stealing a mummified Indian baby and sending it to Chicago for examination, an action that almost precipitates war with the Indians. Other things mentioned include an Indian mound near Spirit Lake, nine miles north of Silver Lake in Dakota Territory; a story in which Pa pretends to fight Indians; and the site of an Indian massacre that had taken place during the Dakota Conflict of 1862.[13]

In comparison to Wilder's autobiography, her nine novels greatly expand the number and extent of references to American Indians. They show up prominently in *Little House on the Prairie,* where they drive much of the plot, and in *By the Shores of Silver Lake.* In the other volumes, they appear sporadically. Spirit Lake gets mentioned in *These Happy Golden Years.* In *Farmer Boy,* young Almanzo Wilder wears Indian moccasins, and his mother bakes "rye'n'injun" bread. Sometimes Indian metaphors get used: Laura and her cousin Lena yell like Indians, young Almanzo Wilder like a Comanche; Mary tells Laura to wear her sunbonnet to keep her skin from turning brown like an Indian's, and little Grace gets a laugh when she repeats the warning at the time of Laura's marriage. Sometimes Wilder's references to Indians are presented in a positive or nonjudgmental manner, as in comments about Indian summer and the first Thanksgiving. In *Farmer Boy*, an Indian performs the remarkable athletic feat of running a mile in two minutes and forty seconds. Other references are pejorative, as in a Fourth of July speech at De Smet in which the orator of the day places "the murdering scalping red-skinned savages" alongside British regulars and their hired Hessians as enemies of the revolutionary patriots.[14]

To frontier families like the Ingallses and Ma's family, the Quiners, fighting Indians seemed to have become a familiar way of life, raising few ethical issues. While visiting the Ingalls family in De Smet, Tom Quiner (Ma's brother) talks matter-of-factly about having fought Indians in the Black Hills with a group of gold miners who entered in violation of a treaty setting the area aside for the Lakota Indians. But he is also honest enough to admit that his own presence in the Black Hills was ethically dubious, and Wilder's insertion of his comment in *These Happy Golden Years* raises an implicit historical issue. "It was Indian country," Tom notes. "Strictly speaking, we had no right there." The Ingalls family's presence in the Osage Diminished Reserve in 1869 was also clearly illegal. Penny T. Linsenmayer, who has done the most thorough job of establishing the historical context for the events described in *Little House on the Prairie*, concludes that it is doubtful that the Ingalls family was unaware that it was intruding illegally on Indian lands.[15] In the dramatic depiction of the conflict in the book, however, the burden of guilt shifts from the encroaching white settlers to a deceptive, arbitrary federal government, which Wilder depicts as having originally invited non-Indians to enter the region.

A central theme of *Little House on the Prairie* is the contest between the settlers and the federal government over the newcomers' right to occupy land set aside as the Osage Diminished Reserve in 1825. This fifty-mile-wide strip along the southern border of Kansas had been reserved for the Osage Indians in return for their relinquishing all other claims to the area. By the late 1860s, approximately 300 full-blood and 750 mixed-blood Osages were living on the reserve. In Montgomery County, where the Ingallses and others had settled, anticipating that the Indians' title to the land would soon be extinguished, the Osages occupied eight villages. The closest one to the Ingalls cabin was apparently located about two or three miles east of them on the east bank of Onion Creek.[16] In editing and revising the manuscript of the family's time in Kansas, Lane referred to it as her mother's "Indian Juvenile," thus installing Indians right in the center of the story.[17]

In this book and others in the series, Wilder depicts her own mother as a stereotypical western woman who was afraid of, ignorant about, and simply disliked Indians. Caroline Quiner Ingalls would have been happy to be rid of them altogether. Today such attitudes and actions would be counted as racist; in the late 1800s, unfortunately, they were nothing unusual. Scholarship has shown them to have been typical—and probably even predominant—among frontier women. While Wilder's account possesses little value as a source of historical information, she no doubt portrayed her mother's reactions toward Indians with considerable accuracy. As described in the novels, Caroline Ingalls reacted to the American Indians she encountered in real life and to the ones she only imagined in her dreams and nightmares by demonizing them and exaggerating the threat they posed to homesteaders like herself.[18] This reaction was not entirely unnatural for a woman who had grown up in frontier Wisconsin, west of Milwaukee, during the 1840s and 1850s when there was still a considerable Indian presence in the area, and who then had further encounters with them at various locations on the frontier as an adult.

Caroline Ingalls had been only four years old when her father died in 1844, and she later told her daughter that friendly Indians had given her struggling family food during the following winter. Encounters like this may have engendered some sympathy in her toward them, but the Black Hawk War of 1832, in which approximately seventy settlers and soldiers died in a dispute over land in Wisconsin and Illinois, was also a recent memory for area residents. News of other outbreaks of racial violence probably had a negative effect on her, as well, just as it did on other frontier women. When the Ingalls family moved west to Walnut Grove, Minnesota, in 1874, they passed near Lake Shetek, where Indians had killed settlers during the Dakota Conflict of 1862, and doubtless heard stories about the scores of others who perished in the area, as well. Experiences like these could only have reinforced whatever fears, prejudices, and animosities had been developing in Caroline Ingalls over the years.[19]

It is important to distinguish between Wilder's own views and the ones she attributed—no doubt accurately—to her mother. A writer is not obligated merely to state approved opinions about different groups of people. Rather, she must describe things as they are, were, or could be, helping readers make ethical distinctions and think seriously about the problems, conundrums, and dilemmas that have always confronted people in their interpersonal relations. Wilder set her mother's attitudes toward Indians off against those of her father, Charles Ingalls, who is presented as having a more enlightened approach, and she places herself as a little girl somewhere in between.[20] Whatever degree of sympathy he may have harbored toward the Indians and their plight, however, was obviated by his assumption—one shared with virtually all of his fellow whites—that Indians would have to give way to white settlers on the land.

If Ma feared and despised Indians, Pa was more empathetic toward them. "There's some good Indians," he insisted in *The Long Winter*. "And they know some things that we don't." Charles Ingalls's more complex understanding of American Indians derived from several sources. Being less tied to home and more able to get out and about, he had greater opportunity to observe and interact with them in different settings. From his boyhood in New York State, he had learned to admire their skills as outdoorsmen, which is reflected in Pa's remark that "you never saw Indians unless they wanted you to see them." Ingalls's optimistic personality made him readier to grant that the Indians' intentions were good, and, being physically stronger and more comfortable with guns than his wife, he had more confidence in his ability to defend himself, if necessary. Also, to a limited extent, he acknowledged the priority of Indians on the land. In *Little House on the Prairie*, after an Indian had threatened to shoot their dog, Jack, for blocking the trail that ran past the Ingallses' cabin, Pa remarked, "Well, it's his path. An Indian trail, long before we came."[21]

Even if the literary character of Charles Ingalls was willing to some extent to recognize an Indian claim on the land, he also believed that they were doomed to retreat in the face of the country's westward expansion. He and his family, of course, stood to benefit from that development. Whether we should attribute this to selfishness, heedlessness, or calculating cupidity, he was operating under the spell of powerful cultural imperatives that had taken root in America as soon as the first European settlers arrived. When a curious Laura questions him about what will happen to the Indians, Pa tries to reassure her, explaining it as part of a vast, impersonal process: "'When white settlers come into a country, the Indians have to move on. The government is going to move these Indians farther west, any time now. That's why we're here, Laura. White people are going to settle all this country, and we get the best land because we get here first and take our pick. Now do you understand?' 'Yes, Pa,' Laura said. 'But, Pa, I thought this was Indian Territory. Won't it make the Indians mad to have to —— ' 'No more questions, Laura,' Pa said, firmly. 'Go to sleep.'"[22] There is a hint here that the question was troubling to Pa and therefore, perhaps, to the author of the book. But the Pa Ingalls character in the books, and presumably Charles Ingalls in real life, like virtually all pioneers, fully accepted the prevailing notion of Manifest Destiny—that Indian tribes were fated to give way to white settlement as it rolled inexorably across the continent, bringing "civilization" in its wake.

Meanwhile, the settlers needed to maintain peaceful relations with their Indian neighbors as long as they remained in place in order to insure their own survival. Pa displays a keen pragmatism in this regard, aware of how to accommodate the Indians he encounters and keep their contacts civil. When Indians enter the family's cabin and squat by the fire, he joins them. He observes that, for the most part, they are perfectly friendly. "If you treat them well and watch Jack, we won't have any trouble," he advises his family. When their neighbor, Mr. Scott, asserts that "the only good Indian is a dead Indian," Pa disagrees. "He figured that Indians would be as peaceable as anybody else if they were let alone," Wilder wrote. "On the other hand they had been moved west so many times that naturally they hated white folks. But an Indian ought to have sense enough to know when he was licked."[23]

Pa especially admires the character of an Osage leader identified in the book as Soldat du Chene, the "tall Indian," who, he believes, prevents his compatriots from attacking the white families living on their land. "That's one good Indian!" Wilder has Pa say at the end of *Little House on the Prairie.* "No matter what Mr. Scott said, Pa did not believe that the only good Indian was a dead Indian."[24] Nevertheless, while Pa generally speaks out opposing those who criticize or— at the extreme—want to kill Indians, he also assumes that the Indians' day is over and that they will eventually have to accommodate themselves to the situation.

Wilder's apparent complacency with regard to the fate of American Indians during the 1930s in the wake of white takeover of their land placed her within the mainstream of the dominant ideology. Three-quarters of a century later, it is impossible to condone such insensitivity, even if we admit that very few white people at the time either gave it any thought or registered any disagreement with it. Moreover, those who objected seldom were able to propose any plausible practical alternatives that might have resolved the issue fairly for both sides.

Wilder can also be criticized for not providing an accurate or thorough historical account in *Little House on the Prairie* of what was happening to the Osage tribe while the family was living in Kansas and again after they left. The Ingallses had joined the post–Civil War rush of settlers determined to push the Osages out of their lands and into Oklahoma, even though the federal government had promised the tribe protection on its reserve in perpetuity. While the government deserved condemnation for not upholding its end of the bargain with the Osages, it had not, in fact, invited settlers to invade the region, and federal troops made at least some attempt to keep them out and expel people who were illegally squatting on Indian land. Profit-oriented railroad executives, scheming townsite promoters, and ambitious homesteaders like the Ingallses who quite knowingly flooded onto the Osage Diminished Reserve during the late 1860s expected the federal government to push the Indians out in short order, thus allowing white settlers to take it over for themselves.[25] "The pressure of settlers was central to the removal of the Kansas tribes," write historians H. Craig Miner and William E. Unrau. The settlers' motivations were complex, but in general, James R. Shortridge notes, "morality was subservient to greed. White Americans wanted agricultural lands, railroad rights-of-way, and townsites. Their desire was overweening enough by 1850 to extinguish a series of solemn treaties made with the eastern Indians between 1825 and 1843." As a result, approximately ten thousand Indians, the Osages among them, were ultimately forced out of Kansas.[26]

If *Little House on the Prairie* does not bear scrutiny as history, Wilder's 1933 trek with Lane to search for the spot where the family had lived in 1869 and 1870 demonstrates that she made some effort, at least, to confirm some of the details of her family's experience. The two never managed to find the homesite that the family had occupied, being actually twenty or thirty miles away from it, an error that comports with Wilder's mistaken statement in the novel that the family settled forty miles from Independence. In reality, they had lived thirteen miles southwest of the town. Wilder and Lane also wrote several letters to historical agencies inquiring about "Soldat du Chene" and about the historical circumstances surrounding the Ingalls family's stay in the area.[27] But from the evidence that has been preserved of those inquiries, their effort to pin down facts and events was short-lived and of little assistance to them.

Wilder's search for the actual homesite and her effort to find out something about Soldat du Chene, which she mistakenly thought was the name of the Indian leader her father had told her had befriended the family, shows her mode of thinking about these events to have been entirely different from that of the New Western Historians, multiculturalists, and other investigators who seek to uncover the broader forces that were operating at the time and their long-term implications. Simple facts can go only partway toward unlocking the broad meaning and significance of the events that were transpiring in southeastern Kansas. Closer attention needs to be paid to the broad forces operating to negotiate relations between opposing groups vying for control.

With regard to the specific facts, it should be kept in mind that Wilder was writing sixty-five years after the events, describing things that had occurred when she was two or three years old, although her fictional persona was several years older than that. She could lay small claim to accuracy about these events. Stories passed down to her by her parents, reinforced by a small amount of research but also refracted through the prism of her own knowledge and preconceptions and faded with the passage of time, made for poor history. Just as she mistook the location of the family's cabin, for instance, she also seems to have mistakenly believed that her father had joined a posse that set out to lynch the legendary "Bloody Bender" clan. For years, these murderous thugs had lured unwary travelers into their roadside store, robbing, killing, and burying them on the premises. In fact, the Benders were not pursued as murder suspects until a couple of years after the Ingalls family had already moved on.[28] Although Wilder did not include the Bender story in her novel of the Kansas experience, it and other stories like it provided grist for her literary imagination.

Little House on the Prairie, then, was more misleading than enlightening on the events transpiring on the Osage Diminished Reserve during the brief time that the Ingalls family lived there, and it contributed to readers' misunderstanding of the underlying forces that were operating during the process that dispossessed the Indians of their land at the time. This has led some educators and cultural analysts to advocate removing the books from libraries and school classrooms and to condemn Wilder for obtuseness, if not perfidy, in her writing about Indians. While one can understand their anger and concern, we should not be too quick to suppress texts that otherwise have considerable strengths and appeal to young readers. Used with caution and supplemented by explanation and further information about historical context, the story of the family's time in Kansas can provide a useful teaching opportunity—one in which teachers, librarians, and parents can have the chance to explain how prevailing concepts and attitudes can blind people to reality. Such a reading also possesses the potential to allow young readers to exercise their own imaginations and increase their empathy in addressing issues of cultural difference. Children can learn how to use research and reason to supplement and, if necessary, to contradict the assumptions and findings that they read in books.

It also needs to be remembered that Wilder's genre was fiction—and children's fiction at that. She was not writing history and should not be judged by its standards. Moreover, she wrote from a viewpoint reflecting the mentality of a child close to the age that she had been at the time the events being described took place. Whenever Lane believed her mother was beginning to edge outside of these parameters, she reminded her to stay within the narrative framework they had established.[29] Wilder's stories were admittedly autobiographical. A major problem for those who would defend her books today is that she and Lane always insisted that everything in them was true. It is unfortunate that mother and daughter vehemently continued to insist upon the factual accuracy of the books because they thereby elevated readers' expectations about their historical usefulness and exposed themselves to critical reaction when it was shown where the stories indeed did not comport with the facts. They were responsible themselves, in other words, for much of the criticism that has rained down upon the books in recent years.

Considering her purposes in writing the books, the resources that were available to her, and self-imposed constraints on her writing style, Wilder can be credited at least with addressing the subject of American Indians in her novels and with posing some of the questions that need answering. Wilder deserves—if not the highest marks by current standards—at least absolution from the charge that she willfully maligned and misrepresented Indians and recognition that she dealt with her material in a generally balanced and aboveboard way. Any fair assessment of her writings has to recognize that on this theme, as on many others, Wilder displayed considerable talent for illustrating some of the complexities of frontier life and realities that settlers experienced on a daily basis.

To put Wilder's attitudes toward Indians in a broader perspective, it is helpful to ask how she reacted to other ethnic groups. While scant evidence exists to answer the question, two points stand out in the infrequent references in her writing along these lines. In the first place, she took a sort of detached, reportorial approach to describing people with whom she was unfamiliar. Secondly, while frequently bossy, cantankerous, and judgmental in her relationships with and attitudes toward other individuals, she tried—more or less successfully—to implement the lessons of benevolence, open-mindedness, and charity that she knew she should practice as a professed Christian.

In the diary that she kept of her and her family's journey to Missouri in 1894, Wilder characterized the unfamiliar groups they encountered in flat, nonjudgmental terms, reflecting an openness to them as human beings without rushing to embrace or reject them. A group of German-Russian immigrants they met in Hutchinson County before they reached Yankton on the Missouri River were described as kind, generous, hospitable, polite, and smiling, though still untutored in English. Wilder recorded, apparently with some surprise but with no additional comment, the presence of "colored" people in Topeka and in several towns in southeastern Kansas. That she was capable of critical comments shone through in her reference to the town of Yankton as "a stick in the mud" and in her comment as they moved into Missouri that "judging from weeds in the gardens and fields, the people are shiftless."[30] She seemed reluctant, however, to make snap judgments about specific groups of people.

Two decades later, while visiting Rose in San Francisco during the 1915 Pan American Exposition, she wrote long letters back to Almanzo in Mansfield with observations and comments on the things and people she saw there. After witnessing a mock Navajo Indian village, she noted, "The Indians are very friendly and good-natured." Of the Samoan village on exhibit, she wrote, "The girls are very pretty and some of the men are fine-looking." With regard to their dances, she enthused, "They were very graceful and I did enjoy every bit of it." A walk through Chinatown a few days later led her to observe, "A good many of them are wearing American dress and are very nice-looking people. Some still wear the Chinese costume as it is in pictures you have seen and the children are the cutest ever. I do not like the Chinese food and shall not try any more of it." A visit to a cannery the following day stimulated her to write about the mainly Italian labor force working there, "They were so kind and nice to us and when they could not talk English they would chatter Italian at us and smile."[31]

But she also observed some nasty behavior while she was in San Francisco. Shortly after returning home she wrote about one of these episodes in the *Missouri Ruralist*. It involved a conversation she had overheard between two women at the exposition: "Said the first woman, 'How do you like San Francisco?' The other replied, 'I don't like San Francisco at all! Everywhere I go there is a Chinaman on one side, a Jap on the other and a n—— behind.'" Wilder criticized the narrow-minded provinciality and bigotry of the pair, urging her readers to remain open-minded in their relations with others and to look for the beauty, charm, and goodness in people, regardless of color.[32] It was a message she thought important to preach to others, even if she did not always find it easy to follow herself.

The lessons she had learned at her parents' knees, as well as in school and at church, she took to heart, and she wanted other people to do so, too. Magnanimity and open-mindedness were the virtues she hoped to illustrate and encourage her readers to practice in what she wrote for a December 1917 column. Recalling the mother of her childhood schoolmate Ida Brown, she noted that Ida's mother frequently left dishes unwashed and the house unkempt. Only later did she discover that Mrs. Brown had been writing stories for the papers to earn some money to buy Ida a new winter outfit. This called to mind a poem entitled "If We Only Understood," whose refrain went, "We would love each other better, / If we only understood." Wilder commented, "The things that people do would look so different to us if we only understood the reasons for their actions, nor would we blame them so much for their faults if we knew all the circumstances of their lives." From this she drew the conclusion, "The safest course is to be as understanding as possible, and, where our understanding fails, to call charity to its aid."[33]

By today's standards, Wilder could be indicted for being deficient in her views on race, gender, and ethnic minorities. Living in southwest Missouri—in the heart of the Ozark Mountains and in a border state—she could hardly have avoided imbibing some of the frequently crude and unenlightened prejudices of her time and place. Local newspaper articles routinely mentioned the race of African American crime suspects and prisoners (referring to them as small-*n* "negroes"), printed crude jokes, ran racially stereotyped cartoons and illustrations, and generally reflected a failure even to consider the possibility that black people deserved or could possibly attain equality with whites.[34] That Wilder might have reflected some of these ideas and behaviors is not to be wondered at. More remarkable was the degree to which she transcended the standard prejudices and attitudes of the time.

Quite telling in this regard is a comment she made in her diary as she and her husband traveled from De Smet to their new home in Mansfield in 1894. Noting the beauty of the James River Valley as they approached the Missouri River, she wrote on July 23, "I wished for an artist's hand or a poet's brain or even to be able to tell in good plain prose how beautiful it was. If I had been the Indians I would have scalped more white folks before I ever would have left it."[35] Only four years after the Wounded Knee massacre, Wilder was aware of and sympathetic enough to the Indians' point of view to speak in rather blunt terms about the injustice that had been done to them. She demonstrated an ability to put herself in the shoes of another, persecuted group of people and to understand why they might have felt animosity toward the dominant group to which she belonged.

The question of how to read and interpret Wilder's books, and especially *Little House on the Prairie*, three-quarters of a century after they were written is by no means easily answered. The comfortable assumptions, ugly prejudice, and blatant discrimination that remained widely prevalent and too often acceptable in the Missouri Ozarks, and more generally in the United States, during the depression decade have considerably receded, although there is still much work that needs to be done in this regard. No longer can ignorance and consensus be trotted out in defense of such attitudes and practices. Since the rise of the civil rights movement, multiculturalism, and concerted efforts to achieve Indian rights, the bar has significantly risen, and the Little House books need to be considered in that light. Careful discrimination, however, is called for in sorting out Wilder's intentions in writing the books from the ways in which they are read and reacted to now; in identifying the voices contained in the books and trying to ascertain who speaks for Wilder in the books, if anybody does; in inquiring into how the books can be used to further readers' knowledge and understanding; and in deciding where the books belong—on library shelves, in school classrooms, in bookstores, in home collections, or elsewhere. In these regards, again, the story of the Osages in Indian Territory stands out.

For commentators such as Frances Kaye, the answer is obvious: the books (at least, *Little House on the Prairie*) should not be read, for they are inaccurate, misleading, and racist. Others, however, have suggested their usefulness in providing teachable moments, in which issues presented by pioneer expansion and Indian removal can profitably be discussed. This is no easy assignment. As Donna Campbell notes, "Defending *Little House on the Prairie* in an age that rightly values cultural sensitivity presents a difficult task, for the book is not free from troubling racial implications." She urges us, however, not to consider it as history but as the literature that it is, and children's literature at that.[36]

Campbell is not the only one to point out the competing voices and narrative ambivalence in the book. Philip Heldrich locates the fictional Laura in the middle ground between her more fearful, racist "Ma" and her more thoughtful, ambivalent, and tolerant "Pa." Heldrich notes that she grows over the course of the prairie journey, though "she has yet to reach a fully mature, self-conscious understanding of her feelings toward the Indians." In similar fashion, Elizabeth Segal sees growth in the fictional Laura as well as courage in her questioning of society's attitudes toward and treatment of Indians. In her view, "Wilder was able in her books to implicitly criticize as well as honor and love those complex and imperfect women and men who settled the American West. Nor did she fail to notice and sympathize with those whose tragedy was unfolding outside the snug walls of the little house."[37]

Scholarship published on this controversial issue during the past decade or so provides useful suggestions for how teachers, librarians, parents, and readers can engage with Wilder's texts and benefit from their reading. Anita Clair Fellman shows how men and women tended to experience and thus to conceptualize two very different Wests. Men, in line with Frederick Jackson Turner's vaunted historical thesis, were inclined to perceive the frontier as "a place of conquest, escape to freedom, lawlessness, individualism, and concern for autonomy." Women, while embracing some of those ideas, tended to focus their attention more on making gardens, improving their homes, and promoting community. Wilder's books, in her view, embody the tensions existing in those two visions and thus can be instructive.[38]

Beyond obtaining a more nuanced understanding of the frontier and Native Americans' place in it, readers can learn other worthwhile things from the books, according to others who have studied them. Ann Romines suggests that in showing his daughters how to analyze the tracks made by Indians and to interpret artifacts from their fireplaces, Pa was modeling the activities of a nineteenth-century ethnologist. "Leading his daughters into the hollows of the complex, convoluted prairie text, he also leads them beyond the limits of prescribed reading for nineteenth-century white American girls," she notes.[39] If reading the Little House books helps make students more observant of and understanding about their cultural surroundings, they will have served a useful purpose.

Some feminist scholars have also suggested that Wilder's perspective as a woman provides an alternative feminist entryway into the study of the frontier, allowing readers to admire her "use of the Osages to represent a freedom that counters Ma's racist—and sexist—gentility." Kaye, however, does not buy into this argument. Only by accepting the Native viewpoint and rejecting all the assumptions, circumlocutions, rationalizations, and contradictions of what she deems to be an imperialist mind-set can justice be done and truth be told, she believes. A balanced approach is not the remedy. Only a thoroughgoing repudiation of the stereotypes that held Wilder and Lane in their thrall, a willingness to call the settlers' impulses for what they were—greed, violence, and racism, and simply a refusal to read the books will suffice to jar our consciences and critical faculties enough to rectify our previous mistakes.[40]

Trying to ascertain the impact of *Little House on the Prairie* and Wilder's other books on their readers is a difficult task and one that has hardly begun to accumulate the empirical evidence that is necessary to answer the question. We are better able to say something useful about the conditions in which Wilder wrote her books and how these volumes came to be issued in the form that they were than we are to talk about how they were received by their readers, except to say that they were hugely popular.[41] Placing Wilder's published writings and private thoughts in their proper context, it should be apparent that she—rather than being guilty of gross insensitivity or blatant prejudice toward Indians—was considerably advanced in her attitudes toward Indians in particular and toward other ethnic groups in general. Considering the circumstances in which she grew up and the conditions in which she lived most of her life, her stance was a substantial accomplishment. The better question to ask is not why she was so bad in this regard but why she was relatively so good.[42]

Condemning racism, false stereotypes, and the bad behavior of historical actors can be helpful, but how much good refusing to read Wilder's books will actually achieve to improve the condition of today's Indian population, promote greater truth-telling in the realm of history, or adequately atone for past wrongdoings is questionable. Historians and biographers will do best by situating people and events within their rightful context, attempting to identify causes and motives, and interpreting and evaluating the outcomes and impacts of human actions. Listening to the insights and lessons being uncovered by students of American Indian history and engaging in dialogue about the past are good ways to begin righting the balance and opening up new paths to follow. We need to listen more carefully to each other, which should also have the effect of toning down the rhetoric. No easy consensus is likely to emerge soon, but history usually does better in the long run than in the short run.

As Wilder and Lane would have been the first to suggest, the right to read a book like *Little House on the Prairie* entails an obligation to do one's utmost to understand correctly the message that is being presented and to question the facts and interpretations that are presented in it. A considerable amount of humility is always in order. The past, in a certain sense, "is something we can never have," John Lewis Gaddis reminds us. "We can only *represent* it. . . . We can perceive shapes through the fog and mist, we can speculate as to their significance, and sometimes we can even argue among ourselves as to what these are. Barring the intervention of a time machine, though, we can never go back there to see for sure."[43]

9

Frontier Nostalgia and Conservative Ideology in the Writings of Wilder and Lane

To writers ranging from Frederick Jackson Turner and Willa Cather to Hamlin Garland and Laura Ingalls Wilder, the American frontier has provided a suggestive and durable theme for their work. Some treated it realistically and many wrote acerbically and ironically about it, but the pioneering period in the West more often stimulated nostalgia and myth-making, frequently with political overtones.[1] It should not be surprising that the writings of Laura Ingalls Wilder and her daughter, Rose Wilder Lane, reflected some of these impulses. They both wrote their major works during the 1930s, the most highly politicized decade of the twentieth century, and the early 1940s. Both wound up their political odysseys on the right end of the ideological spectrum, and in both cases frontier nostalgia operated as a significant factor in the process. Children's literature is generally considered to be a conservative medium, as it is often used to shape its young readers' values and to provide models of proper behavior.[2] To the degree that conservative values found expression in the Little House books, however, they were intended more as a political statement than as an effort to improve children's morality.

Prior to 1932, the year Wilder's first novel appeared, there is relatively little in the historical record that reflects upon her political views. Hints exist that she and her family were attracted to William Jennings Bryan and the Populist banner during the historic election of 1896.[3] She and her husband, Almanzo, apparently continued to cast their votes in the Democratic column until the late 1920s, a period in which Missouri Democrats, for the most part, remained no less conservative than their Republican counterparts.[4] She was elected chair of the Wright County Democratic Committee in 1919, and six years later she ran, unsuccessfully, for collector of Pleasant Valley Township—an action apparently motivated more by the salary attached to the position and by a sense of civic duty than by any ideological purposes. Her acceptance of a legitimate government role in the socioeconomic realm can be seen in her work to establish a Mansfield branch of the National Farm Loan Association in 1918 and her service as its secretary-treasurer for a decade.[5]

For the period after Franklin D. Roosevelt moved into the White House in March 1933 and as the New Deal expanded its activities, the record speaks more plainly. Roosevelt was a polarizing figure, and there is no question where Laura and Almanzo took their stand. They viewed the large hand of the federal government, manifested in a multitude of new "alphabetical agencies" and governmental initiatives, as being far too intrusive in people's lives in ways that seriously threatened personal freedom. Almanzo expressed his feelings in a hilarious—but nevertheless serious—manner when a Department of Agriculture employee appeared at Rocky Ridge farm while he was working in the field one day. The government agent wanted to ask a few questions about the family's farm operation and informed him that federal regulations permitted the planting of no more than two acres of oats there. That prompted him to order the fellow off his property, threatening to go get his shotgun if he didn't. Almanzo made his intentions clear, in a story Lane obviously relished relating afterward. "God damn you, you get the hell off my land and you do it now," the old man warned. "I'll plant whatever I damn please on my own farm, and if you're on it when I get to my gun, by God I'll fill you with buckshot."[6]

Laura took pleasure in reporting that a birthday celebration in Mansfield for the president in 1939 had managed to draw out less than fifty people. "I really should have thought there would have been the whole town there," she wrote Rose, considering all the New Deal largesse that had been showered on the little community. The city was bonding itself for $17,000 to raise its match for a W.P.A.

grant to build a sewer system. "God help the poor taxpayers!" was Laura's comment.[7]

The Wilders' antipathy to the president and his administration officials hardened as foreign policy issues rose to the forefront during the late 1930s. Strongly supportive of the proposed Ludlow Amendment to the U.S. Constitution, which for a time at the end of 1937 became the focus of the foreign policy debate, Wilder joined friends in the Athenean Club, a women's study group, in writing to their congressman to urge him to vote for the war referendum and thereby oppose Roosevelt's veering in the direction of another unwanted conflict (World War I having disillusioned them).[8]

Lane was even more convinced than her mother and father about Roosevelt's dictatorial tendencies and was more outspoken and vitriolic in her hatred of and opposition to "that man in the White House." As early as March 1933, the month the former New York governor was sworn into office, she was casually referring in her diary to Roosevelt as a dictator.[9] Early on in the New Deal, she detected power flowing into the hands of the president, who she perceived was aggressively concentrating decision-making authority in the White House. By 1937, believing that the New Deal was killing the American pioneer spirit, Lane, in one of her more unbalanced moods, actually talked about political assassination. In a letter to her literary agent, George Bye, she wrote, "I hoped that Roosevelt would be killed in 1933. If there were any genuine adherence to American political principles in this country, any man in public life with the simple decency to forget his own personal picayune interests and stand for them, I would make a try at killing FDR now." As with her mother, Lane's frustration with Roosevelt was exacerbated by her fear that he was leading the nation into war, and she, too, strongly supported the Ludlow Amendment, devoting most of the little writing she did in 1939 to the campaign to get it approved.[10] In their strong antipathy—even violent hatred—toward Roosevelt and the New Deal, Wilder and Lane were by no means unique. Although the president retained the admiration and support of a majority of the populace, as the decade wore on a large and growing opposition emerged among a wide variety of businessmen, rural dwellers, intellectuals, journalists, affluent voters, and dissenters of all types.[11]

Trying to pinpoint why mother and daughter harbored their antipathy toward Roosevelt and the New Deal presents a tricky task but one worth attempting. Wilder's case is easier, in a sense, because of her more limited experience and more conventional mind-set. Her views, shaped by her family, childhood, and education, as well as by her Missouri Ozarks milieu, remained more within the mainstream of popular opinion. She left fewer traces of her thoughts on the subject, partly because she was less interested in and concerned about politics than Lane was.

Several factors help explain Wilder's negative reaction to Roosevelt and the New Deal. The values she associated with the new administration in Washington clashed strongly with the ones she connected to her remembered frontier experience, such as self-reliance, individual initiative, frugality, hard work, and personal responsibility. Wilder believed that the New Deal was undermining those qualities and fostering instead dependency, regimentation, loss of initiative, and wastefulness. Her childhood experiences on the farm and in the small towns in which she had grown up, along with her life in Mansfield during the last sixty-three years of her life, led her to be critical of expanding governmental bureaucracy and the urbanized, collectivized, institutionalized culture she thought the New Deal was helping foster during the depression.

In addition, her pacifistic sentiments and disillusionment with the nation's experience in World War I led her to join many other Americans in worrying about Roosevelt's foreign policies and increased her suspicion that he was assuming the role of a dictator. In addition, Wilder, not surprisingly, responded to those living around her, and, although she could be cantankerous and unconventional in her beliefs and behavior, she may have found it comfortable to conform to the political proclivities of her friends and neighbors in and around Mansfield. While Missouri as a whole remained a Democratic state, with Roosevelt easily carrying it by an almost two-to-one margin in 1936, the president garnered only 37 percent of the vote in Mansfield and 41 percent in Wright County that year. Mansfield and the surrounding Ozarks region historically had been Republican strongholds. During the late 1930s, Wilder found herself closely in tune with the staunchly conservative Republican, anti-New Deal stance taken by Seventh District Congressman Dewey Short of Galena, an outspoken Roosevelt "basher."[12]

Rose Wilder Lane's political odyssey, it is not surprising, was much more dramatic and extreme than her mother's. She was, as many people noted, "a piece of work." Brilliant, emotional, mercurial, individualistic, unconventional—Lane never blended into anybody's woodwork. Whether she was clinically manic- depressive is a matter better left to armchair psychologists, but that her mood could shift drastically from day to day and moment to moment and that she harbored intense loves and deep hatreds are incontestable.[13] A thumbnail biography of her would take note of her dropping out of school several times as an adolescent; finishing high school while living with her Aunt Eliza Jane in Crowley, Louisiana; running off to Kansas City at age seventeen to become a telegrapher; winding up in California as an early-day female real estate salesman; divorcing her husband and refusing to marry again in order to retain her complete freedom of action; and wandering the globe from Paris and Rome to Baghdad and Albania before settling down in Mansfield, temporarily, and finally making her home in Danbury, Connecticut.

To suggest that Lane was a nonconformist is to say that the sun rises and sets every day. Her unconventional personality helps explain both her left-wing flirtations in the late teens and early twenties and her later outspoken right-wing views during the thirties and after. She claimed to have once been a communist (though not a card-carrying Communist party member) and to having hung out with the likes of John Reed, the radical left-wing author of *Ten Days That Shook the World*.[14] During the thirties, she wrote that firsthand observations in Soviet Georgia a decade earlier had disillusioned her with communism in action.[15] Politics played a lesser role in her thinking as she moved back and forth between Rocky Ridge and Albania during the middle and late 1920s. She retained a high estimation of Herbert Hoover, the subject of one of her earlier biographies, because she regarded him as a hard-boiled businessman—strong, efficient, and practical as well as generous, loyal, and humane.[16] However, so many people blamed Hoover for the Great Depression that his chances for reelection in 1932 were minuscule, prompting a mad scramble for the Democratic presidential nomination, eventually won by New York governor Franklin Roosevelt. Lane might have been excused for feeling ill about Hoover, too, since her entire nest egg of savings, invested in the Palmer Company, disappeared by the end of 1931. But the resulting trauma did not translate into receptivity to Roosevelt. Between his inauguration on March 4, 1933, and the summer of 1935, she grew increasingly disillusioned with him as a leader and with the policies of his New Deal administration.

In her growing antipathy to the president and her increasing alienation from what she perceived as excessive state intervention in people's affairs, Lane was part of a growing libertarian wing of anti–New Deal thinkers and political activists that included writers and journalists such as Ayn Rand, Isabel Paterson, Henry Hazlitt, John T. Flynn, William Henry Chamberlain, Garet Garrett, *Chicago Tribune* publisher Colonel Robert McCormick, and *Saturday Evening Post* publisher George Horace Lorimer, as well as organizations such as the American Liberty League.[17] But while sociological or intellectual explanations for Lane's political odyssey, taking account of correspondences between her and other like-minded thinkers, are useful, I believe an equally, if not more persuasive, argument can be found in psychology. We need to ask why she, among her wide coterie of friends and colleagues, should have chosen to become a fanatical foe of Roosevelt and the New Deal, while many of them admired the man and the movement or remained on the sidelines.

The process by which Rose Wilder Lane migrated from a squishy, romantic political leftism during the years surrounding World War I to an absorbed and fanatical far-rightism by the 1940s was much more complicated and psychologically charged than the one carrying Laura Ingalls Wilder from a traditional allegiance to the Democrats to a firm alliance with conservative Republicans and a strong dislike for Roosevelt and the New Deal. In the end, Lane would denounce Republicans along with Democrats, rejecting the "me-too" policies of Dwight Eisenhower and aligning herself with extreme libertarians who expected the political system to collapse and be replaced by one in which power devolved to the fifty states. She preferred using the labels "libertarian" or "anarchist," rather than "conservative," to describe herself.[18]

Luckily for us, Lane frequently kept a journal that revealed her deepest and most profound fears, despair, hopes, and dreams. These, along with diary entries and copious letters, allow us to piece together a plausible account of the seismic shift that occurred in her political thinking during the depression decade and to attempt to connect it to her writings during those years. To some degree, her philosophical convictions also found outlet in some of the work she did on her mother's novels.

While it can be safely said that Wilder's opposition to FDR and the New Deal was, like that of many of her fellow citizens, rather conventional in its reflection of her personal value system and even its vehemence, Lane's reaction took place in a maelstrom of psychological upheaval and philosophical doubts. That these all came together and peaked during the several years after 1933, the first year of the Roosevelt administration, adds to the drama as well as to the intensity of the transition.

Along with William Holtz, Anita Clair Fellman and Julia C. Ehrhardt have probed most deeply in their analyses of the political views of mother and daughter.[19] In advancing her thesis that Lane wrote fiction, in part, as a way of advancing her own personal politics, Ehrhardt ably delineates the Missourian's shift toward an extreme brand of conservatism by the end of the thirties. She notes that the Great Depression and the New Deal helped reenergize her faltering writing career and redirect her literary energies to a subject she felt passionate about. The former self-proclaimed leftist emerged as part of an until-now little discussed literary movement—anti–New Deal fiction. Her newfound devotion to right-wing political activism allowed her to escape permanently from the confines of Rocky Ridge, which had come in many ways to seem like a prison for her.

Building upon the insights of Ehrhardt's treatment, I would like to redirect our emphasis toward Lane's profound psychological problems, bordering upon mental illness, which were exacerbated by conditions surrounding the financial debacle of the thirties.[20] While I agree with Ehrhardt that Lane's shifting her intellectual energies to libertarian political ideology was a way to deal with the problems of writer's block and a stagnating career at the same time that it allowed full expression for her personal politics of unrestrained individualism, my emphasis will be upon the way in which, in addition to giving her a chance to escape a whole host of personal problems, it provided a solution for the problem of what biographer William Holtz has called her "metaphysical angst."[21] Lane's eventual escape from her demons and her discovery of comfort and a sense of stability in right-wing libertarian political ideology resulted from a journey down a winding path, marked by numerous retreats and side trips. The extreme political postulates at which she arrived, while not entirely dismissible, were largely unanalyzable in rational terms. Though Lane clothed them in historical and philosophical guise, they were arrived at as much through feeling as through reason.

By the time Lane approached and passed her fortieth birthday in December 1926, she was spending more and more of her time dwelling upon her personal status, her career as a writer, and her future prospects. Highly emotional, hugely ambitious, a workaholic when fully engaged on a writing project, and desperate to do something worthwhile that would be recognized by her peers, she struggled during the 1920s to identify a subject worthy of her talents and one that might allow her to fulfill her potential. Complicating her situation were her concern for and sense of responsibility toward her parents, who turned sixty and seventy, respectively, in February 1927.

Lane's convoluted relationship with her mother—at once solicitous and resentful—lay at the center of her own psychological miseries as they intensified during the early 1930s.[22] Distressed by her indebtedness, a declining market for her writing, and signs of advancing age, lack of love, bad teeth, increasingly flabby body, and personality disorders, Lane poured out her frustrations in long letters written to Fremont Older, her former boss at the *San Francisco Bulletin,* Guy Moyston, a fellow writer whom she professed to love but refused to marry, and others.[23] Finding virtually no one—including her parents—with whom she could have a serious conversation in Mansfield and considering people in that section of the Missouri Ozarks generally to be provincial and worthy of little more than providing inspiration for the hillbilly stories that she wrote for popular magazines, Lane longed to get away from her parents and to experience fully the radical freedom for which she hungered. "What I most want in living is freedom," she wrote Moyston in January 1926. "I intensely want the freedom of liberation from work. Unable to have that, I shall have at least the mental freedom of recognizing the fundamental difference between the activities that are rooted in my *self,* and those that are forced upon me by entirely external conditions."[24]

This intense and highly emotional commitment to personal freedom and self-determination bound Lane to other like-minded "New Women" growing up and maturing during the early twentieth century. Many of her friends and acquaintances shared her desire for personal liberation—Dorothy Thompson, Mary Margaret McBride, and Helen Boylston, among others. The most obvious manifestation of Lane's radical individualism was her refusal to marry again after divorcing Gillette Lane. Her numerous letters to Guy Moyston during the twenties, containing long, involved explanations of her continuing love for him along with the reasons why she could not marry, reflected her commitment to—as well as the cost of—complete freedom of action. After the Stock Market Crash, as the country plunged into economic chaos, politics became scrambled, and millions of Americans faced starvation and despair, Lane could less afford some of the frivolous hopes and fantasies in which she had indulged a few years earlier, such as her plan for building an elaborate dream house in Albania. Though still earning, by the standard of the time, sizable royalties for stories and articles in large-circulation magazines, she continually fretted—even obsessed—about money. But her spendthrift habits insured that she would never have enough to satisfy her.

More to the point, this highly introspective woman came to realize that she lacked a fundamental core of personality that could provide a solid foundation for living. This all spilled out in an agonizing entry in her journal on January 24, 1933, as the United States plunged into the deepest trough of the Great Depression. Just days before Germany installed Adolf Hitler as chancellor and weeks before Roosevelt took over in the White House, Lane was lamenting in her journal, "So far, I am almost superlatively a failure. There has been no success in personal relationships, in adjustments to the world, in work, or in money." She attributed these and her failures in love and marriage to a "fundamental mal-adjustment." She observed candidly, "I know very few people. My acquaintance is not wide, and I have no friends. There is no person upon whose loyalty I could rely." All that she had to look forward to now was death, and during the coming months and years she would frequently express a willingness—even a longing—for it. At bottom, she lacked a firm sense of identity: "I have never really felt that I am I; I feel no identification with myself. My life is not *my* life, but a succession of short stories and one-act plays, all begun by chance and left unfinished." After five years back at Rocky Ridge living near her parents, she felt no pleasure or satisfaction. "I do not like the place, I do not like to live here, and I see no prospect of ever leaving," she wrote. Things only got worse. Two-and-a-half weeks later, her dog, Mr. Bunting, died, killed by a passing automobile. Frequently in the days after that, she could not stop crying. "I can not love," she wrote the day after the accident. "That's what's wrong with me. I give everything except real warmth myself. Living is hell and all life is to be pitied."[25]

Lane's feeling out of place in an alien world reflected not only a sense of social isolation and vocational drift, but also bespoke her much deeper metaphysical angst. She was a serious, if not systematic, reader of philosophical works and kept in tune with new trends in thought and scholarship. In long letters to friends and fellow writers, she expounded at length on her views about religion and the ultimate ends of existence. While calling herself a theist, she rejected Christianity, proclaimed herself agnostic, and declared against all absolutes and certainties. "I still do not believe that there *is* any Good, or any Evil," she wrote Fremont Older in May 1928. "I don't naturally think in moralistic terms, any more than I can instinctively believe, as most persons do, in immortality. I don't believe that there are any abstract Absolutes: Virtue, Sin, Truth, Good, Evil, all the rest of 'em."[26]

Lane enjoyed venturing broad speculations and throwing out controversial ideas, waiting to see what people's reactions would be. Taking her endless pronouncements and pontifications too literally or out of context would not be very helpful, but the drift of her thinking during the late twenties and early thirties was clear enough. To Clarence Day in September 1927 she wrote, "More and more, I am oppressed by the sense of emptiness, of not-worth-whileness. Of all my days going. . . . I can't get rid of this intolerable wanting-to-accomplish. What? What *is* there to accomplish? . . . I, with nothing under the heel, in a world quite happily ignorant that I'm on it, know in advance that nothing can really be accomplished." And she wrote this in a journal entry in April 1928: "Convictions—completely blank!"[27]

Caught up in intellectual trends of the times that questioned all truths and absolutes,[28] grasping wildly for some kind of significant subject matter that would both enhance her reputation and stabilize her bank account, depressed by personal problems and relationships, and avidly longing to break away from the small town of Mansfield, Lane rode the violent tides of her mercurial temperament during the early 1930s, appearing gay and exuberant on the outside to friends and neighbors, seldom revealing the private agonies she was going through.

Into this social-psychological-philosophical vacuum, as the 1930s wore on, conservative political theory gradually emerged as a firm foundation upon which Lane was able to build a sense of meaning and significance for herself. Not incidentally, it also provided her with something new to do with her time. At the outset, her new-found sense of certainty focused *negatively* on what was *wrong* about Franklin Roosevelt and the New Dealers. As time went by, she increasingly invested in libertarian political principles the kind of *positive* moral and epistemological efficacy she had been lacking for so long. The process can be seen occurring in four stages.

The first of these involved the writing in 1931 and 1932 of *Let the Hurricane Roar,* a book describing the courage of a young woman living alone with her baby in a sod house during a terrifically cold Dakota winter, overcoming all the challenges a malign nature hurled at her. Her work on the book coincided with her labors on the first of her mother's books, *Little House in the Big Woods.* For some time, Lane had sought to help her mother find higher paying outlets for her work than the farm newspapers she had been writing for since 1911. In 1930, she had gotten her to write "Pioneer Girl," the autobiographical account of her childhood, but after helping rewrite it into an approximately two-hundred-page manuscript, Lane had been unable to place it as a serial with a major magazine. In May 1931, she spent about a week reworking the manuscript of a children's novel that her mother had written, based on material extracted from the beginning of her autobiography. By the time that book came out in March 1932 as *Little House in the Big Woods,* Wilder had already drafted a second children's novel, *Farmer Boy,* about her husband's boyhood years in Malone, New York. In the meantime, no doubt partially inspired by the work she had been doing on her mother's manuscripts, Lane began writing a book based upon her maternal grandparents' homesteading experience in Dakota Territory during the 1880s. Tentatively titled "Courage," it later took the name of a song her mother remembered singing as a child in Dakota. It took the better part of a year for Lane to complete "Hurricane," partly because she was drawn away from it by working on the second of what she called her mother's "juveniles."

While she was grateful that these children's novels provided a supplemental source of income for her mother, she considered the effort she put into them to be inconsequential and resented the time they took away from her own work, as can be seen in some of her diary entries. At the end of May 1931, she noted, "This whole past month got nothing done but one short story: A Spool of Thread and my mother's 35,000 word Juvenile"—which was *Little House in the Big Woods.* On June 2, 1932, she wrote, "Did nothing worth while: a few pp Farmer Boy." In July and August 1932 she set aside her mother's second book to work on "Hurricane," for which the *Saturday Evening Post* paid her three thousand dollars (out of which her agent

George Bye took his usual 10 percent cut) and which was featured as a two-part serial in the magazine in October. It was republished the following February in book form.[29]

Though gratified by her mother's success as a children's author, Lane was temporarily transformed by the work she did on her own book, because in it she finally had discovered something that she had been seeking for years—a significant subject to write about. In a journal entry on June 8, 1932, she observed that her current despondency had not derived so much from the aging process, dental problems, or financial woes. "My whole trouble," she wrote, "was that I am not master of my material in writing my mother's second juvenile. It was a little job that seemed inconsequential—and is—and therefore it was able to do all this to me without my knowing it. The truth is that for better or worse, no matter how hopelessly a failure, I am a writer. I am a writer. Nothing else in the world is so important to me—to my own inner self—as writing is." Ironically, by the time Lane, at age forty-five, declared this triumphal insight, she had only about five years remaining as a writer of fiction. Moreover, she would plunge even more deeply into personal despair during succeeding months, judging 1933 to be her "worst year yet."[30]

Let the Hurricane Roar constituted a paean to the pioneer virtues of courage, optimism, individualism, self-reliance, and hard work. Its main characters were named Charles and Caroline, the same as her mother's parents, whose stories of hardship and the challenges they had endured on Dakota's prairies had inspired the book. While the plot of the novel coincided with the experiences of the Ingallses only in the loosest sense, they shared themes and circumstances that would have been familiar to any participant in the Great Dakota Boom of the early 1880s. In Lane's working title, "Courage," lay a wealth of emotions and personal references applicable to her own situation, as well as to the one facing the country in 1932.

This was an allegory Americans needed to hear, Lane believed, during a time of great stress and perplexity. It provided a solid American philosophy of living that could engender courage, steadfastness, and resourcefulness to tide the country through its time of troubles. The purpose of the narrative, Rose indicated in *Better Homes and Gardens* in December 1933, was to provide a reply to pessimists who had been paralyzed by the depression. The book had been written from her "feeling that life is never easy, that all human history is a record of achievement in disaster (so that disaster is no cause for

despair), and that our greatest asset is the valor of the American spirit—the undefeated spirit of millions of obscure men and women
who are as valiant today as the pioneers were in the past," she said.
"The story of the American pioneer has not yet been truthfully told,"
she also wrote in her journal. "It is a story of gigantic achievement,
physically, spiritually, morally, which in the telling should reveal the
primal forces which have gone into the making of America. A story
which, rightly told, should lead the world back from the defeatist
thinking of the socialistic, militaristic, caste formula in which European thought is so hopelessly involved."[31]

Rose had come a long way from her belief several years earlier that
American civilization provided little of interest to think or write
about. "I don't like the American spirit," she had written Guy Moyston from Albania in February 1927. "I don't like its energy, its deifi-
cation of work, its insularity, its standardization, its terrific stress on
possessions and comfort, its complacency, its ignorance, its idealism,
and (mental sum-total of these) its unconscious hypocrisy." Admittedly, Americans were building the greatest civilization history had
ever known, but it was one "that has nothing to do with the human-
ities, that has nothing humane in it, nothing static, nothing to do with
form." All of this had made her very uncomfortable at the time.[32]

By 1932, however, Lane was ready to declare *for* America—for the
pioneers, the builders, the doers, and the optimists, as over against
the pessimists, the whiners, the charity-seekers, and the naysayers.
Let the Hurricane Roar was, first of all, a eulogy of the pioneer virtues
of courage, initiative, hard work, self-reliance, and persistence and,
secondarily, a screed against government. Most of its ideological
underpinning remained implicit, subsumed in the general plot of
courageous reaction to stupendous challenge and hardship, although at several points in the story words reflecting Lane's own political viewpoint found their way into the mouths of her characters.
For example, Caroline, who more than her husband, Charles, is the
truly heroic figure of the novel, says, "We aren't going to beg," and
"The country's all right, Mr. Svenson. No country's going to feed you
with a spoon."[33] A letter Caroline writes to her husband but never
mails might as easily have been a political speech delivered during
the election campaign of 1932, when the story was being written:

> We are having hard times now, but we should not dwell upon
> them but think of the future. It has never been easy to build up a

country, but how much easier it is for us, with such great comforts and conveniences, kerosene, cookstoves, and even railroads and fast posts, than it was for our forefathers. I trust that, like our own parents, we may live to see times more prosperous than they have ever been in the past, and we will then reflect with satisfaction that these hard times were not in vain. (93–94)

Lane took aim at people overwhelmed by "shapeless, nameless dread," urging them to buck up and face reality steadfastly and courageously. The challenge of the Dakota blizzards had been not merely physical, but existential, which, in the language she used to describe it, resembled in many ways the diary and journal entries she was using to portray her own fears and obsessions at the time. In the bright glare of whiteness created by the snow blanketing the land around her dugout, Caroline perceives "a world neither alive nor dead, and terrible because it was alien to life and death, and ignorant of them." This language was reminiscent of some of the philosophical musings Lane had spilled into her journals and letters. She continued,

> In that instant she knew the infinite smallness, weakness, of life in the lifeless universe. She felt the vast, insensate forces against which life itself is a rebellion. Infinitely small and weak was the spark of warmth in a living heart. Yet valiantly the tiny heart continued to beat. Tired, weak, burdened by its own fears and sorrows, still it persisted, indomitably it continued to exist, and in bare existence itself, without assurance of victory, even without hope, in its indomitable existence among vast, incalculable, lifeless forces, it was invincible. (99–100)

The words seemed highly applicable to the state of Lane's psyche at the time.

Yet to read entries in Lane's journal and diary during the next year or two would have revealed a woman who more often resembled the weak-kneed, pitiable creatures she was inveighing against than the strong-willed, valiant optimists she was calling for. Day by day, as Caroline and her tiny baby survived in the dugout in the face of raging storms outside, the homesteader used her gaiety as defiance against the challenges facing her. Lane, too, showed a cheerful face to the people around her on the streets of Mansfield, even as she went home to write despairing entries in her diary:

February 12, 1932: "Had another panic all night. Am I trying to do the impossible? And why?"

May 29, 1932: "I am old, I am alone, a failure, forgotten, here in this dull alien place, I am losing my teeth. It is strange horror of dying makes me want to die."

February 13, 1933: "I can't stop crying."

September 24, 1934: "Blue as hell, old, ugly, tired & useless & broke."

February 7, 1935: "Sick at heart & scared because of money. Tired, awfully tired."

September 28, 1935: "No one who's old can be happy. Not really. Never again truly happy."

October 1, 1935: "Dopey. . . . I am not normal in the head. I really shall be glad to die."[34]

Though most of her entries were by no means as morose as these, Lane's wild, roller-coaster moods frequently left her in a state of depression. In imputing to many of her fellow Americans a lack of courage and a sense of defeatism, Lane was surely, knowingly or unknowingly, projecting some of her own psychological weaknesses onto them. And in demanding that people face the future unafraid, she was asking them to do what she all too often was incapable of doing herself. But as time went by, she was discovering a philosophical foundation upon which to reconstruct her life.

The second stage of Lane's ideological odyssey can be located in 1935, when she collected a series of Ozarks stories that she had previously published, inspired by her experience and observations in Mansfield, in a volume called *Old Home Town*. Shortly thereafter, she wrote a polemical article for the *Saturday Evening Post* called "Credo," which was an only slightly disguised diatribe against the New Deal. Lane had always viewed people in Mansfield as provincial, narrow-minded, and excessively moralistic, themes that energized the stories she had originally written for the *Saturday Evening Post* and *Ladies Home Journal*. Lane had rebelled against her childhood circumstances and gotten out of town as quickly as she could, but in 1935 she professed to have discovered redeeming virtues both in the lessons her parents had taught her and in the culture of small-town Missouri. Those lessons included the precepts that "it is impossible to get something for nothing," that "he who does not work can not long continue to eat," and that "chickens come home to roost." America's recent experience provided "unexpected proof that our parents knew what they were talking about," she wrote in her preface to *Old Home Town,* continuing,

> We suspect that, after all, man's life in this hostile universe is not easy and cannot be made so; that facts are seldom pleasant and must be faced; that the only freedom is to be found within the slavery of self-discipline; that everything must be paid for and that putting off the day of reckoning only increases the inexorable bill.
>
> This may be an old-fashioned, middle-class, small-town point of view. All that can be said for it is that it created America.[35]

As an introduction to her collection of stories, the words were not entirely relevant, and as an expression of Lane's own personal philosophy they seemed somewhat strained and artificial. They did, however, reflect the general drift of her thinking at the time toward a celebration of individual effort and self-discipline, a rejection of easy solutions to problems, and an implicit condemnation of governmental interference in people's lives.

Shortly after writing the preface in April 1935, Lane accepted an offer to write a book on Missouri for a series of state volumes focusing on history and important sites. Her research for the assignment soon took her to the State Historical Society in Columbia, where she was visited by her libertarian writer friend Garet Garrett, who was on assignment from the *Saturday Evening Post* to write a series of articles on New Deal farm policy. She decided to travel along with him for two weeks through Illinois, Iowa, Nebraska, and Kansas to observe firsthand how the New Deal was affecting people at the grass roots. In her eyes, what Roosevelt's farm programs were doing to the country was hardly better than Stalin's collectivization of Soviet agriculture and the tyranny she had observed in Soviet Georgia in 1922. Back in Columbia, before returning to work on her book, she pounded out a visceral reaction to the New Deal in an 11,550-word article that she submitted to the *Post* for publication.

For almost three years, Lane's suspicions and concerns about Roosevelt had been escalating, and her opposition to governmental intrusions into people's lives had been growing. "Conditions in this country are really terrible," she had written in January 1935 to Rexh Meta, the Albanian young man she was sponsoring through Cambridge University. "All the Roosevelt ballyhoo has come to nothing whatever except enormous government expenditures, which there is really no way to pay for except by inflation." The Democratic administration, which in 1932 had promised to cut government expenses by a quarter, had instead increased them several times. "Also it has crippled business and agriculture until they could not recover possibly," Lane asserted. She believed the men around the president were trying to convert America to communism. Roosevelt was "the worst type of crooked politician," a man "drunk on his own self-importance." In an article in the *Post* in July 1935, Lane had written that she was now "a fundamentalist American," believing that "individualism, laissez faire and the slightly restrained anarchy of capitalism offer the best opportunities for the development of the human spirit."[36] Already convinced that the New Deal administration was destroying freedom in the United States, Lane's trip with Garet Garrett simply reinforced already preformed opinions and gave her the incentive to write a polemic against it.

Though first rejected by the *Post*, "Credo" was later accepted for fifteen hundred dollars and published as the magazine's lead article on March 7, 1936. Franklin Roosevelt carried all but two states in the presidential election that year, garnering 61 percent of the popular vote, and Democrats swept 77 percent of the seats in Congress, but Rose Wilder Lane was moving in the opposite direction. She began "Credo" by asserting that in 1919 she had been a communist and went on to explain why she now believed that governmental intrusion into people's lives was unacceptable and why anything that undermined personal freedom and self-reliance was un-American. Without mentioning Roosevelt or the New Deal by name, she implicitly linked them with "economic tyranny" and suggested that, by depriving people of their freedom, they were akin to Communists. If the ultimate human value is individual liberty, then the corollary of that principle is individual responsibility for one's self. The old spirit of individualism was still alive and well, she rejoiced. Half the unemployed had stayed off relief, millions of farmers remained "lords on their own land," and countless others were paying off their debts on their own, with no help from government. These were Lane's heroes—people who stood on their own two feet and asked help from no one. "By such personal courage and endurance, the American principle has been successfully defended for more than a century," she stated. Lane's article was a plea that all Americans would continue to carry on in that tradition.[37] Soon published in pamphlet form and reprinted many times as *Give Me Liberty*, the polemic stood as Lane's proudest attempt to summarize her political ideas.

While she continued to crank out magazine stories in 1936 and, at a much reduced pace, in 1937, Lane's next big project was a novel set again in Dakota Territory and inspired by her parents' trials and tribulations in trying to make a living on the land after their marriage. *Free Land,* for which Lane received her biggest payday—twenty-five thousand dollars—had been started several times earlier but was written primarily during 1937. It constituted the third stage in Lane's career path on the way to conservative political polemics and contained more ideological baggage than had *Let the Hurricane Roar.* By the time it was published, Roosevelt's huge popularity consolidated in the 1936 election was rapidly fading, and a conservative coalition had begun to form in Congress, even before the 1938 off-year elections, which reduced Democratic numbers in the House of Representatives by seventy and in the Senate by seven. Upon publication of *Free Land* in eight parts in the *Saturday Evening Post* in March and April 1938 (it came out in book form in May), Lane indicated, "I usually write because I need the money. Sometimes I write because I get mad. I wrote Let the Hurricane Roar and Free Land because I got mad."[38] Her concern in 1932 had been with people who succumbed to fear and lethargy rather than relying on their own courage and energy. Six years later, she was more specifically worried about the public's growing reliance upon government.

The book's title was deliberately ironic, because Lane was insistent upon showing that land in the west had never really been free for the taking, despite the government's willingness to grant settlers 160 acres for a modest filing fee and five years' residence on and improvements of it, under terms of the Homestead Act of 1862. Lane did not want anyone to infer that "free" homesteads in the late 1800s provided a justification for government doles and handouts during the 1930s. In accordance with what historians who had studied the subject had written, and informed by what homesteaders like her parents had told her, Lane observed that it had taken a considerable amount of money to get established on a farm, what with purchasing machinery and tools, putting up a house, barn, and other buildings, erecting fences, digging a well, and meeting other expenses. Her underlying theme in the book was that government was not a solution for people's problems. "I wrote Free Land," she indicated, "because I could no longer bear hearing people say, 'But everything is changed now; there's no more free land.' Everything certainly is changed now, but as to really 'free' land, there never was any."[39]

Antigovernment statements pop up in a number of places in the book. Of James Beaton, father of the book's protagonist, the author says, "He did not believe in giving, or getting, something for nothing. He believed in every man's paying his own way. The Beatons had always done it." The father's antigovernmental leanings rubbed off on his son David, who did not hesitate to lie about his age when he applied for a government homestead, an action which he likened to "paying something on an old grudge." The putative author's comment on the subterfuge: "A man knew instinctively that Government was his natural enemy." David's brother and sister played their own games with government rules, leaving clothes lying around in their shanties while absent from them in order to give the impression that they were occupied, so as to fool any officials who might come snooping around to see if they were fulfilling the letter of the law in meeting requirements for proving up on their homesteads. Again, their intent was to deceive the government. Later on, David expressed his opinion that protective tariffs were not only undesirable but also unconstitutional: "The Constitution says, plain for any man to read, this government's got no right to favor anybody. 'Taxes for revenue only,' is what it says, plain black and white." The underlying assumption was that "every man's got to lift himself by his own bootstraps." Another antigovernmental reference, which would also show up later in her mother's book *Little House on the Prairie*, when the characters involved were her mother's parents, was a story told by Nettie Peters about their family being evicted from Indian Territory by government soldiers, despite the fact that her father "had the word straight from Washington" that it was all right to settle on the land. "David supposed that someone in Washington had an ax to grind," was the spin put on the episode by the author, implying that it was government officials who were at fault, rather than the settlers who had ventured illegally onto Indian land.[40]

It is not so much the specific actions or statements of the characters in the book, however, that set its tone. Rather it is the central underlying theme that "free land" was a misnomer, giving the government credit where none was due and failing to understand that the real heroes of the story were energetic, hardworking, and responsible individuals like the Beatons. By implication, that same kind of spirit continued unabated in America at the end of the depression decade, and people no more needed to rely on government intervention then than they had earlier on.

Lane's basic purpose in writing *Free Land* was apparently too subtle for most of the book's reviewers to grasp, she thought. She was gratified, however, by Burton Rascoe's comments in his column in *Newsweek,* where he referred to it as "one of the most tonic and engrossing novels that has come along in years." His review actually had more to say about Lane's earlier *Give Me Liberty* (originally "Credo"), which in his opinion "might be considered the most eloquent and most revolutionary utterance of the decade in America" because of its American tone and feeling and its contrast with the ideas of so many intellectuals who had come to the conclusion that Americans would be forced to choose between fascism and communism as a way out of the depression.[41]

The final stage of Lane's political odyssey would come after the publication of *Free Land,* when she abandoned fiction writing and during the early 1940s discovered her true vocation in conservative political polemics. Her treatise *The Discovery of Freedom: Man's Struggle against Authority,* published in 1943, along with other activities she engaged in afterward to promote libertarian philosophy, became her lasting legacy to American intellectual life. The book, which was published in 1943 along with Isabel Paterson's *The God of the Machine* and Ayn Rand's *The Fountainhead,* antedated Friedrich Hayek's *The Road to Serfdom* by a year. It has earned a reputation as one of the founding documents of the new American right during the years after World War II. Scholars have noted the conservative or libertarian values implicitly and explicitly contained in Lane's writings. While historians of postwar conservative thought have generally omitted her from their accounts, she has been recognized, along with Rand and Paterson, as one of the founding "godmothers" of modern libertarian political philosophy.[42]

Unlike most of her fellow right-wing polemicists, such as Hayek, Ludwig von Mises, Russell Kirk, and Richard Weaver, Lane was not an academician, but she had acquired a wide-ranging acquaintance with history, social theory, and political philosophy through voracious and eclectic, if unsystematic, reading. In *The Discovery of Freedom* she attempted to provide a philosophical and historical grounding for the kind of deeply felt, emotional criticisms she had been directing against Franklin Roosevelt and the New Deal for a decade.

Interestingly, the president and his minions remained unmentioned in the book, but their presence was implicit throughout. Lane approached her task from two directions. The first quarter of the book adopted a logical and philosophical approach to the meaning of terms such as *freedom, control, responsibility,* and *authority.* The rest of the volume was devoted to a broad-ranging survey of world history in search of antecedents for the kind of freedom she wished to celebrate. Largely unencumbered by the usual scholarly paraphernalia of footnotes and references, Lane's text was a sprightly and readable, if rather idiosyncratic, take on the subject. Her forte in this work, as it always had been as a conversationalist, letter writer, and author of fiction and nonfiction, was clarity, directness, and forcefulness, all served up in a conversational tone that established rapport with the reader. Little or no room for nuance, ambiguity, or complexity remained.

Hovering over Lane's entire presentation was a strict dualism that divided the world and its history into two camps: human freedom versus collective authority; energy, creativity, and the ability to choose versus control, repression, and stultification; change and progress versus stasis and degeneration; limited government or anarchy versus planned economies and despotism; America versus Europe and the rest of the world; the present and the future versus the past; and, ultimately, the individual versus the masses. There was no question on which side of these dichotomies Lane stood. Driving the point home, she declared, "Nothing but your desire, your will, can generate and control your energy. You alone are responsible for your every act; no one else can be." And "Everyone knows that anarchy is the natural relationship of human beings, and that it works perfectly well." And again, "American Government is not an Authority; it has no control over individuals and no responsibility for their affairs."[43]

It is hard to know exactly how to take statements like the last one, since as an assertion of fact it was so obviously literally untrue. Lane, in fact, spent some time in the book cataloging various government interventions and programs she disliked, including protective tariffs, farm subsidies, workmen's compensation, unemployment insurance, Social Security, antitrust laws, and compulsory labor union membership. In fact, Lane thought government should do little more than guarantee public safety and provide for the national defense. She even drew the line at road building, contending that private enterprise was perfectly capable of constructing and financing highways, and she suggested that beyond the eighth grade families should be responsible for funding the further education of their children (63–64, 213, 245, 258–59). Though not using the term, Lane was arguing for about as extreme a laissez-faire form of government as one can contemplate. Associating all economic planning with the kinds of things that happened in totalitarian states such as Hitler's Germany and Stalin's Soviet Union, she left no room for compromise between total state control of people's lives and the kind of anarchic freedom she said had existed in the western United States during the late nineteenth century and which she would have liked to see reestablished (27–28, 220). That last notion reflected a nostalgic re-imagining of the supposed virtues of the kind of frontier society her parents had known in Dakota during the 1880s and about which she had written two novels of her own and had helped her mother in producing her series of children's novels. In fact, the last of Wilder's *Little House* series and the fourth set in Dakota Territory, *These Happy Golden Years*, appeared the same year as Lane's political treatise. Had Lane known more about the history of Western settlement, however, she would have understood that governmental institutions had quickly followed in the wake of settlement and that the kind of romantic, laissez-faire conditions about which she was rhapsodizing had never been a historical reality.[44]

Lane identified several points in human history when freedom began to emerge in opposition to authority. She found them in the Judeo-Christian tradition, from Abraham and Moses through Jesus; the example of Mohammed and the Saracens; and the American Revolution. The last event was her real focus; she traced the beginnings of the movement for freedom to American protests against the first British Navigation Act of 1660. Admitting that not all of the Revolutionaries and Founding Fathers adhered to extreme libertarian views like her own, she nevertheless discovered in the Declaration of Independence and the Constitution, as well as in the state constitutions that were written around that time, affirmation for her contention that complete personal freedom was the ultimate value.

Like many of her fellow libertarian thinkers, Lane found little to recommend in democracy per se.[45] Taking note of the Founding Fathers' aversion to democratic rule and their insistence upon placing strict limits on what government could do, she engaged in an extended discussion of why voting and the right to vote were not only of little importance but also, in many cases, undesirable. In this, she showed how different her temperament was from her mother's. Wilder seemed perfectly content living among her relatively unlettered and unsophisticated Missouri Ozarks neighbors. Though critical of many of their actions and attitudes, she discerned no reason to dissociate herself from them. Her daughter, in contrast, felt totally out of place in Mansfield, and honed in on the foibles and idiosyncrasies of the rural and townsfolk much like an anthropologist or the fiction writer that she had been. While able to be friends with a few of them, she remained fundamentally an elitist—a well-read and somewhat exotic outlander whose interest in people could be likened to a lepidopterist's attraction to butterflies. "Average Americans have common sense," Lane observed:

> They know that there are always enough stupid, ignorant, dishonest voters to carry any election; they know that demagogues, liars, hill-billy bands, popular actors and orators, free picnics and vote-buying can always corral enough voters. They know that these extensions of the franchise have broken down the moral standards of American politics, and have so overcome the moral character of American politicians that both parties use these methods of getting votes. And that therefore an election is merely a sporting event, like a ball game, its outcome depending on luck as well as on skill, and its object being no more than to get ballots into boxes, and men into office. (211)

These observations, which might sound unexceptional to political scientists today,[46] were symptomatic of how little faith Lane retained in democratic politics and of how estranged she had become from her fellow citizens. From her days as a reporter for the *San Francisco Bulletin* during the teens through her fiction-writing career in the twenties and thirties, she had succeeded to the degree that she had been able to keep her finger on the public's pulse and had provided at least a significant segment of the public what it wanted to read. During the last quarter-century of her life she poured most of her energies into trying to transform politics, but she never sensed that she was in the mainstream of opinion or that many people agreed with her or even wanted to read about her ideas.

Reviews of *The Discovery of Freedom* were sparse and less than enthusiastic, which Lane blamed on the liberal biases of New York reviewers. This was her last significant publication. She would go on to influence and help inspire a small coterie of right-wing political thinkers, however, through her editing during the late 1940s of the National Economic Council's monthly *Review of Books*, a task that allowed her to keep informed about new developments in social, political, and economic thought. She touched an even smaller number of individuals through personal contact and her proverbial long, single-spaced typewritten letters, into which she poured her increasingly strident and contentious views and speculations on politics. Among those she influenced through her writings and correspondence were economists Orval Watts and Hans Sennholz, retired Du Pont Corporation executive Jasper Crane, National Economic Council founder Merwin Hart, newspaperman and Freedom School founder Robert LeFevre, Leonard Reed of the Foundation for Economic Education, and the young Roger MacBride, who met her when he was the fourteen-year-old son of a *Reader's Digest* editor who was working with Lane on reprinting *Let the Hurricane Roar*. The two struck up a long correspondence and friendship, and she eventually made him her lawyer, agent, and financial adviser, informally adopted him as her "grandson," and designated him as her heir. MacBride, a graduate of Princeton University and Harvard Law School, won some national notoriety in 1976 when he became the Libertarian party's nominee for president.[47]

The small amount of writing that Lane did during the last two decades of her life was mostly on needlework, to which she managed to impart a conservative political flavor. Her grandmother Caroline Ingalls had been known for her sewing. Lane herself enjoyed the physical activity of the craft, but more important to her were the symbolic and ideological meanings she discovered in it. In several articles for *Woman's Day* magazine between 1940 and 1942, and then again two decades later in 1960 and 1961, when they were collected in a book, she spelled those meanings out for readers, arguing that needlework constituted a way of telling "the American story." It was a distinctively American art, she contended, quite different from traditions and practices that some immigrants had attempted to transport across the Atlantic from desiccated, feudal Europe. It was classless, not aristocratic, in orientation and was dedicated to maintaining individual liberty and self-determination. "In shared hardship and danger," she wrote, the first Americans "learned that every person has the powers of self-control and self-reliance, and the responsibility, that are liberty. They learned that each one makes his own life what it is, and that all alike must struggle to survive and to make human living better than it is." No room here for massive governmental intervention, public assistance, and confiscatory taxes! The conservative political tenets that she was also able, to some degree at least, to highlight in or to intrude into her mother's books were also applicable, as she demonstrated, to a major domestic art. This is the power of strongly held ideology: it can find outlet is almost anything, and in this particular instance it certainly did.[48]

Lane was able to live comfortably after 1938 in her Danbury, Connecticut, home with savings accumulated from her own writing career, supplemented, after her mother's death in 1957, by royalties from the Little House books. That was only fair, since Lane had been so instrumental in originally encouraging her mother to write the books and then in editing and partially rewriting them. But accepting the proceeds was hardly consistent with her philosophy holding that people should stand independently, with no assistance from government or from anyone else. The hypocrisy—or perhaps better, the compartmentalization—of her views was especially blatant in an article she wrote in 1938 advising readers not to pay for their children's college educations. At the time she was generously sending her own "adopted sons," John and Al Turner, through school and financing their trips to Europe and elsewhere.[49]

In assessing the degree to which Wilder's conservative political views did or did not intrude in her writing, we need to keep in mind that her daughter may have had much to do with whatever conservative tinge can be discovered in it. William Holtz judges Lane's work on her mother's Little House series to have been her greatest literary accomplishment.[50] We would like to be able to know exactly what words to attribute to the mother and what to her daughter, but in many specific instances the researcher can only guess at who bore major responsibility for the words on the page.

Considering the vehement political sentiments of both mother and daughter and the strength and quantity of political overtones in Lane's *Let the Hurricane Roar* and *Free Land,* I am more surprised by the paucity of overt political references in the Little House books than I am by their frequency. If one goes looking for something, one is likely to find it, and there is a fair amount of explicit and implicit political messaging to be found in the books.[51]

To the degree that learning—or being socialized to believe in—the virtues and rewards of hard work, deferred gratification, self-control, community, respect for the authority of teachers and parents, deference to the wisdom of elders, and the blessings of harmonious, co-operative families are identified as things associated exclusively with the conservative point of view, I believe that interpreters are misreading and shortchanging liberals. These kinds of values and behaviors need to be considered American ones, or, more broadly, human ones, not exclusively conservative ones. There is no logical inconsistency in adhering to these kinds of values while at the same time contending for full equality between the sexes; human rights; openness to and equal opportunity for different races, nationalities, and ethnic groups; appreciation for different types of family and gender relations; and commitment to assisting individuals and groups in society who need it. These are matters that need to be worked out on the basis of ethical criteria of love, respect, appreciation, opportunity, motivation, responsibility, duty, and so forth, not on the basis of political affiliation.

In Wilder's original "Pioneer Girl" manuscript and in the first five Little House volumes published between 1932 and 1939, explicit political references are few and far between, and what ideological overtones can be detected in the texts remain largely inferential. Wilder was certainly proud of relating a personal story of her family's pluck and persistence on the frontier between the 1860s and 1880s, and she invested it with moral significance. Facing myriad challenges and dangers, ranging from wolves, panthers, and bears to blizzards, hailstorms, and grasshoppers, as well as cheats, robbers, and menacing Indians, the family exhibits bravery and tenacity, ensuring its survival, if not prosperity.[52]

By the time Wilder and Lane were working on *The Long Winter,* the two were well experienced at collaboration. With Lane now living in Danbury, she was more apt to simply rewrite her mother's drafts than to consult extensively with her over how to do it. This volume, which Lane worked on intermittently between June 1939 and May 1940, contains many more episodes and references reflective of conservative ideas and, according to William Holtz, was marked by considerably more revision of and expansion of her mother's manuscript as well as simple insertions of her own material, than in any of the previous books.[53]

Early in the volume, Lane probably added most of the details of the story about the extra-sturdy muskrat house, which suggested that the coming winter would be a hard one. God doesn't tell humans about such things, Pa tells Laura, "Because we're not animals. We're humans, and, like it says in the Declaration of Independence, God created us free. That means we got to take care of ourselves."

Later, the book takes up a theme that Lane had used the year before in *Free Land:* homestead filers who were under the minimum age of twenty-one. "None of the rules worked as they were intended to," the author writes, implying that as a result the rules could justifiably be ignored. It was another swipe at government. When Mr. Edwards shows up again in the story, he explains that he's going further west because the country is getting too crowded: "The politicians are a-swarming in already, and ma'am if'n there's any worse pest than grasshoppers it surely is politicians."[54]

Lane apparently added the scene in which Ma says, "I hope you don't expect to depend on anybody else, Laura. A body can't do that." She probably also added another one, in which Almanzo indicates, "I'm going to run my own business my own way." When Almanzo and Cap Garland drive into the wintry countryside to buy wheat from a man named Anderson, to keep the people in town from starving, the homesteader says it's not his "lookout" to take care of other people. "Nobody's responsible for other folks that haven't got enough forethought to take care of themselves."[55]

Little Town on the Prairie clearly shows Lane's contribution most strongly and contains more frequent and explicit expressions of conservative ideology than any of Wilder's seven other novels. Perhaps the most clear-cut example of this occurs in the chapter on Fourth of July festivities in De Smet. "Every man Jack of us [is] a free and independent citizen of God's country, the only country on earth where a man is free and independent," declares the orator of the day. "Most of us are out here trying to pull ourselves up by our own boot straps."[56] As Laura contemplates the reading of the Declaration of Independence and the singing of "My country, 'tis of thee," she thinks, "God is America's king":

> She thought: Americans won't obey any king on earth. Americans are free. That means they have to obey their own consciences. No king bosses Pa; he has to boss himself. Why (she thought), when I am a little older, Pa and Ma will stop telling me what to do, and there isn't anyone else who has a right to give me orders. I will have to make myself be good.
>
> Her whole mind seemed to be lighted up by that thought. This is what it means to be free. It means you have to be good.[57]

Those thoughts might have been what Wilder was thinking, but the words almost certainly were Lane's. They succinctly expressed her philosophy, as stated earlier in "Credo" and as it later would be expounded in *The Discovery of Freedom.*[58] Lane also may have been responsible later in the book for the following statement, attributed to Ma, because it also comported so directly with her oft-stated views: "This earthly life is a battle. If it isn't one thing to contend with, it's another. It always has been so, and it always will be."[59] Life to Lane was a constant struggle, one in which every individual had to depend upon his or her own resources and tenacity, asking nothing and expecting nothing of anyone else.

Yet as the Little House series advances, especially in the last two books, the narrative becomes more and more social in orientation, as the Ingalls family and Laura herself are shown becoming increasingly involved in community affairs.[60] It was only natural that Laura as an adolescent would become more aware of and become more involved in community affairs outside the home. *Little Town on the Prairie* is by far the most social of the Little House books. But while the other ones do not detail to the same degree the social activities going on in town, readers should not assume that these activities were unimportant or that Laura Ingalls, as a character in the books, or that Laura Ingalls Wilder, as the author of the books, did not consider them significant. It makes sense to consider the wide range of social activities that she describes herself and her family participating in throughout this book as the constant backdrop for the personal and family activities that she describes in the other books. People interact in myriad places and activities: conversations in stores, Fourth of July celebrations, horse races, Ladies Aid Society sociables and New England suppers, Friday night literaries, spelling bees, birthday parties, church services, Sunday School lessons, and a variety of entertainments, musical and nonmusical. It all added up to, as the title of chapter 19 suggests, a "whirl of gaiety." People get news of town doings and their neighbors' activities in stories printed in Jake Hopp's newspaper. A fad of exchanging name cards sweeps through town, further encouraging visiting and social interaction. The school board's visit to Laura's classroom illustrates how the collective citizenry establishes rules for behavior and maintains social order—as well as promotes education.

With all of its description of social groups and the kinds of interactions that tie people together, *Little Town on the Prairie* might just as well be titled "Little Community on the Prairie."[61] The Little House series is best understood, therefore, not simply as a libertarian-oriented text exalting personal freedom, responsibility, self-reliance, and individual striving but rather as one that also describes and affirms community, social relationships, and collective action and responsibility. Without denying that Wilder and Lane sometimes slanted episodes and situations in ways that paralleled their political convictions, the stories were driven primarily by a desire to recapture the past as Wilder remembered it in all of its variety and frequent complexity. There exists a tension, in other words, in the books between the individual and the community, which mirrored the actual relationship that existed between the two in American society during that period of time at all levels, from small towns on the western frontier to large metropolitan population centers that increasingly dominated a modernizing, urbanizing, industrializing, and bureaucratizing nation.[62]

Throughout the series, the image of hearth and home, where warmth, security, and love abound, stand contrasted to the world outside, which is often dangerous and sometimes lethal. The books celebrate the family's independence and self-sufficiency and often exaggerate its distance and isolation from its neighbors.[63] Hard work, delayed gratification, devotion to duty, cheerfulness, and generosity are among the values celebrated in the books. Lessons learned, often put forth in apothegms and preachments, include: people will get their just desserts, children should be seen and not heard, the Lord helps those who help themselves, and there is no great loss without some small gain. Patriotism, illustrated by Fourth of July ceremonies, is honored in the books, as is neighborliness and a sense of community. Driving the narrative line from book to book is Pa Ingalls's continual search for "elbow room," an expression of his free-spirited soul. His daughter Laura inherited some of this independence and wanderlust, sometimes wishing to run naked or be an Indian and other times dreaming of soaring free as a bird.

Summing up, readers need to take care to avoid trying to read too much political significance into many of the stories, references, and language contained in the books. People looking for political overtones will surely find them, but if Lane was inclined sometimes during the editing and rewriting process to inject some of her personal political philosophy into the stories, I am reasonably certain that Wilder was not paying much conscious attention to the political implications of what she was writing. Their frequency in her books is certainly of a different order than is the case in Lane's two 1930s novels.

By the time she got to the manuscript of *These Happy Golden Years,* Lane was working on her own soon-to-be-published political treatise. The following passage in her mother's final book, no doubt added by her, could have come straight out of *The Discovery of Freedom.* Pa advises Laura on how to manage Clarence and the other obstreperous children at the first school she teaches, "Brute force can't do much. Everybody's born free, you know, like it says in the Declaration of Independence. You can lead a horse to water, but you can't make him drink, and good or bad, nobody but Clarence can ever boss Clarence. You better just manage." Later in the book, Almanzo, in words pretty obviously added by Lane, takes a shot at "government experts" who "have got it all planned" on how they are going to cover the prairie with trees. In *The Discovery of Freedom,* Lane made frequent belittling references to similar "intellectuals," despite the fact that, while not an academic herself, she surely was an intellectual.[64]

While mother and daughter were in essential agreement on their conservative political leanings, their dislike of governmental intrusions in people's lives, and their antipathy to Roosevelt and the New Dealers, Wilder remained essentially conventional and predictable in her thinking, while Lane was much more theoretical, vehement, and extreme in her approach. While Wilder's books certainly exhibited a frontier nostalgia and commitment to traditional freedoms and antigovernmental attitudes, the books generally, with the exception of *Little Town on the Prairie,* manifested their ideological leanings in an unobtrusive way. Politics constituted a small part of Wilder's life and one that fit comfortably into other aspects of her personality.

For Lane, on the other hand, politics eventually became an all-consuming passion. Conservative ideology invested a sense of purpose and significance in her life that previously had been lacking. Her political odyssey carried her from one extreme to another. Politics, which constituted merely one relatively minor element in her mother's life, led Lane to discontinue writing fiction at age fifty-two and to embrace political theorizing as her preoccupation for the rest of her life. That activity filled several significant vacuums in her personality—social, psychological, and philosophical—but ironically it found little fulfillment in productive output, since her writing career effectively ended with the publication of a single political book. For many years, Lane would tinker with revisions to it, but they were never published. During the 1960s, *The Discovery of Freedom* would be rediscovered by right-wing theorists and be adjudged by some to be one of the key documents in the development of libertarian political thought in the postwar era. The honor accorded to Lane for that accomplishment, however, paled in comparison to that heaped upon her mother, who, as only a handful of people realized at the time, had depended heavily upon her daughter to bring her series of children's novels to fruition. The ironies inherent in the situation became apparent only much later. Now we can finally appreciate some of those ironies, as well as the complexities, contradictions, and conundrums that make the works of both Wilder and Lane much more interesting and compelling than they were when they were perceived as being far more straightforward and simply derived. All this should make us appreciate all the more their respective accomplishments, although we probably will be less likely as a result to accept their writings and ideas at face value or to praise them uncritically.

Notes

1. Writing the Self: Approaching the Biographies of
Laura Ingalls Wilder and Rose Wilder Lane

1. Catherine Peters, "Secondary Lives: Biography in Context," 44; John Updike, "One Cheer for Literary Biography," 3.

2. Stanley Fish quoted by Martin Rubin in "Biography as a Literary Genre," 315; Elizabeth Hardwick quoted by Mary Titus in "Hardwick Tempers Her Wit with Wisdom"; Joyce Carol Oates noted by Scott Heller in "Despite the Pitfalls, Two Biographers Focus on Living Novelists."

3. Arnold Rampersad, "Design and Truth in Biography," 7; Jay Parini, "Biography Can Escape the Tyranny of Facts."

4. Herbert Leibowitz, *Fabricating Lives: Explorations in American Autobiography,* 3; see also G. Thomas Couser, *Altered Egos: Authority in American Autobiography,* 16–17.

5. Paul John Eakin, *Fictions in Autobiography: Studies in the Art of Self-Invention,* 5; Jerome Bruner, "The Autobiographical Process," 39, 38.

6. Linda Wagner-Martin, *Telling Women's Lives: The New Biography,* 5–8.

7. Estelle C. Jelinek, *The Tradition of Women's Autobiography: From Antiquity to the Present,* 186–87.

8. Peter Holland, "Mystery Man," 36; Norman White, "Pieties and Literary Biography," 214.

9. Terry Eagleton, *After Theory,* 1–2; Robert F. Berkhofer Jr., *Beyond the Great Story: History as Text and Discourse,* 2–4; George Lipsitz, *Time Passages: Collective Memory and American Popular Culture,* viii–ix.

10. Terrence J. McDonald, ed., *The Historic Turn in the Human Sciences;* Peter Novick, *That Noble Dream: The "Objectivity Question" and the American Historical Profession,* 1–17; Richard J. Evans, *In Defense of History.*

11. See, for example, Dennis Smith, *The Rise of Historical Sociology;* Gerald Delanty and Engin F. Isin, eds., *Handbook of Historical Sociology;* Andrew Vincent, *The Nature of Political Theory;* Meg Jacobs, William J. Novak, and Julian E. Zeliz-

er, eds., *The Democratic Experiment: New Directions in American Political History;* and Marshall Sahlins, *Islands of History.*

12. Michael G. Kammen, *Selvages and Biases: The Fabric of History in American Culture,* 62; Keith Windschuttle, *The Killing of History: How Literary Critics and Social Theorists Are Murdering Our Past,* 185; Joyce Appleby, Lynn Hunt, and Margaret Jacob, *Telling the Truth about History,* 250.

13. See especially William T. Anderson's highly useful edited collections *A Little House Sampler* and *A Little House Reader.*

14. Jane M. Subramanian, *Laura Ingalls Wilder: An Annotated Bibliography of Critical, Biographical, and Teaching Studies;* RWL and Helen Dore Boylston, *Travels with Zenobia: Paris to Albania by Model T Ford.* On the question of authorship, see William Holtz, ed., *Dorothy Thompson and Rose Wilder Lane: Forty Years of Friendship Letters, 1921–1980;* William Holtz, *The Ghost in the Little House: A Life of Rose Wilder Lane;* Rosa Ann Moore, "Laura Ingalls Wilder's Orange Notebooks and the Art of the Little House Books"; Rosa Ann Moore, "The Little House Books: Rose-Colored Classics"; Rosa Ann Moore, "Laura Ingalls Wilder and Rose Wilder Lane: The Chemistry of Collaboration"; and John E. Miller, *Laura Ingalls Wilder's Little Town: Where History and Literature Meet.* The great range of studies on Wilder and her writings includes, for example, Fred Erisman, "*Farmer Boy:* The Forgotten 'Little House' Book"; Margaret Mackey, "Growing with Laura: Time, Space, and the Reader in the 'Little House' Books"; Ellen Simpson Novotney, "Shattering the Myth: Mary and Laura as Antagonists in *Little House in the Big Woods, Little House on the Prairie,* and *On the Banks of Plum Creek*"; Jan Susina, "The Voice of the Prairie: The Use of Music in Laura Ingalls Wilder's *Little House on the Prairie.*"

15. William T. Anderson, *Laura Ingalls Wilder: A Biography;* Donald Zochert, *Laura: The Life of Laura Ingalls Wilder;* Janet Spaeth, *Laura Ingalls Wilder;* Virginia L. Wolf, *Little House on the Prairie: A Reader's Companion;* Ann Romines, *Constructing the Little House: Gender, Culture, and Laura Ingalls Wilder,* 8; John E. Miller, *Becoming Laura Ingalls Wilder: The Woman behind the Legend.* On consumption and consumerism, see also Lizabeth Cohen, *A Consumer's Republic: The Politics of Mass Consumption in Postwar America;* and Gary Cross, *An All-Consuming Century: Why Commercialism Won in Modern America.*

16. Dwight M. Miller, ed., *Laura Ingalls Wilder and the American Frontier: Five Perspectives.*

17. Anita Clair Fellman, "Laura Ingalls Wilder and Rose Wilder Lane: The Politics of a Mother-Daughter Relationship"; Julia C. Ehrhardt, *Writers of Conviction: The Personal Politics of Zona Gale, Dorothy Canfield Fisher, Rose Wilder Lane, and Josephine Herbst.* See also Anita Clair Fellman's studies "'Don't Expect to Depend on Anybody Else': The Frontier as Portrayed in the Little House Books" and "Everybody's 'Little Houses': Reviewers and Critics Read Laura Ingalls Wilder."

18. Suzanne Rahn, "What Really Happens in the Little Town on the Prairie"; Claudia Mills, "From Obedience to Autonomy: Moral Growth in the Little House Books"; Ann Romines, "Writing the Little House: The Architecture of a Series"; Donna M. Campbell, "'Written with a Hard and Ruthless Purpose': Rose Wilder Lane, Edna Ferber, and Middlebrow Regional Fiction." For the articles mentioned on the subject of Indians in Wilder's fiction, see the notes to Chapter 8.

19. Ann Romines, "*The Long Winter:* An Introduction to Western Womanhood"; Elizabeth Jameson, "In Search of the Great Ma."

20. Anita Clair Fellman, *Little House, Long Shadow: Laura Ingalls Wilder's Impact on American Culture*; Pamela Smith Hill, *Laura Ingalls Wilder: A Writer's Life*.

21. Stephen W. Hines, ed., *Laura Ingalls Wilder, Farm Journalist: Writings from the Ozarks*; Amy Mattson Lauters, ed., *The Rediscovered Writings of Rose Wilder Lane, Literary Journalist*.

Section I. Authorship: Who Wrote the Books?

1. Henry James, "The Art of Fiction," 170; Wayne C. Booth, *The Rhetoric of Fiction*, 23–64.

2. RWL to Mary Margaret McBride, [August 1927?], Box 6, Lane Papers.

2. The Mother-Daughter Collaboration That Produced the Little House Series

1. RWL to LIW, [November 12, 1930], George T. Bye to RWL, April 6, 1931, Box 13, Lane Papers.

2. Marion Fiery to LIW, February 12, March 3, 1931, RWL to LIW, February 16, 1931, Box 13, Lane Papers.

3. RWL to Marion Fiery, May 27, 1931, Marion Fiery to RWL, November 3, December 4, 1931, Box 13, RWL, Diary, November 26, 1931, Box 22, Lane Papers; Virginia Kirkus, "The Discovery of Laura Ingalls Wilder"; William T. Anderson, "The Literary Apprenticeship of Laura Ingalls Wilder," 326–28.

4. "Pioneer Girl" is available on microfilm at the Missouri State Historical Society and in two different typed versions in the Laura Ingalls Wilder segment of the Rose Wilder Lane Papers at the Herbert Hoover Presidential Library in West Branch, Iowa.

5. RWL, Diary, May 21–27, 1931, Box 22, Lane Papers.

6. RWL to Marian Fiery, May 27, 1931, Box 13, Lane Papers.

7. RWL to George T. Bye, September 25, October 5, 1931, Bye to RWL, October 2, 1931, Box 13, Lane Papers.

8. Fellman, "Laura Ingalls Wilder and Rose Wilder Lane," 546–54.

9. RWL, Diary, July 31, 1930, Box 21, Lane Papers; LIW, "Detroit Book Fair Speech," in LIW and RWL, *A Little House Sampler*, ed. William T. Anderson, 217.

10. Lane spent the better part of two years between 1935 and 1937 in Columbia working first on her abortive Missouri book and then on *Free Land*.

11. RWL, Diary, March 6–11, May 9–22, June 2–21, August 12–16, 1932, January 22–30, February 1–5, 22–29, March 2, 1933, Box 22, Lane Papers.

12. Anderson, *Laura Ingalls Wilder*, 201; Holtz, *Ghost in the Little House*, 253; Grant Foreman to RWL, March 26, 27, 1933, Helen McFarland to LIW, June 19, 1933, R. B. Selvidge to LIW, July 5, 1933, Box 14, Lane Papers.

13. RWL, Journal, January 25, 27, 1933, RWL, Diary, May 10, 1936, Box 23, Lane Papers.

14. Campbell, "Written with a Hard and Ruthless Purpose."

15. See, for example, Tyrus Miller, *Late Modernism: Politics, Fiction, and the Arts between the World Wars*.

16. Holtz traces Lane's writing career in detail in *Ghost in the Little House*. The grandiose plan for the ten-volume historical novel is discussed on page 240.

17. Ibid., 257–59, 285–86; see also chapter 6.

18. RWL to Guy Moyston, May 30, 1925, Box 9, Lane Papers.

19. RWL, Journal, April 10, 1933, Box 23, Lane Papers.

20. Fellman, "Laura Ingalls Wilder and Rose Wilder Lane," 546.

21. LIW to George T. Bye, July 16, 1949, Box 7, William Holtz Papers, Herbert Hoover Presidential Library, West Branch, Iowa.

22. LIW to RWL, February 5, 1937, October 8, 1938, Box 13, Lane Papers.

23. LIW to RWL, August 17, 1938, Box 13, Lane Papers.

24. RWL to LIW, [late October 1937], December 19, 1937, Box 13, Lane Papers.

25. LIW to RWL, January 25, 1938, Box 13, Lane Papers.

26. LIW to RWL, January 28, 1938, Box 13, Lane Papers.

27. LIW to RWL, [undated letter with the heading "Silver Lake"], Box 13, Lane Papers.

28. LIW to RWL, [response to Lane's letter of December 19, 1937], Box 13, Lane Papers.

29. LIW to RWL, February 15, August 17, 1938, March 17, 1939, Box 13, Lane Papers.

30. Holtz, *Ghost in the Little House,* 301–2.

31. Ibid., 66, 88, 223–24, 302.

32. Ibid., 379–80; see also Holtz's articles "The Ghost in the Little House Books" and "Ghost and Host in the Little House Books."

33. Caroline Fraser, "The Prairie Queen," 43–45; Rosa Ann Moore first demonstrated the significant role played by Lane in constructing her mother's books in "Laura Ingalls Wilder's Orange Notebooks," "Little House Books," and "Laura Ingalls Wilder and Rose Wilder Lane." William T. Anderson dealt with the question much more extensively in "Literary Apprenticeship" and "Laura Ingalls Wilder and Rose Wilder Lane: The Continuing Collaboration."

34. Fred Erisman, *Laura Ingalls Wilder,* 10; Romines, *Constructing the Little House,* 48, 259–60n28–29; Hill, in *Laura Ingalls Wilder,* 2, 135, 137–38, 159–60, 165, 166, 169, 170–71. Hill, while insisting that within the world of children's book publishing Lane's contribution was "not unusual" and "simply part of an editor's job," also uses the "C" word ("collaboration") more than once to describe the work that Lane did on Wilder's manuscripts.

35. Holtz, "Ghost and Host."

36. Holtz, *Ghost in the Little House,* 306–7, 382–84.

37. LIW to RWL, January 27, 1939, Box 13, Lane Papers.

38. On Lane's and Wilder's assertion of the factual accuracy of the Little House books, see Anderson, "Literary Apprenticeship," 287–89; and Holtz, *Ghost in the Little House,* 352–53.

39. Miller, *Laura Ingalls Wilder's Little Town,* 85–87.

Section II. Place: What Attracted Wilder and Lane to Little Houses?

1. Dolores Hayden, *The Power of Place: Urban Landscapes as Public History,* 15; Eudora Welty, "Place in Fiction," 118.

2. Pauline Dewan, *The House as Setting, Symbol, and Structural Motif in Children's Literature,* 5. Home obviously holds great resonance for authors at every stage of their lives. See Stephanie Kraft, *No Castles on Main Street: American Authors and Their Homes,* with pp. 152–57 on Laura Ingalls Wilder; Frederick Turner, *Spirit of Place: The Making of an American Literary Landscape;* David E. Scherman and Rosemarie Redlich, *Literary America: A Chronicle of American Writers from 1607–1952 with 173 Photographs of the America That Inspired Them.*

3. Gwendolyn Wright, *Moralism and the Model Home,* 1; Daphne Spain, *Gendered Spaces*, 111.

3. The Place of "Little Houses" in the Lives and Imaginations of Wilder and Lane

1. In "Vastness and Contraction of Space in *Little House on the Prairie*," Hamida Bosmajian notes the special symbolic value of the china shepherdess in the books, signifying continuity through all of the family's travels and what might have been experienced as disorienting change (59). He contrasts the vastness of the prairie, which is primarily a man's world, with the contracted space of the little house, which is primarily the domain of women and children. Despite its small size, the house represents the most positive image of civilization in *Little House on the Prairie* (53).

2. LIW, "The Story of Rocky Ridge Farm," *Missouri Ruralist,* July 22, 1911.

3. Ibid.

4. Anderson, *Laura Ingalls Wilder,* 171–75; Miller, *Becoming Laura Ingalls Wilder,* 96, 98–100, 109, 112–13.

5. RWL to Fremont Older, April 12, 1929, April 17, 1930, Box 10, RWL to Guy Moyston, March 3–4, 1924, Box 9, Lane Papers.

6. LIW, "My Ozark Kitchen"; LIW, "The Farm Dining Room"; RWL to LIW, November 12, 23, [1924], undated [November 1924], Box 13, Lane Papers.

7. Louise Erdrich, "A Writer's Sense of Place," 43.

8. John F. Case, "Let's Visit Mrs. Wilder," *Missouri Ruralist,* February 20, 1918.

9. On Ozarks culture, see Milton D. Rafferty, *Missouri: A Geography;* Vance Randolph, *The Ozarks: An American Survival of Primitive Society;* and Russel L. Gerlach, *Immigrants in the Ozarks: A Study in Ethnic Geography.* On the New England stream of migration across the northern tier of states, see John C. Hudson, "Yankeeland in the Middle West."

10. Romines, "Writing the Little House," 107.

11. Fred Erisman, "The Regional Vision of Laura Ingalls Wilder," 166. His reference is to Eleanor Cameron.

12. Diane Dufva Quantic, *The Nature of the Place: A Study of Great Plains Fiction;* Annette Kolodny, *The Lay of the Land: Metaphor as Experience and History in American Life and Letters;* Leonard Lutwack, *The Role of Place in Literature;* Robert Thacker, *The Great Prairie Fact and Literary Imagination;* Susan Naramore Maher, "Deep Mapping the Great Plains: Surveying the Literary Cartography of Place."

13. Yi-Fu Tuan, *Topophilia: A Study of Environmental Perception, Attitudes, and Values,* 4, 93, 99. On the evolving meaning of *nostalgia,* see Susan J. Matt, "You Can't Go Home Again: Homesickness and Nostalgia in U.S. History."

14. Tuan, *Topophilia,* 16; Dolores Rosenblum, "'Intimate Immensity': Mythic Space in the Works of Laura Ingalls Wilder," 73–74; Wolf, *Little House on the Prairie,* 58, 61–65, 91–94.

15. Spain, *Gendered Spaces,* 140. Among the many who have noted that frontier farmwomen often worked outside the home as well as inside is Joan M. Jensen, *Calling This Place Home: Women on the Wisconsin Frontier, 1850–1925,* 239–40.

16. Quantic, *Nature of the Place,* 97.

17. LIW, *These Happy Golden Years,* chap. 7; LIW, *Little Town on the Prairie,* chap. 5.

18. Winifred Gallagher, *The Power of Place: How Our Surroundings Shape Our Thoughts, Emotions, and Actions,* 12; Tony Hiss, *The Experience of Place,* 90; Christo-

pher Alexander, Sara Ishikawa, and Murray Silverstein, *A Pattern Language: Towns, Buildings, Construction,* xvii.

19. Welty, "Place in Fiction," 130.

20. Her biggest payday would be $25,000 for *Free Land* (1938). See Holtz, *Ghost in the Little House,* 177, 188, 268–69, 277–78; Files in Manuscript Series, Box 28, Lane Papers.

21. RWL to Berta and Elmer Hader, [probably December 1924], Box 5, Lane Papers; RWL to Guy Moyston, April 12, 1925, January 23, 1926, Box 9, Lane Papers; RWL, Diary entries, Box 21, Lane Papers.

22. RWL to Guy Moyston, May 18, 1925, Box 9, Lane Papers.

23. RWL to Clarence Day, June 19, 1926, Box 1, Lane Papers.

24. Sketch of Lane's proposed house in Albania, attached to RWL to Guy Moyston, July 4, 1926, Box 9, Lane Papers; Lane may have inherited some of her compulsion to envision and to build houses from her mother, who wrote in March 1920, "When the days are growing longer and the sun shines warm, on the south slopes, with the promise of golden hours to come, my thoughts persist in arranging building plans; for always in the springtime I want to build a house." LIW, "The Farm Home," *Missouri Ruralist,* March 5, 1920. Lane's wild imaginings and bravado shone through in a letter to Guy Moyston in which she wrote, "The place is primarily built for adequate defense with rifles." She explained that it had to be a fortress: "It's right at the point where the next Balkan war will rage, and while officially nobody'd do anything to an American citizen, just the same lots of things can happen unofficially to property that isn't easily protected with rifles." RWL to Guy Moyston, August 1, 1926, Box 9, Lane Papers.

25. "The place really isn't so large," Lane protested in a letter. "In the main court there are only a library, a reception room, a large living-room, a dining-room, a terrasse overlooking the Adriatic, and a small dining-room. You can't call that an enormous house. The kitchen and large store-rooms are in the servants' court, with the servants' quarters. Our own court has two suites; sitting-room, bedroom, dressing room, study, and sleeping porch each, connected by the bath. And there's nothing more to the house except the guests' rooms in the guests' court. It is the courts that make the place look large." The swimming pool court, she admitted, would be expensive, but it would be the last thing completed, as they planned to build the complex, part by part, as finances became available over perhaps twenty years' time. RWL to Guy Moyston, August 1, 1926, Box 9, Lane Papers.

26. RWL to Clarence Day, September 3, 1927, Box 1, Lane Papers.

27. Ehrhardt, *Writers of Conviction,* 113–14. To say that Lane was a dreamer is not to imply that her mother was not. Wilder was just more consistently committed to acting out her dreams than her daughter was. "It is necessary that we dream now and then," Wilder wrote in one of her columns in February 1918. "No one ever achieved anything, from the smallest object to the greatest, unless the dream was dreamed first, yet those who stop at dreaming never accomplish anything. We must first see the vision in order to realize it; we must have the ideal or we cannot approach it; but when once the dream is dreamed it is time to wake up and 'get busy.' We must 'do great deeds; not dream them all day long.'" LIW, "Make Your Dreams Come True," *Missouri Ruralist,* February 5, 1918.

28. RWL to Guy Moyston, February 16, 1927, Box 9, Lane Papers.

29. RWL to Guy Moyston, October 16, 1926, Box 9, Lane Papers.

30. LIW, "Thoughts Are Things," *Missouri Ruralist,* November 5, 1917.

31. LIW to Fremont Older, April 20, 1928, Box 10, Lane Papers; Fellman, "Laura Ingalls Wilder and Rose Wilder Lane," 528n38.

32. RWL Journal, "My Albanian Garden," entry for November 8, 1926, Box 1, Lane Papers.

33. Ibid., November 2, 1926.

34. See letters, invoices, pictures, floor plans, and other materials in folder 146, Box 10, Lane Papers; Holtz, *Ghost in the Little House*, 187, 194–95; Miller, *Becoming Laura Ingalls Wilder*, 176–78.

35. RWL to Mr. Briggs, October 15, 1928, Box 10, Lane Papers.

36. RWL, Diary, December 22, 1928, Box 21, RWL to Fremont Older, October 31, 1928, January 23, 1929, Box 10, Lane Papers.

37. Holtz, *Ghost in the Little House*, 155; RWL to Guy Moyston, August 30, September 6, 1925, Box 9, Lane Papers; John F. Case, "Let's Visit Mrs. Wilder," *Missouri Ruralist*, February 20, 1918.

38. LIW, "The Farm Home," *Missouri Ruralist*, March 5, 1920.

39. Holtz, *Ghost in the Little House*, 259, 284.

40. Ibid., 284; RWL, Diary, April 14, 1938, Box 23, Lane Papers.

41. Norma Lee Browning, "Introspections of an Individualist."

42. RWL, "My House in the Country."

43. RWL, "Come into My Kitchen."

44. RWL, "The Perfect House" (draft), [1934], Box 41, Diary entries, April 19–28 and monthly memorandum, May 5, 10, June 15, 1934, Box 22, Lane Papers.

45. RWL, "A Place in the Country," 26.

46. RWL to Guy Moyston, May 7, 1925, Box 9, Lane Papers; RWL, "Place in the Country," 26; RWL to Guy Moyston, July 11, 1925, Box 9, Lane Papers.

Section III. Time: What Does History Teach?

1. Ann Lawson Lucas, *The Presence of the Past in Children's Literature,* xiii; Daniel Gilbert, *Stumbling on Happiness,* 141.

2. Lawrence W. Levine, *The Unpredictable Past: Explorations in American Cultural History,* 280–81.

3. Robert F. Berkhofer Jr., *A Behavioral Approach to Historical Analysis,* 5, 11; David Hackett Fischer, *Historians' Fallacies: Toward a Logic of Historical Thought,* 68, 70, 172.

4. Gould quoted in John Lewis Gaddis, *The Landscape of History: How Historians Map the Past,* 140–41.

4. A Perspective from 1932, the Year Wilder Published Her First Little House Book

1. The latter quotation is from John A. Garraty in "The Nature of Biography," 123.

2. Freeman Tilden, *Interpreting Our Heritage,* 29; Pierre Nora, "Between Memory and History: *Les Lieux de Memoire,*" 8–9.

3. LIW, "Laura's Book Fair Speech," in Anderson, *Little House Sampler,* 217.

4. Hill, *Laura Ingalls Wilder,* 1–2, 7, 10–11, 160; Spaeth, *Laura Ingalls Wilder,* 1–2, 21, 69, 76–77, 94–95; Miller, *Laura Ingalls Wilder's Little Town,* 83–88.

5. Terry Eagleton, "Buried in the Life: Thomas Hardy and the Limits of Biographies," 89; John Batchelor, ed., *The Art of Literary Biography,* 3.

6. Morton White, *Foundations of Historical Knowledge,* 221, 223–25.

7. Richard S. Kirkendall, *A History of Missouri: Volume V, 1919 to 1953,* 131–33.

8. Holtz, *Ghost in the Little House,* 226–27.

9. RWL, Journal, May 28, 1932, Box 22, Lane Papers; Holtz, *Ghost in the Little House,* 245.

10. Steven Kesselman, "The Frontier Thesis and the Great Depression"; David M. Wrobel, *The End of American Exceptionalism: Frontier Anxiety from the Old West to the New Deal,* chap. 10.

11. Quoted in Arthur M. Schlesinger Jr., *The Crisis of the Old Order, 1919–1933,* 425.

12. Herbert Stein, *The Fiscal Revolution in America: Policy in Pursuit of Reality,* 55–73, 91–130, 147–51, 165–68; Elliot A. Rosen, *Roosevelt, the Great Depression, and the Economics of Recovery,* 71–93, 172–91; Alan Brinkley, *The End of Reform: New Deal Liberalism in Recession and War,* 25–30, 65–85, 250–53, 259–71.

13. On frontier myths, see Robert G. Athern, *The Mythic West in Twentieth-Century America.*

14. A. Scott Berg, *Lindbergh,* chap. 14.

15. Miller, *Becoming Laura Ingalls Wilder,* 227–28.

16. *Mansfield Mirror,* April 21, September 29, December 15, 22, 1932.

17. Ibid., November 10, 1932.

18. William L. Leuchtenburg, *Franklin D. Roosevelt and the New Deal, 1932–1940,* 159n58.

19. Richard Schickel, *Intimate Strangers: The Culture of Celebrity in America;* Lynn Dumenil, *The Modern Temper: American Culture and Society in the 1920s,* 81–97; Gary Dean Best, *The Nickel and Dime Decade: American Popular Culture during the 1930s;* Robert Sklar, *Movie-Made America: A Social History of American Movies.*

20. Warren I. Susman, *Culture as History: The Transformation of American Society in the Twentieth Century,* chaps. 8–9; Christopher Lasch, *The Culture of Narcissism: American Life in an Age of Diminishing Expectations,* 21–22, 59–61, 84–86; Dixon Wecter, *The Hero in America: A Chronicle of Hero-Worship,* chap. 16.

21. Holtz, *Ghost in the Little House,* 67–71, 87–88, 104–5, 112, 158, 163–66, 223–24.

22. Robert W. Creamer, *Babe: The Legend Comes to Life,* 231–33, 361–65; Tom Seaver, *Great Moments in Baseball,* 101–6. The statistics are from *The Baseball Encyclopedia.* The pitcher Charlie Root went on to compile an excellent career record of 201 victories against 160 losses, although he stood 0–3 in World Series play.

23. Creamer, *Babe,* 86.

24. The material on Carl Mays is from various articles in the *Mansfield Mirror;* Mays's personal file at the Baseball Hall of Fame and Museum, Cooperstown, New York; Mike Sowell, *The Pitch That Killed;* and Bob McGarigle, *Baseball's Great Tragedy: The Story of Carl Mays.*

25. LIW to RWL, October 8, 1938, Lane Papers.

26. For examples of the artistry involved in her books and a discussion of the influences on Wilder's writing, see Miller, *Laura Ingalls Wilder's Little Town,* chaps. 5–6.

27. Edmund Blair Bolles, *Remembering and Forgetting: An Inquiry into the Nature of Memory,* 181.

28. Frederic C. Bartlett, *Remembering: A Study in Experimental and Social Psychology,* 197, 201, 205, 213; Henry L. Roediger III and Charles P. Thompson, "Two Views of Remembering," 488–93.

29. Bartlett, *Remembering,* 312.

30. J. D. Salinger, *The Catcher in the Rye*, 238; Ray Bradbury, "Coda," in *Fahrenheit 451*, 178–79; Maurice Mandelbaum, "A Note on History as Narrative," 56.

31. Jacques Barzun, *Clio and the Doctors: Psycho-History, Quanto-History, and History*, 94–94; Thomas Babington Macaulay, "History and Literature," 83.

32. Wagner-Martin, *Telling Women's Lives*, 5–7.

5. Laura Ingalls Wilder, Frederick Jackson Turner, and the Enduring Myth of the Frontier

1. On the myth of the frontier, see Henry Nash Smith, *Virgin Land: The American West as Symbol and Myth*; Athern, *Mythic West*; William H. Goetzmann and William N. Goetzmann, *The West of the Imagination*; Gerald D. Nash, "The West as Utopia and Myth, 1890–1990"; Richard W. Etulain, "Myths and the American West: An Introduction."

2. Erisman, *Laura Ingalls Wilder*, 43; Fellman, "Everybody's 'Little Houses,'" 5; Gail Schmunk Murray, *American Children's Literature and the Construction of Childhood*, 147–48. See also William Holtz, "Closing the Circle: The American Optimism of Laura Ingalls Wilder," 89n3; and Miller, *Laura Ingalls Wilder's Little Town*, 38–39, 103, 113–24, 167.

3. Jameson, "In Search of the Great Ma," 44.

4. Fellman, "Don't Expect to Depend," 105–6.

5. There have been two major biographies of Turner: Ray Allen Billington, *Frederick Jackson Turner: Historian, Scholar, Teacher*; and Allan G. Bogue, *Frederick Jackson Turner: Strange Roads Going Down*. A huge bibliography exists on the controversy over Turner's frontier thesis; see especially Ray Allen Billington, ed., *The Frontier Thesis: Valid Interpretation of American History?*; Ray Allen Billington, *The Genesis of the Frontier Thesis: A Study in Historical Creativity*; and George Rogers Taylor, ed., *The Turner Thesis: Concerning the Role of the Frontier in American History*.

6. See Ray Allen Billington, "Why Some Historians Rarely Write History: A Case Study of Frederick Jackson Turner."

7. Bogue, *Frederick Jackson Turner*, 3–6; Andrew Jackson Turner to Frederick Jackson Turner, undated letter, Box K, Frederick Jackson Turner Papers, Huntington Library, San Marino, Calif. (hereinafter cited as Turner Papers).

8. Quoted in Anderson, *Little House Sampler*, 217.

9. Frederick Jackson Turner to Constance Lindsay Skinner, March 15, 1922, in Billington, *Genesis of the Frontier Thesis*, 208. On Turner's emphasis on the Midwest, see Billington, *Frederick Jackson Turner*, 46, 365, 418, 436–36.

10. Frederick Jackson Turner, "The Significance of the Frontier in American History," in *The Frontier in American History*, 1.

11. Turner, *Frontier in American History*, 22–23, 29–30, 37–38, 209–14.

12. Elizabeth Jameson notes that Wilder's story provides a "family-centered" approach, in contradistinction to Turner's "state-centered" narratives, showing what can be gained by adding the feminine role to frontier history; see Jameson's "Unconscious Inheritance and Conscious Striving: Laura Ingalls Wilder and the Frontier Narrative," 71. See also Romines, *Constructing the Little House*; Fellman, "Laura Ingalls Wilder and Rose Wilder Lane"; and Kathryn Adam, "Laura, Ma, Mary, Carrie, and Grace: Western Women as Portrayed by Laura Ingalls Wilder."

13. On Turner's approach to history, see Billington, *Frederick Jackson Turner*, chaps. 18–19; Bogue, *Frederick Jackson Turner*, 228–33, 326, 368; 380–82, 419–29;

Carl L. Becker, "Frederick Jackson Turner"; Merle E. Curti, "The Section and the Frontier in American History: The Methodological Concepts of Frederick Jackson Turner," 353–67; and Avery Craven, "Frederick Jackson Turner."

14. Turner to Constance Lindsay Skinner, March 15, 1922, in Billington, *Genesis of the Frontier Thesis*, 216.

15. Robert V. Hine, *Community on the American Frontier: Separate but Not Alone*, 247; Alexis de Tocqueville, *Democracy in America*, 489–92.

16. Everett E. Edwards, "Bibliography of the Writings of Frederick Jackson Turner."

17. Turner to Arthur M. Schlesinger, May 5, 1925, in Wilbur R. Jacobs, *The Historical World of Frederick Jackson Turner*, 164. Patricia Nelson Limerick's *The Legacy of Conquest: The Unbroken Past of the American West* served as the outstanding manifesto of the New Western Historians. Exemplary collections of their writings are Patricia Nelson Limerick, Clyde A. Milner II, and Charles E. Rankin, eds., *Trails: Toward a New Western History* and William Cronon, George Miles, and Jay Gitlin, eds., *Under an Open Sky: Rethinking America's Western Past*.

18. Howard W. Lamar, "Frederick Jackson Turner," 74, 419n1.

19. Florence Porter Robinson, undated comments on Turner's teaching methods at the time of his retirement from Harvard, Volume 1, Turner Papers.

20. William Cronon, "Revisiting the Vanishing Frontier: The Legacy of Frederick Jackson Turner," 160. Richard Hofstadter had made a similar point two decades earlier: "Even Turner's sharpest critics have rarely failed to concede the core merit of his thesis, and wisely so. For over two hundred and fifty years the American people shaped their lives with the vast empty interior of the continent before them. Their national existence up to Turner's day had been involved with conquering, securing, occupying, and developing their continental empire" (*The Progressive Historians: Turner, Beard, Parrington*, 119).

21. Hofstadter, *Progressive Historians*, 114. On Turner's shift to sectionalism, see Michael C. Steiner, "From Frontier to Region: Frederick Jackson Turner and the New Western History"; Michael C. Steiner, "The Significance of Turner's Sectional Thesis"; and Richard Jensen, "On Modernizing Frederick Jackson Turner: The Historiography of Regionalism."

22. Cronon, "Revisiting the Vanishing Frontier," 161.

23. Turner, "The Significance of History," in John Mack Faragher, ed., *Rereading Frederick Jackson Turner: "The Significance of the Frontier in American History" and Other Essays*, 18, 28.

24. Jacobs, *Historical World*, 79.

25. LIW to RWL, October 8, 1938, Box 13, Lane Papers.

26. RWL to LIW, December 19, 1937, Lane Papers.

27. Billington, *Frederick Jackson Turner*, 435–42; Bogue, *Frederick Jackson Turner*, 277, 337, 363–66, 413.

28. The most detailed treatment of Wilder's origins, growth, and development as a writer is Hill, *Laura Ingalls Wilder*.

29. On Turner's artistic bent, see Merrill E. Lewis, "The Art of Frederick Jackson Turner: The Histories"; on Wilder's poetry, see Hill, *Laura Ingalls Wilder: A Writer's Life*, 61, 104.

30. Handwritten copy of poem located in Turner's files, File Drawer 15B, Turner Papers (emphasis Turner's).

31. LIW, *These Happy Golden Years*, 289.

6. Rose Wilder Lane and Thomas Hart Benton:
A Turn toward History during the 1930s

1. John Bodnar, *Remaking America: Public Memory, Commemoration, and Patriotism in the Twentieth Century*, 126–35; Karal Ann Marling, *Wall-to-Wall America: A Cultural History of Post-Office Murals in the Great Depression*, chap. 4. On the growing interest in history during the 1930s, see Richard H. Pells, *Radical Visions and American Dreams: Culture and Social Thought in the Depression Years*, 314–16; Susman, *Culture as History*, 175–76; and Michael G. Kammen, *Mystic Chords of Memory: The Transformation of Tradition in American Culture*, chap. 11.

2. General works on Thomas Hart Benton and on his Missouri mural include Henry Adams, *Thomas Hart Benton: An American Original*; Erika L. Doss, *Benton, Pollock, and the Politics of Modernism: From Regionalism to Abstract Expressionism*; Karal Ann Marling, *Tom Benton and His Drawings*; Matthew Baigell, *Thomas Hart Benton*; Matthew Baigell and Allen Kaufman, "The Missouri Murals: Another Look at Benton"; James Gordon Rogers Jr., "Thomas Hart Benton's Mural *The Social History of Missouri*"; Bob Priddy, *Only the Rivers Are Peaceful: Thomas Hart Benton's Missouri Mural*; and Nancy Edelman, *The Thomas Hart Benton Murals in the Missouri State Capitol*. Benton himself published two autobiographies: *An Artist in America* and *An American in Art*.

3. Information on Lane and her Missouri history book is contained in the Rose Wilder Lane Papers at the Herbert Hoover Presidential Library. They contain correspondence and two typed manuscript versions of the book and notebooks she compiled while doing the research for it.

4. Highly influential essays by Carl Becker and Charles A. Beard on history as a construct led many of their fellow historians toward a more relativistic view of their subject during the thirties. Becker, "Everyman His Own Historian"; Beard, "Written History as an Act of Faith." See also Novick, *That Noble Dream*, 252–58; and James O. Robertson, *American Myth, American Reality*.

5. Benton, *Artist in America*, 258–76; Adams, *Thomas Hart Benton*, chaps. 8–10, 14.

6. Edelman, *Thomas Hart Benton Murals*, 8.

7. RWL, Diary, May 10, 1935, Box 22, Lane Papers; Holtz, *Ghost in the Little House*, 258–59.

8. Holtz, *Ghost in the Little House*, 194–95, 244–45, 263–64, 293.

9. RWL, Journal, January 11, 1933, in American Novel Outline file. See also her diary for June 25, 1933 and her regular Journal entry for June 26, 1933, Boxes 22–23, Lane Papers.

10. RWL, Journal, January 30, 1933, Diary, January 15, June 7, 10–11, 16–18, 1933, Boxes 22–23, Lane Papers.

11. See the dozen or so notebooks that Lane used in the Missouri Book file, Boxes 36–37, Lane Papers.

12. RWL, Diary, July 23–Aug. 9, 1935 (passim), Box 22, Lane Papers; Holtz, *Ghost in the Little House*, 260.

13. Quoted in Holtz, *Ghost in the Little House*, 261.

14. RWL, "Credo"; Roger L. MacBride, ed., *The Lady and the Tycoon*, 340.

15. Matthew Baigell, ed., *A Thomas Hart Benton Miscellany*, 33; Baigell and Kaufman, "Missouri Murals," 314, 319–20; Adams, *Thomas Hart Benton*, 79–80, 225–34; Holtz, *Ghost in the Little House*, 235–37, 246–47, 260–63, 267–68, 270–71, 325.

16. Adams, *Thomas Hart Benton*, 241, 243; Benton, *Artist in America*, 259–62;

Holtz, *Ghost in the Little House,* chaps. 16–19, Doss, *Benton, Pollock, and the Politics of Modernism,* 126.

17. *Kansas City Journal-Post,* Feb. 2, 1937; RWL, Diary, May–July, 1935 (passim), Box 22, Lane Papers.

18. Benton, *Artist in America,* 273; *Kansas City Star,* June 18, 1936. The notebook is 7 by 8 1/2 inches and contains fifteen pages. The Thomas Hart Benton Trust is at the United Missouri Bank of Kansas City. See also Priddy, *Only the Rivers,* 43–45.

19. Holtz, *Ghost in the Little House,* 259; RWL, notebooks in Missouri Book File, Boxes 36–37, Lane Papers.

20. Maxwell Aley to RWL, Aug. 28, 1936, Maxwell Aley to RWL, Nov. 9, 1936, Walter D. Edmunds to RWL, May 22, 1938, Missouri Book File, Box 36, Lane Papers; Holtz, *Ghost in the Little House,* 285–86.

21. On the interpenetration of history and myth, see Peter Heehs, "Myth, History, and Theory."

22. RWL, "We Say Missoury," draft, version one, p. 3, Missouri Book File, Box 39, Lane Papers.

23. Ibid., 1, 242 and RWL, "The Name Is Missoury," draft, version two, p. 38, Missouri Book File, Box 38, Lane Papers.

24. RWL, "We Say Missoury," draft, version one, p. 76 and RWL, "Name Is Missoury," draft, version two, pp. 160, 215, Missouri Book File, Boxes 38–39, Lane Papers.

25. Benton explicitly linked the regionalist movement with a historical turn of mind in *An American in Art,* 70, where he associated his and the work of Wood and Curry with the popular histories of Charles Beard and James Truslow Adams.

26. See Lane's manuscripts in Missouri Book File, Boxes 38–39, Lane Papers.

27. Thomas Hart Benton, "The Thirties," in Priddy, *Only the Rivers,* 233, 254–56.

28. Ibid., 212.

29. Observations about the mural are based on personally viewing it and on detailed accounts of it in Rogers, "Thomas Hart Benton's Mural"; Priddy, *Only the Rivers;* and Edelman, *Thomas Hart Benton Murals.*

30. Adams, *Thomas Hart Benton,* 261; Doss, *Benton, Pollock, and the Politics of Modernism,* 2.

31. Quoted in Priddy, *Only the Rivers,* 175.

32. *Columbia Missourian,* Apr. 15, 1937.

33. Priddy, *Only the Rivers,* 243.

34. Ibid., 272–75.

35. Adams, *Thomas Hart Benton,* 259–60; Edelman, *Thomas Hart Benton Murals,* 1–4; Benton, *Artist in America,* 271–73.

36. Doss, *Benton, Pollock, and the Politics of Modernism,* 126.

Section IV. Culture: How Should People Live, and How Should Society Function?

1. Mills, "Obedience to Autonomy," 127. See Jean Piaget, *The Moral Judgment of the Child;* and Lawrence Kohlberg, *The Philosophy of Moral Development.* Briefly stated, Kohlberg's six-part developmental scheme consists of three stages: preconventional, conventional, and postconventional morality. Each stage contains two levels, progressing from obedience to rules and responsiveness to punishment at the first level, to self-interest at the second, followed by conformity to

the expectations of others, responsiveness to authority and social order, a social contract orientation, and finally adherence to universal ethical principles.

7. Wilder's Apprenticeship as a Farm Journalist

1. Quotations in *Book Review Digest, 1932*, 1021.

2. Holtz, *Ghost in the Little House*, 380. See also Holtz, "Ghost in the Little House Books"; and Holtz, "Ghost and Host."

3. Hill, *Laura Ingalls Wilder*.

4. LIW, in Anderson, *Little House Reader*; LIW, *Laura Ingalls Wilder's Fairy Poems*; *De Smet News*, June 20, 1930.

5. Information on the *Missouri Ruralist* is taken from Billy C. Brantley, "History of the *Missouri Ruralist*, 1902 through 1955." On Capper, who was frequently mentioned during the 1920s as a potential Republican candidate for the presidency, see Homer E. Socolofsky, *Arthur Capper: Publisher, Politician, and Philanthropist*.

6. LIW, "Favors the Small Farm Home," *Missouri Ruralist*, February 18, 1911. These *Missouri Ruralist* articles have been collected in Hines, *Laura Ingalls Wilder, Farm Journalist*. See also Miller, *Becoming Laura Ingalls Wilder*, 114–16; Anderson, *Laura Ingalls Wilder*, 176–78; John F. Case, "Let's Visit Mrs. Wilder," *Missouri Ruralist*, February 20, 1918.

7. The population of Rea, Missouri, Case's home, was only three hundred, but during the 1920s, as editor of the *Missouri Ruralist*, Case would go on to ghostwrite some of Arthur Capper's speeches, direct the Missouri State Fair, become president of the Missouri State Board of Agriculture and of the Missouri State Plant Board, serve as a member of the University of Missouri Board of Visitors and of the Missouri Conservation Commission, and in 1931 was elected president of the American Agricultural Editors' Association. Brantley, "History of the *Missouri Ruralist*," 82, 127; Socolofsky, *Arthur Capper*, 250n35.

8. LIW, *Little House in the Ozarks: A Laura Ingalls Wilder Sampler: The Rediscovered Writings*; LIW, *Laura Ingalls Wilder, Farm Journalist: Writings from the Ozarks*. See also Richard Marshall, ed., *Laura Ingalls Wilder: A Family Collection*; and Stephen W. Hines, ed., *I Remember Laura*.

9. This judgment is based on a line-by-line comparison between Wilder's original manuscript for *Little House in the Big Woods* and the final version published by Harper and Row in 1932. The manuscript for *Little Town on the Prairie* is held by the Pomona, California, Public Library. Those for *The Long Winter* and *These Happy Golden Years* are in the Rare Book Room of the Detroit Public Library. The other five are available in microfilm at the State Historical Society of Missouri.

10. Wilder's first effort at writing her autobiography, an unpublished manuscript called "Pioneer Girl," was a straightforward, unembellished account that lacked the fuller development, dramatization, and interesting dialog that characterized *Little House in the Big Woods* and the later novels. The handwritten draft of "Pioneer Girl" is held by the State Historical Society of Missouri.

11. LIW, "As a Farm Woman Thinks," *Missouri Ruralist* (cited as *MR* throughout the rest of this chapter), May 15, 1923.

12. LIW, "What Makes My County Great," *MR*, December 1, 1923. See also "When Is a Settler an Old Settler?" *MR*, June 6, 1916; and "Pioneering on An Ozark Farm," *MR*, June 1, 1921.

13. "Our Fair and Other Things," *MR*, November 5, 1916; "Haying While the

Sun Shines," *MR,* July 20, 1916; "Without Representation," *MR,* July 5, 1917; "What Makes My County Great," *MR,* December 1, 1923.

14. "Getting the Worst of It," *MR,* March 5, 1917; "To Buy or Not to Buy," *MR,* September 20, 1917.

15. "The Farm Home," *MR,* November 5, 1919, February 5, April 20, 1920. See also "Women's Duty at the Polls," *MR,* April 20, 1919.

16. On the latter, see E. F. Schumacher, *Small Is Beautiful: Economics as If People Mattered.*

17. "Favors the Small Farm Home," *MR,* February 18, 1911. See also "A Home-maker in the Ozarks," *MR,* June 20, 1914; "Visit 'Show You' Farm," *MR,* March 20, 1918.

18. "Good Times on the Farm," *MR,* February 5, 1914; "Folks Are 'Just Folks,'" *MR,* May 5, 1916; "Learning to Work Together," *MR,* December 5, 1916; "As a Farm Woman Thinks," *MR,* April 1, 1924.

19. "The Farm Home," *MR,* March 20, 1920.

20. "Good Times on the Farm," *MR,* February 5, 1914. See also "Folks Are 'Just Folks,'" MR, May 5, 1916; "Facts versus Theories," *MR,* June 20, 1916; and "The Farm Home," *MR,* July 5, 1919.

21. "As a Farm Woman Thinks," *MR,* March 1, 1922. See also "We Must Not Be Small Now," *MR,* April 20, 1918.

22. "Opportunity," *MR,* November 5, 1918; "How About the Home Front?" *MR,* May 20, 1918; "Are You Helping or Hindering?" *MR,* July 5, 1918.

23. "The Farm Home," *MR,* November 5, 1919.

24. "The Farm Home," *MR,* January 5, 1920.

25. "The Farm Home," *MR,* December 5, 1919.

26. "What Days in Which to Live!" *MR,* September 20, 1918.

27. "What Makes My County Great," *MR,* December 1, 1923.

28. "Favors the Small Farm Home," *MR,* February 18, 1911; "Let's Revive the Old Amusements," *MR,* January 20, 1919; "Does 'Haste Make Waste'?" *MR,* April 20, 1917.

29. LIW, "Whom Will You Marry?" 8, 62.

30. "What the War Means to Women," *MR,* May 5, 1918.

31. "A Bouquet of Wild Flowers," *MR,* July 20, 1917; "As a Farm Woman Thinks," *MR,* April 15, August 1, 1923, May 15, 1924.

32. "The Farm Home," *MR,* June 5, 1919; "Thanksgiving Time," *MR,* November 20, 1916; "According to Experts," *MR,* February 5, 1917; "As a Farm Woman Thinks," *MR,* December 15, 1924.

33. "Let's Revive the Old Amusements," *MR,* January 20, 1919.

34. "A Bouquet of Wild Flowers," *MR,* July 20, 1917; "As a Farm Woman Thinks," *MR,* June 15, 1921.

35. "The Farm Home," *MR,* May 5, 1919, March 20, 1920; "As a Farm Woman Thinks," *MR,* August 1, 1923; "Chasing Thistledown," *MR,* June 20, 1917; "We Must Not Be Small Now," *MR,* April 20, 1918; "When Is a Settler an Old Settler?" *MR,* June 5, 1916.

36. "As a Farm Woman Thinks," *MR,* November 15, 1921, November 15, 1923, May 15, 1924; "The Farm Home," *MR,* December 20, 1919.

37. "As a Farm Woman Thinks," *MR,* February 1, 1922.

38. See, for example, William Jay Jacobs, "Frontier Faith Revisited: The Little House Books of Laura Ingalls Wilder"; Anita Clair Fellman, "Making Meaning of the Past through the Little House Books"; and Murray, *American Children's Literature,* 147.

39. "The Farm Home," *MR,* September 5, 1919, January 20, 1920; "As a Farm

Woman Thinks," *MR*, July 1, November 1, 1922, November 1, 1923; "What's in a Word?" *MR*, January 5, 1917; "Chasing Thistledown," *MR*, June 20, 1917; "Keep Journeying On," *MR*, March 5, 1918; "Do the Right Thing Always," *MR*, June 20, 1918; "Make Your Dreams Come True," *MR*, February 5, 1918.

40. "What Makes My County Great," *MR*, December 1, 1923.

41. "As a Farm Woman Thinks," *MR*, June 15, 1921, September 1, 1922, April 1, 1923; "Learning to Work Together," *MR*, December 5, 1916; "Make Your Dreams Come True," *MR*, February 5, 1918.

42. "Are You Going Ahead?" *MR*, February 20, 1917.

43. "Everyone Can Do Something," *MR*, November 20, 1917.

44. "So We Moved the Spring," *MR*, April 20, 1916; "Are You Going Ahead?" *MR*, February 20, 1917; "As a Farm Woman Thinks," *MR*, November 1, 1921, March 1, 1922, July 1, 1923; "The Farm Home," *MR*, October 20, November 20, 1919.

45. "When Proverbs Get Together," *MR*, September 5, 1918; "The Farm Home," *MR*, January 5, 1920.

46. "Does It Pay to Be Idle?" *MR*, February 20, 1916; "The Farm Home," *MR*, March 20, 1920.

47. "Women's Duty at the Polls," *MR*, April 20, 1919; "Make Every Minute Count," *MR*, March 20, 1918.

48. "My Apple Orchard," *MR*, June 1, 1912; "Make Your Dreams Come True," *MR*, February 5, 1918; "So We Moved the Spring," *MR*, April 20, 1916;

49. "Do Not Waste Your Strength," *MR*, September 5, 1916; "The Farm Home," *MR*, May 5, October 20, 1919; "Let's Be Just," *MR*, September 5, 1917.

50. "Do Not Waste Your Strength," *MR*, September 5, 1916.

51. "Look for Faeries Now," *MR*, April 5, 1916.

8. "They Should Know When They're Licked": American Indians in Wilder's Fiction

1. On the New Western History, see note 18 in chapter 5.

2. Violet J. Harris, *Teaching Multicultural Literature in Grades K–8*, 140; Magda Lewis, "'Are Indians Nicer Now?': What Children Learn from Books about Native North Americans," quotation from 144–45.

3. Robert F. Berkhofer Jr., *The White Man's Indian: Images of the American Indian from Columbus to the Present*, 28–30; Wolfgang Mieder, "'The Only Good Indian Is a Dead Indian': History and Meaning of a Proverbial Stereotype."

4. See, for example, Elizabeth Cook-Lynn, "Indian Studies—How It Looks Back at Us after Twenty Years"; Jack Weaver, "More Light than Heat: The Current State of Native American Studies"; Duane Champagne, "In Search of Theory and Method in American Indian Studies."

5. Melissa Kay Thompson, "A Sea of Good Intentions: Native Americans in Books for Children," 353; see also Arlene Hirschfelder, Paulette Fairbanks Molin, and Yvonne Wakim, eds., *American Indian Stereotypes in the World of Children: A Reader and Bibliography*; Beverly Slapin and Doris Seale, eds., *Through Indian Eyes: The Native Experience in Books for Children*; and Jon C. Stott, *Native Americans in Children's Literature*.

6. Sharon Smulders, "'The Only Good Indian': History, Race, and Representation in Laura Ingalls Wilder's *Little House on the Prairie*," 191; Frances W. Kaye, "Little Squatter on the Osage Diminished Reserve: Reading Laura Ingalls Wilder's Kansas Indians," 123.

7. Donna M. Campbell, "'Wild Men' and Dissenting Voices: Narrative Disruption in *Little House on the Prairie*," quotation on 111; Wolf, *Little House on the Prairie*, 83–84, 118; RWL, "The American Revolution, 1939," 23.

8. Quoted in John F. Case, "Let's Visit Mrs. Wilder," *Missouri Ruralist*, February 20, 1918.

9. LIW, *Little House in the Big Woods*, 1–2; Michael Dorris, "Trusting the Words," 1820; James Axtell, *The Invasion Within: The Contest of Cultures in Colonial North America*; Francis Jennings, *The Invasion of America: Indians, Colonialism, and the Cant of Conquest*; Dorris, "Trusting the Words," 1820. For more on Dorris's point of view, see *Minneapolis Star-Tribune*, April 17, 1996, A1.

10. Dennis McAuliffe Jr., *The Deaths of Sybil Bolton: An American History*, 110–13.

11. Ibid.; Zochert, *Laura*, 49–50.

12. LIW, "Pioneer Girl," 1930, unpaginated, Box 14, Lane Papers; LIW, *The First Four Years*.

13. LIW, *By the Shores of Silver Lake*, 63–65; LIW, *Long Winter*, 59–62; LIW, "Pioneer Girl." Suffering under adverse conditions on their reservation along the Minnesota River, the Santee Dakota revolted and killed more than seven hundred non-Indians in 1862. After a military campaign of reprisal, many of the prominent leaders were hung, and most Santee were expelled from the state. Howard R. Lamar, ed., *The New Encyclopedia of the American West*, 1052.

14. LIW, *These Happy Golden Years*, 171, 283; *Farmer Boy*, 4, 79–80, 93, 266; *By the Shores of Silver Lake*, 52; *On the Banks of Plum Creek*, 81, 143; *Little House on the Prairie*, 122; *Long Winter*, 58; LIW, *Little Town on the Prairie*, 72.

15. LIW, *These Happy Golden Years*, 108–9; Penny T. Linsenmayer, "Kansas Settlers on the Osage Diminished Reserve: A Study of Laura Ingalls Wilder's *Little House on the Prairie*," 169, 173–74. In agreement with her are Kaye, "Little Squatter," 137; and Smulders, "Only Good Indian," 192–93.

16. Linsenmayer, "Kansas Settlers," 168–85; L. Wallace Duncan, *History of Montgomery County, Kansas, by Its Own People*, 7; Paul F. Harper, "*Surely It Flowest with Milk and Honey*": A History of Montgomery County, Kansas, to 1930, 3–5. See also Willard H. Rollings, *The Osage: An Ethnohistorical Study of Hegemony on the Prairie-Plains*; and John J. Mathews, *The Osages: Children of the Middle Waters*.

17. RWL, Diary, 1931–1935, February 1, May 19–June 25, 1934, Box 22 and Journal, June 5, 1934, Box 23, Lane Papers.

18. See, for example, LIW, *Little House on the Prairie*, 229 and *Long Winter*, 64. On the relationship between frontier women and Indians, see Glenda Riley, *Women and Indians on the Frontier, 1825–1915*; Julie Roy Jeffrey, *Frontier Women: The Trans-Mississippi West, 1840–1880*, 46–49, 54–55; and Carol Fairbanks, *Prairie Women: Images in American and Canadian Fiction*, 118–56. On relations between Indians and non-Indians in general, see Berkhofer, *White Man's Indian*; Richard Drinnon, *Facing West: The Metaphysics of Indian-Hating and Empire-Building*; and Brian W. Dippie, *The Vanishing American: White Attitudes and U.S. Indian Policy*.

19. Anderson, *Laura Ingalls Wilder*, 20–21; Lamar, *New Encyclopedia of the American West*, 108; LIW, "Pioneer Girl."

20. Miller, *Becoming Laura Ingalls Wilder*, 25, 31, 47–48. Wolf, *Little House on the Prairie*, likewise emphasizes the complex vision of American Indians in Wilder's novels. Wolf calls Wilder's descriptions realistic, indicates that she provides a full range of opinions, and notes that the stereotypes derive largely from Wilder's stylistic approach of using the narrative voice of a young girl (83–84).

21. LIW, *Long Winter*, 64; LIW, *Little House on the Prairie*, 55, 231.

22. LIW, *Little House on the Prairie*, 237.

23. Ibid., 228–30, 284–85.

24. Ibid., 301.

25. Ibid., 47, 237, 273, 316.

26. H. Craig Miner and William E. Unrau, *The End of Indian Kansas: A Study of Cultural Revolution, 1854–1871*, 107 (see pp. 121–32 of the same volume for a detailed discussion of the struggle over Osage lands); James R. Shortridge, *Peopling the Plains: Who Settled Where in Frontier Kansas*, 16.

27. Wilder probably heard of Soldat du Chene from her father, who appears to have mistakenly believed that an Osage by that name had been involved in the events the family experienced. Librarian Helen M. McFarland of the Kansas State Historical Society wrote Wilder: "I have been unable to find a reference to your story of the Indian chief who was friendly to the white settlers. It is evident that during the years 1870–71 the Indians were greatly disturbed by the white invasion, but no place do I find even a remote suggestion of your story nor of a gathering of tribes in the locality of your father's home." McFarland to LIW, June 19, 1933, Box 14, Lane Papers. Soldat du Chene had lived in the area earlier, and a letter from R. B. Selvidge of Muskogee, Oklahoma, may have encouraged Wilder to believe that he was present at the time her family lived there. Selvidge wrote, "The chief of the Osages at the time was named Le-Soldat-du-Chene. This man was very friendly to the white people." Selvidge to LIW, July 5, 1933, Box 14, Lane Papers. See also Grant Foreman to RWL, March 26, 27, 1933, Box 14, Lane Papers; Anderson, *Laura Ingalls Wilder*, 201; Holtz, *Ghost in the Little House*, 253.

28. LIW and RWL, in Anderson, *Little House Sampler*, 220–22; Edith Connelley Ross, "The Bloody Benders." On Wilder's use of memory in the writing of her books, see Miller, *Laura Ingalls Wilder's Little Town*, 98–99, 106–8.

29. RWL to LIW, December 19, 1937, Box 13, Lane Papers.

30. LIW, *On the Way Home: The Diary of a Trip from South Dakota to Mansfield, Missouri, in 1894*, 20–22, 25, 51, 55, 63–64.

31. LIW, *West from Home: Letters of Laura Ingalls Wilder, San Francisco 1915*, 38, 39, 41–42, 46.

32. LIW, "Life Is an Adventure," *Missouri Ruralist*, March 5, 1916.

33. LIW, "If We Only Understood," *Missouri Ruralist*, December 5, 1917.

34. See issues of the weekly *Mansfield Mirror* during this period.

35. LIW, *On the Way Home*, 23–24.

36. Campbell, "'Wild Men' and Dissenting Voices," 119.

37. Ibid., 111–12; Philip Heldrich, "'Going to Indian Territory': Attitudes toward Native Americans in *Little House on the Prairie*," 100; Elizabeth Segel, "Laura Ingalls Wilder's America: An Unflinching Assessment," 66, 70.

38. Fellman, "Don't Expect to Depend," 105.

39. Romines, *Constructing the Little House*, 62–63.

40. Kaye, "Little Squatter," 124–25, 139n5, 126, 138–39. Kaye makes the point about the books' feminist perspectives with reference to the writings of Ann Romines, Elizabeth Segel, Virginia L. Wolf, and Janet Spaeth.

41. Anita Clair Fellman's chapter "The Little House Books in American Culture," in Miller, *Laura Ingalls Wilder and the American Frontier*, was an excellent move toward analyzing the books' impact upon their readers. See also Fellman's new book *Little House, Long Shadow*.

42. Trying to answer that question is risky and necessarily inferential. Her fa-

ther's influence would seem pertinent, and her reading of the Bible also taught her tolerance and love for others. For more, see Miller, *Becoming Laura Ingalls Wilder,* 29, 33–35, 42, 56–58, 62, 131–32.

43. Gaddis, *Landscape of History,* 3.

9. Frontier Nostalgia and Conservative Ideology
in the Writings of Wilder and Lane

1. See note 1 in Chapter 5.

2. Murray, *American Children's Literature,* xvi.

3. RWL, *Old Home Town,* 8–9.

4. Miller, *Becoming Laura Ingalls Wilder,* 199, 274n20.

5. Anderson, *Little House Reader,* 119–21; *Mansfield Mirror,* February 26, March 19, April 2, 1925; Rose Wilder Lane to Guy Moyston, February 17, March 9, 22, 31, April 1, 1925, Box 9, Lane Papers.

6. Lane told the story in a letter to Mark Sullivan, August 16, 1938, Box 11, Lane Papers.

7. LIW to RWL, February 20, 1939, Box 13, Lane Papers.

8. LIW to RWL, September 26, 1938, Box 13, Lane Papers; Miller, *Becoming Laura Ingalls Wilder,* 227–28, 233. Democratic Congressman Louis Ludlow of Indiana got his name attached to the proposed amendment, the idea of which had been floating around for a number of years. The amendment would have required a public referendum before a declaration of war in every instance except cases in which American soil was directly attacked by an invading foe, thereby effectively removing the power to declare war from Congress.

9. RWL, Diary, 1931–1935, March 1933 Memoranda section, Box 22, Lane Papers; see also Lane's Journal entries for March 5 and 24, 1933, ibid.

10. RWL, quoted in Holtz, *Ghost in the Little House,* 271; see also 287–88.

11. George A. Wolfskill and John A. Hudson, *All but the People: Franklin D. Roosevelt and His Critics, 1933–39.*

12. *Official Manual of the State of Missouri* (1937–1938), 227, 332; *Mansfield Mirror,* November 5, 12, 1936; Robert S. Wiley, *Dewey Short: Orator of the Ozarks.* When I lived in Monett, Missouri, a hundred miles west of Mansfield on Highway 60, between 1961 and 1966, our Congressman, Durward Hall, carried on the strong right-wing political tradition represented earlier by Short.

13. "I am supposed to be the manic-depressive type," she once wrote Fremont Older, November 3, 1929, Box 10, Lane Papers. A number of studies have shown that poets and writers are particularly susceptible to periodic depression or manic- depressive illness. The list includes Samuel Taylor Coleridge, Edgar Allen Poe, Alfred Tennyson, Sylvia Plath, Hart Crane, Randall Jarrell, and Robert Lowell. See Anthony Storr, "Psychiatry and Literary Biography," 84.

14. RWL to Floyd Dell, May 9, 1948, Box 5, RWL to Frank S. Meyer, September 24, 1953, Box 9, Lane Papers; RWL, "Credo," 5; Holtz, *Ghost in the Little House,* 86–8, 261.

15. RWL, "Credo," 6–7.

16. RWL to Fremont Older, November 16, 1928, Box 10, Lane Papers.

17. George H. Nash, *The Conservative Intellectual Movement in America since 1945,* 10; Brian Doherty, *Radicals for Capitalism: A Freewheeling History of the Modern American Libertarian Movement,* 59–65; George Wolfskill, *The Revolt of the Conservatives: A History of the American Liberty League.*

18. RWL to Jasper Crane, February 4, 1954, Box 3, October 16, 1967, Box 4, Lane Papers.

19. Ehrhardt, *Writers of Conviction,* chap. 3; Fellman, "Don't Expect to Depend," 107–8; Fellman, "Little House Books." Others who have noted the conservative political inclinations of Wilder and Lane include Miller, *Becoming Laura Ingalls Wilder,* 197–99, 220–21, 227–28, 233, 254; Holtz, *Ghost in the Little House,* 10, 246–47, 261, 267–68, 287–88, 315–21, 326–34; 48–50; and Romines, *Constructing the Little House,* 37, 201, 259n16, 262n21, 264n13.

20. In emphasizing the role that libertarian political ideology played in providing a welcome respite from the philosophical doubts and terrors that plagued Lane in the thirties, I am also departing somewhat from the interpretation advanced in Anita Clair Fellman's hugely insightful article "Laura Ingalls Wilder and Rose Wilder Lane," which emphasizes her intense and stormy relationship with her mother as well as her periodic psychological depressions, faltering career, and simple disgust with her Missouri Ozarks surroundings.

21. Ehrhardt, *Writers of Conviction,* 95–96, 115–16. On Lane's "metaphysical angst," see Holtz, *Ghost in the Little House,* 133–34, 191–92, 229–30, 257–58.

22. On mother-daughter relationships, see Nancy Chodorow, *The Reproduction of Mothering: Psychoanalysis and the Sociology of Gender;* Rozsika Parker, *Mother Love, Mother Hate: The Power of Maternal Ambivalence;* Sharon Hays, *The Cultural Contradictions of Motherhood;* Linda Rosenzweig, *The Anchor of My Life: Middle-Class American Mothers and Daughters, 1880–1920.*

23. See also her Journal entries for May 28–29, 1932, Box 22, Lane Papers.

24. RWL to Guy Moyston, January 12, 1926, Box 9, Lane Papers.

25. RWL, Journal, January 24, 1933, February 11, 1933, Box 23, Lane Papers.

26. RWL to Fremont Older, May 30, 1928, Box 10, Lane Papers.

27. RWL to Clarence Day, September 3, 1927, Box 1, Lane Papers; the April 1928 entry is quoted in Holtz, *Ghost in the Little House,* 187.

28. See, for example, Walter Lippmann, *A Preface to Morals;* Joseph Wood Krutch, *The Modern Temper: A Study and a Confession;* Robert M. Crunden, *From Self to Society.*

29. RWL, Diary, Memoranda for end of May 1931, June 2, 1932, Box 22, Lane Papers; RWL, *Let the Hurricane Roar.*

30. RWL, Journal, June 8, 1932, Diary, Memoranda for end of year 1933, Lane Papers.

31. RWL to Eleanor Garst, reprinted in *Better Homes and Gardens* 12 (December 1933), 19; RWL, Journal, December 23, 1932, Box 22, Lane Papers.

32. RWL to Guy Moyston, February 16, 1927, Box 9, Lane Papers.

33. RWL, *Let the Hurricane Roar,* 58, 67; hereinafter page citations are given parenthetically in the text.

34. RWL, Diary entries, Box 22, Lane Papers.

35. RWL, preface to *Old Home Town,* 23–24.

36. RWL to Rexh Meta, January 5, 1935, Box 8, Lane Papers; RWL, "Who's Who—And Why," 30.

37. RWL, "Credo," 5–7, 30–31, 34–35.

38. RWL, "Keeping Posted," 104.

39. Ibid.

40. RWL, *Free Land,* 7, 29, 41, 230–31, 25.

41. Burton Rascoe, "We, the People," 30; William Holtz, "Rose Wilder Lane's *Free Land:* The Political Background."

42. For example, George H. Nash does not include her in his comprehensive study *The Conservative Intellectual Movement in America.* Jim Powell calls the book

one of the founding documents of the modern libertarian movement in "Three Women Who Inspired the Modern Libertarian Movement," and Brian Doherty also includes Lane along with Isabel Paterson and Ayn Rand as one of the three to whom the modern American libertarian movement "can convincingly be traced" in chapter 3 of his massive *Radicals for Capitalism.*

43. RWL, *The Discovery of Freedom,* xi, 78, 190; hereinafter page citations are given parenthetically in the text.

44. See Earl S. Pomeroy, *The Territories and the United States, 1861–1890;* Howard R. Lamar, *Dakota Territory, 1861–1889: A Study of Frontier Politics.*

45. In an article published earlier, Lane had written, "The American revolution rejected democracy, because Athens had proved that democracy—majority rule—is not freedom but a form of dictatorship." Lane, "American Revolution, 1939," 23. H. L. Mencken's distaste for democracy was frequently cited by Lane's anarcho-libertarian fellow thinkers. Doherty, *Radicals for Capitalism,* 63.

46. Journalist Michael Kinsley starkly makes the same point about the average voter's general lack of knowledge about politics when he writes, "It's not just that Americans are scandalously ignorant. It's that they seem to believe they have a democratic right to their ignorance" ("The Intellectual Free Lunch," 5). Philip E. Converse's classic article "The Nature of Belief Systems in Mass Publics" continued a long tradition among political scientists on the subject and helped stimulate further research on it. See, for example, Bernard R. Berelson, Paul F. Lazarsfeld, and William A. McPhee, *Voting: A Study of Opinion Formation in a Presidential Campaign;* Angus Campbell, Philip E. Converse, Warren E. Miller, and Donald E. Stokes, *The American Voter;* and W. Russell Neuman, *The Paradox of Mass Politics: Knowledge and Opinion in the American Electorate.*

47. Holtz, *Ghost in the Little House,* 313, 323, 325, 334, 336, 351; Andrew Ward, "The Libertarian Party."

48. RWL, "The Story of American Needlework"; Lane told Merwin Hart in 1962 that three decades earlier the needlework series had been her "only chance of getting Americanism into print." RWL to Hart, January 1, 1962, Box 5, Lane Papers; Holtz, *Ghost in the Little House,* 348–49.

49. RWL, "Don't Send Your Son to College"; Holtz, *Ghost in the Little House,* 271–72, 276, 288, 291, 297–98.

50. Holtz, *Ghost in the Little House,* 220, 313.

51. I detect more political undertones in the Little House series than does Pamela Smith Hill, who contends that "Wilder never took an overtly political stance in her books" (*Laura Ingalls Wilder,* 151). However, I do not find the books shot through with political messages either, as some interpreters suggest.

52. The original "Pioneer Girl" manuscript, written in 1930, was almost entirely devoid of overt political references. About the only ones I could find are related to Wilder's disgruntlement regarding federal soldiers removing white settlers from Indian land—first in Indian Territory (as discussed in *Little House on the Prairie*) and later when gold prospectors were kicked out of the Black Hills. In both cases, whether Wilder realized it or not, the whites were illegally present on the land. See LIW, "Pioneer Girl" (Bye Version), 10–11, 162–63, Box 14, Lane Papers.

53. Holtz, *Ghost in the Little House,* 294, 301–2.

54. LIW, *Long Winter,* 13, 99, 112.

55. Ibid., 127, 166, 277.

56. LIW, *Little Town on the Prairie,* 73.

57. Ibid., 76.

58. See RWL, *Discovery of Freedom*, xi–xii, 158–59, 190; see also Holtz, *Ghost in the Little House*, 306–7.

59. LIW, *Little Town on the Prairie*, 89.

60. In "Big House in American Literature," 24, Chilton Williamson Jr. notes, "The last two volumes—*Little Town on the Prairie* and *These Happy Golden Years*—are social books, whose themes (apart from her courting by Almanzo) are Laura's accommodation to town life, which she learns to enjoy and appreciate, and her acceptance of the duty to become a schoolteacher." Suzanne Rahn, in "What Really Happens," contends that *Little Town on the Prairie* describes an "isolated young girl becoming thoroughly socialized" (125). Virginia L. Wolf also notes that, starting with *On the Banks of Plum Creek* and peaking in the last two volumes in the series, community becomes an important feature in the books (*Little House on the Prairie*, 9, 18, 126). See also Miller, *Laura Ingalls Wilder's Little Town*, chaps. 2 and 9.

61. John E. Miller, "The Places We Treasure and Their Contribution to Our Lives," 7; John E. Miller, "Place and Community in the 'Little Town on the Prairie': De Smet in 1883."

62. See, for example, Alan Trachtenberg, *The Incorporation of America: Culture and Society in the Gilded Age*; Olivier Zunz, *Making America Corporate, 1870–1920*; Robert H. Wiebe, *The Search for Order, 1877–1920*; Rowland Berthoff, *An Unsettled People: Social Order and Disorder in American History*; Max Lerner, *America as a Civilization*; Michael G. Kammen, "Biformity: A Frame of Reference"; and Robert N. Bellah, Richard Madsen, William M. Sullivan, Ann Swidler, and Steven M. Tipton, eds. *Individualism and Commitment in American Life: Readings on the Themes of Habits of the Heart*.

63. Fellman, "Little House Books," 49–50.

64. LIW, *These Happy Golden Years*, 54, 171; RWL, *Discovery of Freedom*, 124, 156, 161, 171.

Bibliography

Manuscript Collections

Detroit Public Library, Rare Book Room. It holds Wilder's original handwritten manuscripts of *The Long Winter* and *These Happy Golden Years*.

Holtz, William, Papers. Herbert Hoover Presidential Library, West Branch, Iowa.

Lane, Rose Wilder, Papers. Herbert Hoover Presidential Library, West Branch, Iowa. This collection contains more primary materials on Laura Ingalls Wilder and Rose Wilder Lane than any other source, including numerous versions of Wilder's book manuscripts and letters between Wilder and Lane.

Mays, Carl, File. Baseball Hall of Fame and Museum, Cooperstown, N.Y.

Pomona, California, Public Library. It holds the handwritten manuscript of *Little Town on the Prairie*.

Thomas Hart Benton Trust. United Missouri Bank of Kansas City, Kansas City, Mo.

Turner, Frederick Jackson, Papers. Huntington Library, San Marino, Calif.

Wilder, Laura Ingalls, Papers. Joint Collection, University of Missouri, Western Historical Manuscripts Collection, State Historical Society of Missouri. It has microfilm copies of the handwritten manuscripts of Wilder's autobiography "Prairie

Girl" and the first five books in the Little House series. The originals are located in the Laura Ingalls Wilder Memorial Association, Mansfield, Mo.

Newspapers

Columbia (Mo.) Missourian, various issues.
De Smet (S. Dak.) News, various issues.
Mansfield (Mo.) Mirror, 1908–1960.
Missouri Ruralist, 1911–1924.

Laura Ingalls Wilder's Writings

"The Farm Dining Room." *Country Gentleman* 90 (June 13, 1925): 21–22.

Laura Ingalls Wilder, Farm Journalist: Writings from the Ozarks. Ed. Stephen W. Hines. Columbia: University of Missouri Press, 2007. [A collection of her *Missouri Ruralist* columns]

Laura Ingalls Wilder's Fairy Poems. Ed. Stephen W. Hines. New York: Doubleday, 1998.

Little House in the Ozarks: A Laura Ingalls Wilder Sampler: The Rediscovered Writings. Ed. Stephen W. Hines. Nashville: Thomas Nelson, 1991.

A Little House Reader: A Collection of Writings by Laura Ingalls Wilder. Ed. Wiliam T. Anderson. New York: HarperCollins, 1998.

A Little House Sampler. With Rose Wilder Lane. Ed. William T. Anderson. Lincoln: University of Nebraska Press, 1988.

"My Ozark Kitchen." *Country Gentleman* 90 (January 17, 1925): 19, 22.

On the Way Home: The Diary of a Trip from South Dakota to Mansfield, Missouri, in 1894. New York: Harper and Row, 1962.

"Pioneer Girl." 1930, unpaginated, Lane Papers. [This is Wilder's unpublished handwritten autobiography. It is available on microfilm at the Missouri State Historical Society and in two different typed versions in the Lane Papers at the Hoover Library.]

West from Home: Letters of Laura Ingalls Wilder, San Francisco 1915. New York: HarperCollins, 1974.

"Whom Will You Marry?" *McCall's* 49 (June 1919): 8, 62.

Wilder's eight original Little House Books were reprinted in a Harper Trophy Book edition by Harper and Row, New York, in 1971. The First Four Years *came out at the same time.* The original publication of the books occurred in the following years:

> *Little House in the Big Woods,* 1932
> *Farmer Boy,* 1933
> *Little House on the Prairie,* 1935
> *On the Banks of Plum Creek,* 1937
> *By the Shores of Silver Lake,* 1939
> *The Long Winter,* 1940
> *Little Town on the Prairie,* 1941
> *These Happy Golden Years,* 1943
> *The First Four Years,* 1971

Rose Wilder Lane's Writings

"The American Revolution, 1939." *Saturday Evening Post* 211 (January 7, 1939): 23, 50–52.

"Come into My Kitchen." *Woman's Day* 23 (October 1960): 61, 98–99.

"Credo." *Saturday Evening Post* 208 (March 7, 1936): 5–7, 30–35.

The Discovery of Freedom: Man's Struggle against Authority. 1943. Reprint, New York, Arno Press, 1972.

"Don't Send Your Son to College." *Woman's Day* 1 (August 1938): 4–5, 44.

Free Land. 1938. Reprint, Lincoln: University of Nebraska Press, 1984.

"I, Rose Wilder Lane . . ." *Cosmopolitan* 80 (June 1926): 42–43, 140.

"Keeping Posted." *Saturday Evening Post* 210 (March 5, 1938): 104.

Lauters, Amy Mattson, ed. *The Rediscovered Writings of Rose Wilder Lane, Literary Journalist.* Columbia: University of Missouri Press, 2007.

Let the Hurricane Roar. 1933. Reprint, New York: Harper and Row, 1961.

A Little House Sampler. With Laura Ingalls Wilder. Ed. William T. Anderson. Lincoln: University of Nebraska Press, 1988.

"My House in the Country." *Woman's Day* 5 (May 1942): 12–13, 66–67.

"The Name Is Missoury." 1935. Draft manuscript, version 2, Lane Papers.

Old Home Town. 1935. Reprint, Lincoln: University of Nebraska Press, 1985.

"A Place in the Country." *Country Gentleman* 90 (March 14, 1925): 3–4, 26.

"The Story of American Needlework." *Woman's Day* 5 (March 1942), 19; and 24 (February 1961), 41, 88.

Travels with Zenobia: Paris to Albania by Model T Ford. With Helen Dore Boylston. Ed. William Holtz. Columbia: University of Missouri Press, 1983.

"We Say Missoury." 1935. Draft manuscript, version 1, Lane Papers.

"Who's Who—And Why." *Saturday Evening Post* 208 (July 6, 1935): 30.

References

Adam, Kathryn. "Laura, Ma, Mary, Carrie, and Grace: Western Women as Portrayed by Laura Ingalls Wilder." In *The Women's West,* ed. Susan Armitage and Elizabeth Jameson, 95–110. Norman: University of Oklahoma Press, 1987.

Adams, Henry. *Thomas Hart Benton: An American Original.* New York: Knopf, 1989.

Alexander, Christopher, Sara Ishikawa, and Murray Silverstein. *A Pattern Language: Towns, Buildings, Construction.* New York: Oxford University Press, 1977.

Alpern, Sara, Joyce Antler, Elisabeth Israels Perry, and Ingrid Winther Scobie, eds. *The Challenge of Feminist Biography: Writing the Lives of Modern American Women.* Urbana: University of Illinois Press, 1992.

Anderson, William T. *Laura Ingalls Wilder: A Biography.* New York: HarperCollins, 1992.

———. "Laura Ingalls Wilder and Rose Wilder Lane: The Continuing Collaboration." *South Dakota History* 16 (summer 1986): 89–143.

———. "The Literary Apprenticeship of Laura Ingalls Wilder." *South Dakota History* 13 (winter 1983): 285–331.

Anderson, William T., ed. *A Little House Reader: A Collection of Writings by Laura Ingalls Wilder.* New York: HarperCollins, 1998.

———. *A Little House Sampler.* Lincoln: University of Nebraska Press, 1988.

Appleby, Joyce, Lynn Hunt, and Margaret Jacob. *Telling the Truth about History.* New York: W. W. Norton, 1994.

Athern, Robert G. *The Mythic West in Twentieth-Century America.* Lawrence: University Press of Kansas, 1986.

Axtell, James. *The Invasion Within: The Contest of Cultures in Colonial North America.* New York: Oxford University Press, 1985.

Baigell, Matthew. *Thomas Hart Benton.* New York: Abrams, 1973.

Baigell, Matthew, ed. *A Thomas Hart Benton Miscellany.* Lawrence: University Press of Kansas, 1971.

Baigell, Matthew, and Allen Kaufman. "The Missouri Murals: Another Look at Benton." *Art Journal* 36 (summer 1977): 314–21.

Bartlett, Frederic C. *Remembering: A Study in Experimental and Social Psychology.* Cambridge: Cambridge University Press, 1932.

Barzun, Jacques. *Clio and the Doctors: Psycho-History, Quanto-History, and History.* Chicago: University of Chicago Press, 1974.

Baseball Encyclopedia. 10th ed. New York: Macmillan, 1996.

Batchelor, John, ed. *The Art of Literary Biography.* Oxford: Clarendon Press, 1995.

Beard, Charles A. "Written History as an Act of Faith." *American Historical Review* 39 (January 1934): 219–29.

Becker, Carl L. "Everyman His Own Historian." *American Historical Review* 37 (January 1932): 221–36.

———. "Frederick Jackson Turner." In *American Masters of Social Science: An Approach to the Study of the Social Sciences through a Neglected Field of Biography,* ed. Howard W. Odum, 273–318. New York: Henry Holt, 1927.

Bellah, Robert N., Richard Madsen, William M. Sullivan, Ann Swidler, and Steven M. Tipton, eds. *Individualism and Commitment in American Life: Readings on the Themes of Habits of the Heart.* New York: Harper and Row, 1987.

Benton, Thomas Hart. *An American in Art.* Lawrence: University Press of Kansas, 1969.

———. *An Artist in America.* 4th rev. ed. Columbia: University of Missouri Press, 1983.

Berelson, Bernard R., Paul F. Lazarsfeld, and William A. McPhee. *Voting: A Study of Opinion Formation in a Presidential Campaign.* Chicago: University of Chicago Press, 1954.

Berg, A. Scott. *Lindbergh.* New York: Putnam's Sons, 1998.

Berkhofer, Robert F., Jr. *A Behavioral Approach to Historical Analysis.* New York: Free Press, 1969.

———. *Beyond the Great Story: History as Text and Discourse.* Cambridge: Harvard University Press, 1995.

———. *The White Man's Indian: Images of the American Indian from Columbus to the Present.* New York: Random House, 1978.

Berthoff, Rowland. *An Unsettled People: Social Order and Disorder in American History.* New York: Harper and Row, 1971.

Best, Gary Dean. *The Nickel and Dime Decade: American Popular Culture during the 1930s.* Westport, Conn.: Praeger, 1993.

Billington, Ray Allen. *Frederick Jackson Turner: Historian, Scholar, Teacher.* New York: Oxford University Press, 1973.

————. *The Genesis of the Frontier Thesis: A Study in Historical Creativity.* San Marino, Calif.: Huntington Library, 1971.

————. "Why Some Historians Rarely Write History: A Case Study of Frederick Jackson Turner." *Mississippi Valley Historical Review* 50 (June 1963): 3–27.

Billington, Ray Allen, ed. *The Frontier Thesis: Valid Interpretation of American History?* New York: Holt, Rinehart and Winston, 1966.

Bodnar, John. *Remaking America: Public Memory, Commemoration, and Patriotism in the Twentieth Century.* Princeton: Princeton University Press, 1992.

Bogue, Allan G. *Frederick Jackson Turner: Strange Roads Going Down.* Norman: University of Oklahoma Press, 1998.

Bolles, Edmund Blair. *Remembering and Forgetting: An Inquiry into the Nature of Memory.* New York: Walker, 1988.

Book Review Digest, 1932. New York: H. W. Wilson, 1933.

Booth, Wayne C. *The Rhetoric of Fiction.* Chicago: University of Chicago Press, 1961.

Bosmajian, Hamida. "Vastness and Contraction of Space in *Little House on the Prairie*." *Children's Literature* 11 (1983): 49–63.

Bradbury, Ray. "Coda." In *Fahrenheit 451.* 50th anniversary edition, 175–79. New York: Ballantine Books, 2003.

Brantley, Billy C. "History of the *Missouri Ruralist*, 1902 through 1955." Master's thesis, University of Missouri, 1958.

Brinkley, Alan. *The End of Reform: New Deal Liberalism in Recession and War.* New York: Knopf, 1995.

Browning, Norma Lee. "Introspections of an Individualist." *Chicago Tribune*, March 16, 1947.

Bruner, Jerome. "The Autobiographical Process." In *The Culture of Autobiography: Constructions of Self-Representation*, ed. Robert Folkenflik, 38–56. Stanford, Calif.: Stanford University Press, 1993.

Campbell, Angus, Philip E. Converse, Warren E. Miller, and Donald E. Stokes. *The American Voter.* New York: Wiley, 1960.

Campbell, Donna M. "'Wild Men' and Dissenting Voices: Narrative Disruption in *Little House on the Prairie*." *Great Plains Quarterly* 20 (spring 2000): 111–22.

————. "'Written with a Hard and Ruthless Purpose': Rose Wilder Lane, Edna Ferber, and Middlebrow Regional Fiction." In *Middlebrow Moderns: Popular American Women Writers of the 1920s*, ed. Lisa Botshon and Meredith Goldsmith, 25–44. Boston: Northeastern University Press, 2003.

Champagne, Duane. "In Search of Theory and Method in American Indian Studies." *American Indian Quarterly* 31 (summer 2007): 353–72.

Chodorow, Nancy. *The Reproduction of Mothering: Psychoanalysis and the Sociology of Gender.* Berkeley and Los Angeles: University of California Press, 1978.

Cohen, Lisabeth. *A Consumer's Republic: The Politics of Mass Consumption in Postwar America.* New York: Knopf, 2003.

Converse. Philip E. "The Nature of Belief Systems in Mass Publics." In *Ideology and Discontent,* ed. David E. Apter, 206–61. New York: Free Press, 1964.

Cook-Lynn, Elizabeth. "Indian Studies—How It Looks Back at Us after Twenty Years." *Wicazo Sa Review* 20 (spring 2005): 179–87.

Couser, G. Thomas. *Altered Egos: Authority in American Autobiography.* New York: Oxford University Press, 1989.

Craven, Avery. "Frederick Jackson Turner." In *The Marcus W. Jernegan Essays in American Historiography,* ed. William T. Hutchinson, 252–70. Chicago: University of Chicago Press, 1937.

Creamer, Robert W. *Babe: The Legend Comes to Life.* New York: Pocket Books, 1976.

Cronon, William. "Revisiting the Vanishing Frontier: The Legacy of Frederick Jackson Turner." *Western Historical Quarterly* 18 (April 1987): 157–76.

Cronon, William, George Miles, and Jay Gitlin, eds. *Under an Open Sky: Rethinking America's Western Past.* New York: W. W. Norton, 1992.

Cross, Gary. *An All-Consuming Century: Why Commercialism Won in Modern America.* New York: Columbia University Press, 2000.

Crunden, Robert M. *From Self to Society.* Englewood Cliffs, N.J.: Prentice-Hall, 1972.

Curti, Merle E. "The Section and the Frontier in American History:

The Methodological Concepts of Frederick Jackson Turner." In *Methods in Social Science: A Case Book,* ed. Stuart A. Rice, 353–67. Chicago: University of Chicago Press, 1931.

Dahl, Ann Weller. "Laura Ingalls Wilder: An Elementary School Teacher's Perspective." In *Laura Ingalls Wilder and the American Frontier: Five Perspectives,* ed. Dwight M. Miller, 95–103. Lanham, Md.: University Press of America, 2002.

Delanty, Gerald, and Engin F. Isin, eds. *Handbook of Historical Sociology.* London: Sage, 2003.

Dewan, Pauline. *The House as Setting, Symbol, and Structural Motif in Children's Literature.* Lewiston, N.Y.: Edwin Mellon, 2004.

Dippie, Brian W. *The Vanishing American: White Attitudes and U.S. Indian Policy.* Middleton, Conn.: Wesleyan University Press, 1982.

Doherty, Brian. *Radicals for Capitalism: A Freewheeling History of the Modern American Libertarian Movement.* New York: Public Affairs, 2007.

Dorris, Michael. "Trusting the Words." *Booklist* 89 (June 1 / 15, 1993): 1820–22.

Doss, Erika L. *Benton, Pollock, and the Politics of Modernism: From Regionalism to Abstract Expressionism.* Chicago: University of Chicago Press, 1991.

Drinnon, Richard. *Facing West: The Metaphysics of Indian-Hating and Empire-Building.* New York: Shocken Books, 1990.

Dumenil, Lynn. *The Modern Temper: American Culture and Society in the 1920s.* New York: Hill and Wang, 1995.

Duncan, L. Wallace. *History of Montgomery County, Kansas, by Its Own People.* Iola, Kans.: Press of the Iola Register, 1903.

Eagleton, Terry. *After Theory.* New York: Basic Books, 2003.

———. "Buried in the Life: Thomas Hardy and the Limits of Biographies." *Harper's* 315 (November 2007): 89–94.

Eakin, Paul John. *Fictions in Autobiography: Studies in the Art of Self-Invention.* Princeton: Princeton University Press, 1985.

Edelman, Nancy. *The Thomas Hart Benton Murals in the Missouri State Capitol.* Jefferson City: Missouri State Council on the Arts, 1975.

Edwards, Everett E. "Bibliography of the Writings of Frederick Jackson Turner." In *The Early Writings of Frederick Jackson Turner,* 233–72. Madison: University of Wisconsin Press, 1938.

Ehrhardt, Julia C. *Writers of Conviction: The Personal Politics of Zona*

Gale, Dorothy Canfield Fisher, Rose Wilder Lane, and Josephine Herbst. Columbia: University of Missouri Press, 2004.

Erdrich, Louise. "A Writer's Sense of Place." In *A Place of Sense: Essays in Search of the Midwest,* ed. Michael Martone, 34–44. Iowa City: University of Iowa Press, 1988.

Erisman, Fred. "*Farmer Boy:* The Forgotten 'Little House' Book." *Western American Literature* 28 (1993): 123–30.

———. *Laura Ingalls Wilder.* Boise, Idaho: Boise State University, 1994.

———. "The Regional Vision of Laura Ingalls Wilder." In *Studies in Medieval, Renaissance, American Literature: A Festschrift,* ed. Betsy F. Colquitt, 165–71. Fort Worth: Texas Christian University Press, 1971.

Etulain, Richard W. "Myths and the American West: An Introduction." *Journal of the West* 37 (April 1998): 5–9.

Evans, Richard J. *In Defense of History.* New York: W. W. Norton, 1999.

Fairbanks, Carol. *Prairie Women: Images in American and Canadian Fiction.* New Haven: Yale University Press, 1986.

Faragher, John Mack, ed. *Rereading Frederick Jackson Turner: "The Significance of the Frontier in American History" and Other Essays.* New York: Henry Holt, 1994.

Fellman, Anita Clair. "'Don't Expect to Depend on Anybody Else': The Frontier as Portrayed in the Little House Books." *Children's Literature* 24 (1996): 101–16.

———. "Everybody's 'Little Houses': Reviewers and Critics Read Laura Ingalls Wilder." *Publishing Research Quarterly* 12 (spring 1996): 3–19.

———. "Laura Ingalls Wilder and Rose Wilder Lane: The Politics of a Mother-Daughter Relationship." *Signs: Journal of Woman in Culture and Society* 15 (spring 1990): 535–61.

———. *Little House, Long Shadow: Laura Ingalls Wilder's Impact on American Culture.* Columbia: University of Missouri Press, 2008.

———. "The Little House Books in American Culture." In *Laura Ingalls Wilder and the American Frontier: Five Perspectives,* ed. Dwight M. Miller, 45–67. Lanham, Md.: University Press of America, 2002.

———. "Making Meaning of the Past through the Little House Books." Paper delivered at Western History Association Conference, Portland, October 8, 1999.

Fischer, David Hackett. *Historians' Fallacies: Toward a Logic of Histori-cal Thought*. New York: Harper and Row, 1970.

Fraser, Caroline. "The Prairie Queen." *New York Review of Books* 41 (December 22, 1994): 38–45.

Gaddis, John Lewis. *The Landscape of History: How Historians Map the Past*. New York: Oxford University Press, 2002.

Gallagher, Winifred. *The Power of Place: How Our Surroundings Shape Our Thoughts, Emotions, and Actions*. New York: Poseidon Press, 1993.

Garraty, John A. "The Nature of Biography." *Centennial Review* 1 (spring 1957): 123–41.

Gerlach, Russel L. *Immigrants in the Ozarks: A Study in Ethnic Geogra-phy*. Columbia: University of Missouri Press, 1976.

Gilbert, Daniel. *Stumbling on Happiness*. New York: Knopf, 2006.

Goetzmann, William H., and William N. Goetzmann. *The West of the Imagination*. New York: W. W. Norton, 1986.

Harper, Paul F. *"Surely It Flowest with Milk and Honey": A History of Montgomery County, Kansas, to 1930*. Independence, Kans.: In-dependence Community College Press, 1988.

Harris, Violet J. *Teaching Multicultural Literature in Grades K–8*. Nor-wood, Mass.: Christopher-Gordon Publishers, 1993.

Hayden, Dolores. *The Power of Place: Urban Landscapes as Public His-tory*. Cambridge, Mass.: MIT Press, 1995.

Hays, Sharon. *The Cultural Contradictions of Motherhood*. New Haven: Yale University Press, 1996.

Heehs, Peter. "Myth, History, and Theory." *History and Theory* 33 (1994): 1–19.

Heldrich, Philip. "'Going to Indian Territory': Attitudes toward Na-tive Americans in *Little House on the Prairie*." *Great Plains Quar-terly* 20 (spring 2000): 99–109.

Heller, Scott. "Despite the Pitfalls, Two Biographers Focus on Living Novelists." *Chronicle of Higher Education*, April 24, 1998, A16.

Hill, Pamela Smith. *Laura Ingalls Wilder: A Writer's Life*. Pierre: South Dakota State Historical Society Press, 2007.

Hine, Robert V. *Community on the American Frontier: Separate but Not Alone*. Norman: University of Oklahoma Press, 1980.

Hines, Stephen W., ed. *Laura Ingalls Wilder, Farm Journalist: Writings from the Ozarks*. Columbia: University of Missouri Press, 2007.

———. *Little House in the Ozarks: A Laura Ingalls Wilder Sampler: The Rediscovered Writings*. Nashville: Thomas Nelson, 1991.

————. *I Remember Laura.* Nashville: Thomas Nelson, 1994.

Hirschfelder, Arlene, Paulette Fairbanks Molin, and Yvonne Wakim, eds. *American Indian Stereotypes in the World of Children: A Reader and Bibliography.* 2d. ed. Latham, Md.: Scarecrow Press, 1999.

Hiss, Tony. *The Experience of Place.* New York: Knopf, 1990.

Hofstadter, Richard. *The Progressive Historians: Turner, Beard, Parrington.* New York: Knopf, 1968.

Holland, Peter. "Mystery Man." *New York Review of Books* 51 (December 16, 2004): 34–38.

Holtz, William. "Closing the Circle: The American Optimism of Laura Ingalls Wilder." *Great Plains Quarterly* 4 (spring 1984): 79–90.

————. "Ghost and Host in the Little House Books." *Studies in the Literary Imagination* 29 (fall 1996): 41–51.

————. *The Ghost in the Little House: A Life of Rose Wilder Lane.* Columbia: University of Missouri Press, 1993.

————. "The Ghost in the Little House Books." *Liberty* 5 (March 1992): 51–54.

————. "Rose Wilder Lane's *Free Land:* The Political Background." *South Dakota Review* 30 (spring 1992): 56–67.

Holtz, William, ed. *Dorothy Thompson and Rose Wilder Lane: Forty Years of Friendship Letters, 1921–1980.* Columbia: University of Missouri Press, 1991.

Hudson, John C. "Yankeeland in the Middle West." *Journal of Geography* 85 (September–October 1986): 195–200.

Jacobs, Meg, William J. Novak, and Julian E. Zelizer, eds. *The Democratic Experiment: New Directions in American Political History.* Princeton: Princeton University Press, 2003.

Jacobs, Wilbur R. *The Historical World of Frederick Jackson Turner.* New Haven: Yale University Press, 1968.

Jacobs, William Jay. "Frontier Faith Revisited: The Little House Books of Laura Ingalls Wilder." *Horn Book* 41 (October 1965), 466–69.

James, Henry. "The Art of Fiction." In *The Art of Criticism: Henry James on the Theory and the Practice of Fiction,* ed. William Veeder and Susan M. Griffin, 165–83. Chicago: University of Chicago Press, 1986.

Jameson, Elizabeth. "In Search of the Great Ma." *Journal of the West* 37 (April 1998): 42–52.

————. "Unconscious Inheritance and Conscious Striving: Laura Ingalls Wilder and the Frontier Narrative." In *Laura Ingalls Wilder and the American Frontier: Five Perspectives*, ed. Dwight M. Miller, 69–93. Lanham, Md.: University Press of America, 2002.

Jeffrey, Julie Roy. *Frontier Women: The Trans-Mississippi West, 1840–1880*. New York: Hill and Wang, 1979.

Jelinek, Estelle C. *The Tradition of Women's Autobiography: From Antiquity to the Present*. Boston: Twayne, 1986.

Jennings, Francis. *The Invasion of America: Indians, Colonialism, and the Cant of Conquest*. Chapel Hill: University of North Carolina Press, 1975.

Jensen, Joan M. *Calling This Place Home: Women on the Wisconsin Frontier, 1850–1925*. St. Paul: Minnesota Historical Society Press, 2006.

Jensen, Richard. "On Modernizing Frederick Jackson Turner: The Historiography of Regionalism." *Western Historical Quarterly* 11 (July 1980): 307–22.

Kammen, Michael G. "Biformity: A Frame of Reference." In *People of Paradox: An Inquiry Concerning the Origins of American Civilization*, 97–116. New York: Random House, 1977.

————. *Mystic Chords of Memory: The Transformation of Tradition in American Culture*. New York: Knopf, 1991.

————. *Selvages and Biases: The Fabric of History in American Culture*. Ithaca: Cornell University Press, 1987.

Kaye, Frances W. "Little Squatter on the Osage Diminished Reserve: Reading Laura Ingalls Wilder's Kansas Indians." *Great Plains Quarterly* 20 (spring 2000): 123–40.

Kesselman, Steven. "The Frontier Thesis and the Great Depression." *Journal of the History of Ideas* 29 (1968): 253–68.

Kinsley, Michael. "The Intellectual Free Lunch." *New Yorker* 70 (February 6, 1995): 4–5.

Kirkendall, Richard S. *A History of Missouri: Volume V, 1919 to 1953*. Columbia: University of Missouri Press, 1986.

Kirkus, Virginia. "The Discovery of Laura Ingalls Wilder." *Horn Book Magazine* 29 (December 1953): 428–29.

Kohlberg, Lawrence. *The Philosophy of Moral Development*. Vol. 1 of *Essays on Moral Development*. New York: Harper and Row, 1981.

Kolodny, Annette. *The Lay of the Land: Metaphor as Experience and His-*

tory in American Life and Letters. Chapel Hill: University of North Carolina Press, 1975.

Kraft, Stephanie. *No Castles on Main Street: American Authors and Their Homes.* Chicago: Rand McNally, 1979.

Krutch, Joseph Wood. *The Modern Temper: A Study and a Confession.* New York: Harcourt, Brace, 1929.

Lamar, Howard R. *Dakota Territory, 1861–1889: A Study of Frontier Politics.* New Haven: Yale University Press, 1956.

Lamar, Howard R., ed. *The New Encyclopedia of the American West.* New Haven: Yale University Press, 1998.

Lamar, Howard W. "Frederick Jackson Turner." In *Pastmasters: Some Essays on American Historians,* ed. Marcus Cunliffe and Robin W. Winks, 74–109. New York: Harper and Row, 1969.

Lasch, Christopher. *The Culture of Narcissism: American Life in an Age of Diminishing Expectations.* New York: W. W. Norton, 1978.

Lauters, Amy Mattson, ed. *The Rediscovered Writings of Rose Wilder Lane, Literary Journalist.* Columbia: University of Missouri Press, 2007.

Leibowitz, Herbert. *Fabricating Lives: Explorations in American Autobiography.* New York: Knopf, 1989.

Lerner, Max. *America as a Civilization.* New York: Simon and Schuster, 1957.

Leuchtenburg, William L. *Franklin D. Roosevelt and the New Deal, 1932–1940.* New York: Harper and Row, 1963.

Levine, Lawrence W. *The Unpredictable Past: Explorations in American Cultural History.* New York: Oxford University Press, 1993.

Lewis, Magda. "'Are Indians Nicer Now?': What Children Learn from Books about Native North Americans." In *How Much Truth Do We Tell the Children?* ed. Betty Bacon, 135–48. Minneapolis: MEP Publications, 1988.

Lewis, Merrill E. "The Art of Frederick Jackson Turner: The Histories." *Huntington Library Quarterly* 35 (May 1972): 241–55.

Limerick. Patricia Nelson. *The Legacy of Conquest: The Unbroken Past of the American West.* New York: W. W. Norton, 1987.

Limerick, Patricia Nelson, Clyde A. Milner II, and Charles E. Rankin, eds. *Trails: Toward a New Western History.* Lawrence: University Press of Kansas, 1991.

Linsenmayer, Penny T. "Kansas Settlers on the Osage Diminished Reserve: A Study of Laura Ingalls Wilder's *Little House on the Prairie.*" *Kansas History* 24 (autumn 2000): 168–85.

Lippmann, Walter. *A Preface to Morals.* New York: Macmillan, 1929.

Lipsitz, George. *Time Passages: Collective Memory and American Popular Culture.* Minneapolis: University of Minnesota Press, 1990.

Lucas, Ann Lawson. *The Presence of the Past in Children's Literature.* Westport, Conn.: Praeger, 2003.

Lutwack, Leonard. *The Role of Place in Literature.* Syracuse: Syracuse University Press, 1984.

Macaulay, Thomas Babington. "History and Literature." In *The Varieties of History: From Voltaire to the Present,* ed. Fritz Stern, 71–89. New York: Vintage Books, 1972.

MacBride, Roger L., ed. *The Lady and the Tycoon.* Caldwell, Idaho: Caxton, 1973.

Mackey, Margaret. "Growing with Laura: Time, Space, and the Reader in the 'Little House' Books." *Children's Literature in Education* 23 (1992): 59–74.

MacLeod, Ann Scott. *American Childhood: Essays on Children's Literature of the Nineteenth and Twentieth Centuries.* Athens: University of Georgia Press, 1994.

Maher, Susan Naramore. "Deep Mapping the Great Plains: Surveying the Literary Cartography of Place." *Western American Literature* 36 (spring 2001): 4–24.

Mandelbaum, Maurice. "A Note on History as Narrative." In *The History and Narrative Reader,* ed. Geoffrey Roberts, 52–58. London: Routledge, 2001.

Marling, Karal Ann. *Tom Benton and His Drawings.* Columbia: University of Missouri Press, 1985.

———. *Wall-to-Wall America: A Cultural History of Post-Office Murals in the Great Depression.* Minneapolis: University of Minnesota Press, 1982.

Marshall, Richard, ed. *Laura Ingalls Wilder: A Family Collection.* New York: Barnes and Noble, 1993.

Martin, Theodore. *The Sound of Our Own Voices: Women's Study Clubs, 1860–1910.* Boston: Beacon Press, 1987.

Mathews, John J. *The Osages: Children of the Middle Waters.* Norman: University of Oklahoma Press, 1961.

Matt, Susan J. "You Can't Go Home Again: Homesickness and Nostalgia in U.S. History." *Journal of American History* 94 (September 2007): 469–97.

McAuliffe, Dennis. Jr. *The Deaths of Sybil Bolton: An American History.* New York: Times Books, 1994.

McDonald, Terrence J., ed. *The Historic Turn in the Human Sciences.* Ann Arbor: University of Michigan Press, 1996.

McGarigle, Bob. *Baseball's Great Tragedy: The Story of Carl Mays.* New York: Exposition Press, 1972.

Mieder, Wolfgang. "'The Only Good Indian Is a Dead Indian': History and Meaning of a Proverbial Stereotype." *Journal of American Folklore* 106 (winter 1993): 38–60.

Miller, Dwight M., ed. *Laura Ingalls Wilder and the American Frontier: Five Perspectives.* Lanham, Md.: University Press of America, 2002.

Miller, John E. "Approaching Laura Ingalls Wilder: Challenges and Opportunities." In *Laura Ingalls Wilder and the American Frontier: Five Perspectives,* ed. Dwight M. Miller, 13–27. Lanham, Md.: University Press of America, 2002.

———. *Becoming Laura Ingalls Wilder: The Woman behind the Legend.* Columbia: University of Missouri Press, 1998.

———. *Laura Ingalls Wilder's Little Town: Where History and Literature Meet.* Lawrence: University Press of Kansas, 1994.

———. "Place and Community in the 'Little Town on the Prairie': De Smet in 1883." *South Dakota History* 16 (winter 1986): 351–72.

———. "The Places We Treasure and Their Contribution to Our Lives." In *Peril and Promise: Essays on Community in South Dakota and Beyond,* ed. Charles L. Woodard, 5–20. Brookings: South Dakota State Agricultural Heritage Museum, 2007.

Miller, Tyrus. *Late Modernism: Politics, Fiction, and the Arts between the World Wars.* Berkeley and Los Angeles: University of California Press, 1999.

Mills, Claudia. "From Obedience to Autonomy: Moral Growth in the Little House Books." *Children's Literature* 24 (1996): 127–40.

Miner, H. Craig, and William E. Unrau. *The End of Indian Kansas: A Study of Cultural Revolution, 1854–1871.* Lawrence: Regents Press of Kansas, 1978.

Moore, Rosa Ann. "Laura Ingalls Wilder and Rose Wilder Lane: The Chemistry of Collaboration." *Children's Literature in Education* 2 (autumn 1980): 101–9.

———. "Laura Ingalls Wilder's Orange Notebooks and the Art of the Little House Books." *Children's Literature* 4 (1975): 105–19.

———. "The Little House Books: Rose-Colored Classics." *Children's Literature* 7 (1978): 7–16.

Murray, Gail Schmunk. *American Children's Literature and the Construction of Childhood.* New York: Twayne, 1998.

Nash, George H. *The Conservative Intellectual Movement in America since 1945.* New York: Basic Books, 1979.

Nash, Gerald D. "The West as Utopia and Myth, 1890–1990." In *Creating the West: Historical Interpretations, 1890–1990,* 197–257. Albuquerque: University of New Mexico Press, 1991.

Neuman, W. Russell. *The Paradox of Mass Politics: Knowledge and Opinion in the American Electorate.* Cambridge: Harvard University Press, 1992.

Nora, Pierre. "Between Memory and History: *Les Lieux de Memoire.*" *Representations* 26 (spring 1989): 7–25.

Novick, Peter. *That Noble Dream: The "Objectivity Question" and the American Historical Profession.* Cambridge: Cambridge University Press, 1988.

Novotney, Ellen Simpson. "Shattering the Myth: Mary and Laura as Antagonists in *Little House in the Big Woods, Little House on the Prairie,* and *On the Banks of Plum Creek.*" *Heritage of the Great Plains* 28 (fall/winter 1995): 48–64.

Official Manual of the State of Missouri. Jefferson City, 1933–1934, 1937–1938.

Parini, Jay. "Biography Can Escape the Tyranny of Facts." *Chronicle of Higher Education,* February 4, 2000, A72.

Parker, Rozsika. *Mother Love, Mother Hate: The Power of Maternal Ambivalence.* New York: Basic Books, 1996.

Pells, Richard H. *Radical Visions and American Dreams: Culture and Social Thought in the Depression Years.* New York: Harper and Row, 1973.

Peters, Catherine. "Secondary Lives: Biography in Context." In *The Art of Literary Biography,* ed. John Batchelor, 43–56. Oxford: Clarendon Press, 1995.

Piaget, Jean. *The Moral Judgment of the Child.* New York: Free Press, 1932.

Pomeroy, Earl S. *The Territories and the United States, 1861–1890.* Philadelphia: University of Pennsylvania Press, 1947.

Powell, Jim. "Three Women Who Inspired the Modern Libertarian Movement." *Freeman* 46 (May 1996): 324.

Priddy, Bob. *Only the Rivers Are Peaceful: Thomas Hart Benton's Missouri Mural.* Independence, Mo.: Bob Priddy, 1989.

Quantic, Diane Dufva. *The Nature of the Place: A Study of Great Plains Fiction.* Lincoln: University of Nebraska Press, 1995.

Rafferty, Milton D. *Missouri: A Geography*. Boulder, Colo.: Westview Press, 1983.

Rahn, Suzanne. "What Really Happens in the Little Town on the Prairie." *Children's Literature* 24 (1996): 117–26.

Rampersad, Arnold. "Design and Truth in Biography." *South Central Review* 9 (summer 1992): 1–19.

Randolph, Vance. *The Ozarks: An American Survival of Primitive Society*. New York: Vanguard Press, 1931.

Rascoe, Burton. "We, the People." *Newsweek* 11 (May 9, 1938): 30.

Riley, Glenda. *Women and Indians on the Frontier, 1825–1915*. Albuquerque: University of New Mexico Press, 1984.

Robertson, James O. *American Myth, American Reality*. New York: Hill and Wang, 1981.

Roediger, Henry L., III, and Charles P. Thompson. "Two Views of Remembering." *Contemporary Psychology* 42 (1997): 488–93.

Rogers, James Gordon, Jr. "Thomas Hart Benton's Mural *The Social History of Missouri*." Ph.D. diss., University of Missouri, 1989.

Rollings, Willard H. *The Osage: An Ethnohistorical Study of Hegemony on the Prairie-Plains*. Columbia: University of Missouri Press, 1992.

Romines, Ann. *Constructing the Little House: Gender, Culture, and Laura Ingalls Wilder*. Amherst: University of Massachusetts Press, 1997.

———. "The Frontier of the Little House." In *Laura Ingalls Wilder and the American Frontier: Five Perspectives*, ed. Dwight M. Miller, 29–44. Lanham, Md.: University Press of America, 2002.

———. "*The Long Winter:* An Introduction to Western Womanhood." *Great Plains Quarterly* 10 (winter 1990): 36–47.

———. "Writing the Little House: The Architecture of a Series." *Great Plains Quarterly* 14 (spring 1994): 107–15.

Rosen, Elliot A. *Roosevelt, the Great Depression, and the Economics of Recovery*. Charlottesville: University of Virginia Press, 2005.

Rosenblum, Dolores. "'Intimate Immensity': Mythic Space in the Works of Laura Ingalls Wilder." In *Where the West Begins: Essays on Middle Border and Siouxland Writing*, ed. Arthur R. Huseboe and William Geyer, 72–79. Sioux Falls: Center for Western Studies Press, 1978.

Rosenzweig, Linda. *The Anchor of My Life: Middle-Class American Mothers and Daughters, 1880–1920*. New York: New York University Press, 1993.

Ross, Edith Connelley. "The Bloody Benders." *Kansas Historical Collections* 17 (1926–1928): 464–79.

Rubin, Martin. "Biography as a Literary Genre." *World and I* 15 (January 2000): 314–15.

Sahlins, Marshall. *Islands of History.* Chicago: University of Chicago Press, 1985.

Salinger, J. D. *The Catcher in the Rye.* New York: Little, Brown, 1951.

Scherman, David E., and Rosemarie Redlich. *Literary America: A Chronicle of American Writers from 1607–1952 with 173 Photographs of the America That Inspired Them.* New York: Dodd, Mead, 1952.

Schickel, Richard. *Intimate Strangers: The Culture of Celebrity in America.* 1985. Reprint, Chicago: Ivan R. Dee, 2000.

Schlesinger, Arthur M., Jr. *The Crisis of the Old Order, 1919–1933.* Boston: Houghton Mifflin, 1957.

Schumacher, E. F. *Small Is Beautiful: Economics as If People Mattered.* New York: Harper and Row, 1975.

Seaver, Tom. *Great Moments in Baseball.* New York: Carol Publishing Group, 1995.

Segel, Elizabeth. "Laura Ingalls Wilder's America: An Unflinching Assessment." *Children's Literature in Education* 8 (summer 1977): 63–70.

Shortridge, James R. *Peopling the Plains: Who Settled Where in Frontier Kansas.* Lawrence: University Press of Kansas, 1995.

Sklar, Robert. *Movie-Made America: A Social History of American Movies.* New York: Vintage, 1976.

Slapin, Beverly, and Doris Seale, eds. *Through Indian Eyes: The Native Experience in Books for Children.* Philadelphia: New Society Publishers, 1992.

Smith, Dennis. *The Rise of Historical Sociology.* Oxford: Polity Press, 1991.

Smith, Henry Nash. *Virgin Land: The American West as Symbol and Myth.* Cambridge: Harvard University Press, 1950.

Smulders, Sharon. "'The Only Good Indian': History, Race, and Representation in Laura Ingalls Wilder's *Little House on the Prairie.*" *Children's Literature Association Quarterly* 27 (winter 2002–2003): 191–202.

Socolofsky, Homer E. *Arthur Capper: Publisher, Politician, and Philanthropist.* Lawrence: University of Kansas Press, 1962.

Sowell, Mike. *The Pitch That Killed.* New York: Macmillan, 1989.

Spaeth, Janet. *Laura Ingalls Wilder.* Boston: Twayne, 1987.

Spain, Daphne. *Gendered Spaces*. Chapel Hill: University of North Carolina Press, 1992.

Stein, Herbert. *The Fiscal Revolution in America: Policy in Pursuit of Reality*. 2d ed. Washington, D.C.: AEI Press, 1996.

Steiner, Michael C. "From Frontier to Region: Frederick Jackson Turner and the New Western History." *Pacific Historical Review* 64 (November 1995): 479–501.

———. "The Significance of Turner's Sectional Thesis." *Western Historical Quarterly* 10 (October 1979): 437–66.

Storr, Anthony. "Psychiatry and Literary Biography." In *The Art of Literary Biography*, ed. John Batchelor, 73–86. Oxford: Clarendon Press, 1995.

Stott, Jon C. *Native Americans in Children's Literature*. Phoenix: Oryx, 1995.

Subramanian, Jane M. *Laura Ingalls Wilder: An Annotated Bibliography of Critical, Biographical, and Teaching Studies*. Westport, Conn.: Greenwood Press, 1997.

Susina, Jan. "The Voice of the Prairie: The Use of Music in Laura Ingalls Wilder's *Little House on the Prairie*." *Lion and the Unicorn* 16 (June 1992): 58–66.

Susman, Warren I. *Culture as History: The Transformation of American Society in the Twentieth Century*. New York: Pantheon, 1984.

Taylor, George Rogers, ed. *The Turner Thesis: Concerning the Role of the Frontier in American History*. Lexington, Mass.: D.C. Heath, 1972.

Thacker, Robert. *The Great Prairie Fact and Literary Imagination*. Albuquerque: University of New Mexico Press, 1989.

Thompson, Melissa Kay. "A Sea of Good Intentions: Native Americans in Books for Children." *Lion and the Unicorn* 25 (September 2001): 353–74.

Tilden, Freeman. *Interpreting Our Heritage*. 3d ed. Chapel Hill: University of North Carolina Press, 1977.

Titus, Mary. "Hardwick Tempers Her Wit with Wisdom." *Minneapolis Star Tribune*, August 23, 1998.

Tocqueville, Alexis de. *Democracy in America*. Ed. and trans. Harvey C. Mansfield and Delba Winthrop. Chicago: University of Chicago Press, 2000.

Trachtenberg, Alan. *The Incorporation of America: Culture and Society in the Gilded Age*. New York: Hill and Wang, 1982.

Tuan, Yi-Fu. *Topophilia: A Study of Environmental Perception, Attitudes, and Values*. Englewood Cliffs, N.J.: Prentice-Hall, 1974.

Turner, Frederick. *Spirit of Place: The Making of an American Literary Landscape.* San Francisco: Sierra Club Books, 1989.

Turner, Frederick Jackson. *The Frontier in American History.* New York: Henry Holt, 1920.

Updike, John. "One Cheer for Literary Biography." *New York Review of Books* 46 (February 4, 1999): 3–5.

Vincent, Andrew. *The Nature of Political Theory.* Oxford: Oxford University Press, 2004.

Wagner-Martin, Linda. *Telling Women's Lives: The New Biography.* New Brunswick, N.J.: Rutgers University Press, 1994.

Ward, Andrew. "The Libertarian Party." *Atlantic* 238 (November 1976): 24–33.

Weaver, Jack. "More Light Than Heat: The Current State of Native American Studies." *American Indian Quarterly* 31 (spring 2007): 233–55.

Wecter, Dixon. *The Hero in America: A Chronicle of Hero-Worship.* Ann Arbor: University of Michigan Press, 1963.

Welty, Eudora. "Place in Fiction." In *The Eye of the Story: Selected Essays and Reviews,* 116–33. New York: Vintage, 1990.

White, Morton. *Foundations of Historical Knowledge.* New York: Harper and Row, 1965.

White, Norman. "Pieties and Literary Biography." In *The Art of Literary Biography,* ed. John Batchelor, 213–26. Oxford: Clarendon Press, 1995.

Wiebe, Robert H. *The Search for Order, 1877–1920.* New York: Hill and Wang, 1967.

Wiley, Robert S. *Dewey Short: Orator of the Ozarks.* Cassville, Mo.: Litho Printers, 1985.

Williamson, Chilton, Jr. "Big House in American Literature." *Chronicles* (November 1991): 20–25.

Windschuttle, Keith. *The Killing of History: How Literary Critics and Social Theorists Are Murdering Our Past.* New York: Free Press, 1997.

Wolf, Virginia L. *Little House on the Prairie: A Reader's Companion.* New York: Twayne, 1996.

Wolfskill, George. *The Revolt of the Conservatives: A History of the American Liberty League.* Boston: Houghton Mifflin, 1962.

Wolfskill, George A., and John A. Hudson. *All but the People: Franklin D. Roosevelt and His Critics, 1933–39.* New York: Macmillan, 1969.

Wright, Gwendolyn. *Moralism and the Model Home.* Chicago: University of Chicago Press, 1980.

Wrobel, David M. *The End of American Exceptionalism: Frontier Anxiety from the Old West to the New Deal.* Lawrence: University Press of Kansas, 1993.

Zochert, Donald. *Laura: The Life of Laura Ingalls Wilder.* New York: Avon, 1976.

Zunz, Olivier. *Making America Corporate, 1870–1920.* Chicago: University of Chicago Press, 1990.

Index

255